Season Review 1999-2000

MATCH CLUB GUIDE

MANAGING EDITOR: Chris Hunt
ART DIRECTOR: Darryl Tooth
ASSISTANT EDITOR: Ian Foster
SUB-EDITOR: James Bandy

CHELSEA BOOK COMPILED BY: Alistair Phillips
CONTRIBUTORS: Hugh Sleight, Kev Hughes, Phil Smith, Bev Ward, Nick Gibbs, Martin Barry, Becky Booth, David Houghton & the correspondents of **MATCHFACTS**.
SPECIAL THANKS TO: Neil Bedingfield, Paul Ewen, Clint Davis, Ian Leach, Tony Warner & Wai Wong at Chelsea.

First published in Great Britain in 2000 by Hayden Publishing Ltd

Produced under licence from Chelsea Village Merchandising Limited,
Mail Order Number: 0870 603 0005
www.chelseafc.co.uk

Colour Origination: Gildenburgh Ltd.
Printed and bound in Italy by LEGO, Vicenza
ISBN 0 9533683 6 X
MATCH MAGAZINE, Bretton Court, Bretton,
Peterborough PE3 8DZ, England

contents

Guide to symbols and ratings

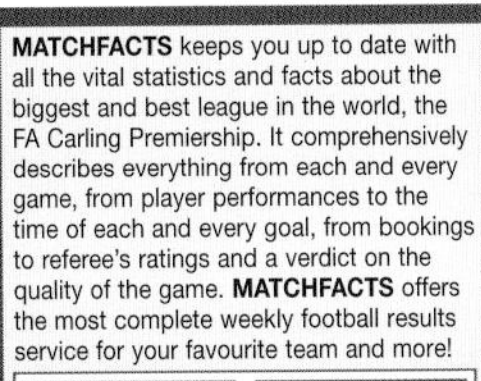

MATCHFACTS keeps you up to date with all the vital statistics and facts about the biggest and best league in the world, the FA Carling Premiership. It comprehensively describes everything from each and every game, from player performances to the time of each and every goal, from bookings to referee's ratings and a verdict on the quality of the game. **MATCHFACTS** offers the most complete weekly football results service for your favourite team and more!

PLAYER RATINGS		MATCH RATINGS	
10	Out of this world	★★★★★	Unbelievable
9	Outstanding	★★★★	Great game
8	Impressive	★★★	Not bad
7	Good	★★	Pretty dull
6	Average	★	Terrible
5	Below par		
4	Poor		

REFEREE: Name and rating of the match official in charge.

GAME NUMBER: Shows the type of competition played in.

Competition: **FA Carling Premiership**
Date: **Saturday April 1, 2000**
Attendance: **40,162**
Referee: **J Winter** (Stockton) 7
Game 46

MATCH RATING: ★★★ **LEAGUE POSITION:** 4th

MATCH RATING: This mark out of five shows how good the game was.

LEAGUE POSITION: Current place in the league – also given for European games to show any place changes.

SYMBOLS: A quick way of identifying how many cards were received or goals scored during the game, explained in detail in the description below.

TEAM: Who were Chelsea playing? If you were in any doubt, it tells you right here!

STAR RATING: Given to the one player from each team who made the greatest impact or contribution to their team's performance.

CHELSEA
Wise ⚽ ▭ ☆ 9
Goal: 44 mins; Booked: 80 mins (foul)
Subbed: 81 mins (Morris)
***sub:** Morris*

PLAYER NAME

SUBSTITUTION: Did the player last the whole game? If not, you can see who he was replaced by and after how long into the game it was.

SUB: Name of player that came on, with a rating if they played 20 minutes or more.

PLAYER RATING: An overall rating out of ten for performance, based on the impact made by the individual during the game.

THAT WAS THE YEAR THAT WAS...

1999-2000

"The trouble is, success is like a drug. The more you get, the more you want, the more you need."
KEN BATES

THAT CHELSEA FOOTBALL CLUB WENT INTO THE FA CUP Final, their 61st and last game of 1999-2000, needing victory to save their campaign says everything about the progress over the last decade of London's most fashionable club.

As they made their way to Wembley for the biggest domestic game of the year, Gianluca Vialli's team were under pressure. They had ended the league season a disappointing fifth in the Premiership, 26 points behind Manchester United. More importantly, despite reaching the Champions League quarter-finals, missing out on a top-four place in the league meant the club failed to secure even a UEFA Cup slot for the following season. "The trouble is, success is like a drug," said Chelsea chairman Ken Bates, on the eve of the final. "The more you get, the more you want, the more you need."

At that moment, Chelsea craved European football more than anything and Vialli, their Italian manager, knew his job was on the line. Winning the FA Cup would ensure a place in the UEFA Cup, but if The Blues failed to beat Aston Villa on May 21 they would be forced into the Intertoto Cup, alongside relegation candidates Bradford City, in a last-ditch bid for European football. For a club who just five weeks earlier had come within a whisker of knocking the mighty Barcelona out of the Champions League, defeat to Villa was unthinkable. "We had to win the FA Cup, it was crucial," admitted Vialli over the summer. "We had put in so much effort over so many months of the season. We entertained the supporters and gave them something to cheer about, especially in Europe, but we'd won nothing. If we hadn't won the FA Cup, we would have entered the Intertoto Cup because European football is vital to this club. But that would have meant more games for my players and I didn't want that. That's why we knew we had to win."

The expectation should have weighed heavily on Vialli and his players as they stepped out onto the hallowed turf for the old Wembley's last ever Cup Final, but from the very first minute the result was never in doubt. Unlike the novices who had succumbed 4-0 to Man. United at Wembley in 1994, this was a Chelsea team packed with international stars, players who'd achieved everything on the world stage, a side that included three World Cup winners and a former World Footballer Of The Year. Roberto Di Matteo's strike won the FA Cup for Chelsea, The Blues were back in Europe and Gianluca Vialli's job was safe!

But it was merely a stay of execution. Premiership failure coupled with the huge financial blow of missing out on another season of Champions League football had left Bates with serious doubts over his manager. Moreover, without the glamour of Champions League football, the chairman knew Chelsea needed the 2000-01 Premiership title to continue their development and establish themselves among Europe's elite. Unfortunately for Vialli, a mediocre start to the league campaign left Bates fearful that the trophy he most desired was already slipping away. Never one to shirk responsibility, he made up his mind and, just five games into the season, Chelsea's most successful ever manager was sacked.

NOW STOP! FORGET FOR A MOMENT THE CHELSEA OF THE new millennium and cast your minds back ten years to the summer of 1990. With Bobby Campbell at the helm, a newly-promoted Chelsea had just finished fifth in their first season back in the top flight. After racing to the Division Two title the season before, The Blues had Kerry Dixon and Kevin Wilson to thank for firing them to their highest league finish for 20 years. The fans may have been disappointed by a League Cup defeat to Fourth Division Scarborough and an FA Cup exit at the hands of Division Three side Bristol City, but league form made up for that. They finished 19 points behind champions Liverpool, but the Anfield club had won the title six times in the 1980s. They were European giants. Chelsea couldn't be expected to compete with that, could they?

By the start of the 1999-2000 season, just nine years later, levels of expectation at Stamford Bridge had changed to such a degree that Chelsea were not only supposed to compete with Europe's top sides, they now began every season under pressure to collect at least one trophy and to do well in every competition they entered. This was a different club, imbued from top to bottom with the need to succeed.

The winning attitude started with Ken Bates, but nowhere was it better embodied than in the manager, Gianluca Vialli. As a player, the Italian had won all three European trophies, two Serie A titles, three Italian Cups, the FA Cup and the League Cup, and demanded nothing less than victory. "I am used to winning games and winning things," said Vialli, as he led his team into the new campaign. "That is my mentality. That's what Chelsea must have. Maybe years ago the club had an inferiority complex, but that doesn't exist for me."

Nor did it exist for the supporters as they took their seats at Stamford Bridge for the opening Premiership fixture against Sunderland. Where the Shed End had happily celebrated winning the Zenith Data Systems Cup in 1990, a decade of growth had given the Chelsea faithful a changed outlook as the 1999-2000 season began. Four different trophies – the FA Cup, Cup-Winners' Cup, League Cup and European Super Cup – had been collected for The Bridge's trophy cabinet during the previous three years and the fans entered the new season confident of more silverware.

Such confidence was understandable. Chelsea had finished third in the 1998-99 Premiership campaign, just four points behind treble winners Man. United and having lost the same number of games, three. The arrival of France's World Cup-winning skipper Didier Deschamps to bolster The Blues' midfield and the belief that United would struggle in the wake of their historic efforts gave Chelsea's fans real belief that this was to be their season. And when Vialli splashed out

Gus Poyet scored a wonder goal on the opening day and grabbed a fine brace in the 5-0 thrashing of Man. United.

a club record £10 million on Blackburn striker Chris Sutton, it seemed the next step would be the club's first League Championship since 1955.

Initially the players did little to dampen the enthusiasm, beginning the season with a 4-0 demolition of Premiership new boys Sunderland. A wonder goal from Gus Poyet was the highlight of a performance in which Chelsea tore apart the Wearsiders' defence with their slick passing. But in hindsight, Vialli felt victory may have done more harm than good. "When we scored four goals, we maybe thought we were better than we really were," he reflected at the season's end. "Perhaps it would have been better if we had made a few mistakes. Then we would have known we needed to improve."

Not that it was immediately obvious that Chelsea had much to correct. Five games into the season, they had dropped only two points – in a 2-2 draw at Leicester – as they racked up wins over Villa, Wimbledon and Newcastle to lie second behind Man. United, who had played more games. The first real test of Chelsea's championship credentials would come with the visit of Sir Alex Ferguson's team.

BOTH CHELSEA AND UNITED HAD STARTED THE SEASON impressively, so when they lined up against each other in early October the game was already being billed as a title showdown. The treble winners swaggered into Stamford Bridge unbeaten in the Premiership since December 19, 1998, a mighty 29-game run, but Chelsea were ready. It took Poyet just 27 seconds to put The Blues ahead and Chelsea ran amok, inflicting a stinging 5-0 defeat on the European Cup holders. Sutton had already bagged his first league goal for the club by the time United's Nicky Butt was sent-off after 22 minutes. Poyet grabbed his second, Henning Berg put through his own net and Jody Morris rounded things off in what seemed like a huge boost to Chelsea's title hopes.

Strange then that the manager should single out such a magnificent result as the moment when his title dreams began to fade. "We beat United 5-0 but they used that match better than us," explained Vialli. "They rolled up their sleeves and hardly lost again. For the rest of the season, they were by far the best team. They were so consistent and so effective."

By contrast, Chelsea took inconsistency to a whole new level as stunning performances when facing the strongest teams in Europe were followed within days by abject displays against teams they should have beaten comfortably.

In fact, by the time United were dismantled, there were signs that it would not be Chelsea's year in the league. The two major problems that would haunt Vialli all season had already surfaced – balancing Champions League football with the demands of the Premiership, and scoring goals.

Between the 4-0 defeat of Sunderland and the 5-0 victory over United, Chelsea had netted just six times in six games, their four victories all coming by a 1-0 scoreline. Even as early as October, a potential problem had been noted. "When we were at home, teams like Aston Villa and Newcastle were putting all their players behind the ball and playing for a draw, and that was presenting new problems," recalled first team coach Ray Wilkins. "In our first 12 games we kept nine clean sheets, but we were finding it difficult to score."

"We beat United 5-0 but they used that match better than we did. For the rest of the season, they were by far the best team."

GIANLUCA VIALLI

"When you go to Derby four days after playing in Milan, you still have the picture of the San Siro in your head and it can be a shock."

MARCEL DESAILLY

By the season's end, a strikeforce that boasted players of the calibre of Gianfranco Zola, Tore Andre Flo, Chris Sutton and George Weah had managed just 53 goals in 38 league games and only 18 away from home. Man. United, in stark contrast, scored a total of 97 league goals and Arsenal 73.

The failure of £10 million signing Chris Sutton didn't help. A title-winner at Blackburn, he had been expected to score the goals that would push Chelsea up the table, but his header against United was his only strike in 28 league games. Zola also suffered a loss of form. Chelsea's 1998-99 Player Of The Year scored against Sunderland, but had to wait two months for his next goal – away to Galatasaray – and didn't score again in the Premiership until mid-April. George Weah's arrival on loan from Milan in January threatened to solve the problem when he bagged the winner against Tottenham on his debut, but by May the former World Footballer Of The Year had managed just three league goals.

Yet back in October, fresh from smashing five past the champions, Chelsea could not have believed that scoring goals would be a major difficulty. More worrying at the time was that European football was already taking its toll on the team's league form. The 2-2 draw at Leicester came days after a 3-0 win over Skonto Riga had virtually booked a place in the group stages of the Champions League. Similarly, an impressive performance in drawing at home to Italian giants AC Milan was followed, three days later, by a 1-0 defeat at the hands of Premiership whipping boys Watford.

Man. United's Ryan Giggs had warned it would take time to adjust to playing top-level European games and picking up league points, but when The Blues convincingly beat United five days after victory over Galatasaray, Vialli and his team must have thought they had things under control.

They hadn't. Nine times during the season The Blues followed European adventures with a poor league result as 21 points were squandered. Wrapped up in the excitement of weekly games against the best teams in Europe, Chelsea found it hard to motivate themselves for run-of-the-mill league games. "When you go to Derby four days after playing in Milan, you still have the picture of the San Siro in your head and it can be a shock," mused Marcel Desailly after another Premiership aberration, a 3-1 defeat at Pride Park.

Looking back, midfielder Jody Morris agreed. "We really suffered at the start of the season," he said. "It's a different state of football in the Premier League, a different approach, and it was a learning process for everyone here, even the manager. Although he's won the European Cup as a player, it's different when you're the manager and you've got to find different ways of motivating players. We all found it tough, but we got better at it as the season went on."

Unfortunately, the damage was done by then. When the Champions League took its winter break, Chelsea were two games into the second group stage and proudly topped Group D ahead of Lazio, Feyenoord and Marseille. But when they lost their next Premiership game to leaders Leeds, The Blues were languishing in tenth place, 17 points behind David O'Leary's young team and 15 behind Man. United, the team they had beaten so convincingly two months earlier.

By January, after a draw at Bradford, Vialli accepted defeat in his team's Premiership challenge. "We are too far away to think about winning the title," he said. "We've got to be realistic. The gap is too big, but it's our duty to win as many matches as possible between now and the end of the season." By May the gap would be bigger as Man. United, also in the Champions League, ran away with the league title.

IF FAILING TO WIN THE LEAGUE WAS A DISAPPOINTMENT for Chelsea, it was brilliantly compensated by their thrilling European exploits. When Latvia's Skonto Riga were defeated and The Blues reached the first group stage of the Champions League, they could scarcely have imagined what lay in store. Drawn to play Germany's Hertha Berlin, Galatasaray of Turkey and Italy's Milan, Chelsea set about

Chelsea ended the season by defeating Aston Villa to win the FA Cup at Wembley.

proving they could hold their own in such elite company. Responding magnificently to a 2-1 defeat in Berlin, Chelsea beat Galatasaray 1-0 at home and followed it up with a 5-0 annihilation of the Turks in Istanbul. But it was two draws with Milan that announced Chelsea's arrival as a European force. Unlucky not to take all three points at Stamford Bridge, Chelsea more than matched their illustrious opponents in the famous San Siro stadium, coming back from a goal down to equalise through Dennis Wise and force a 1-1 draw.

For Wise, it was proof that Chelsea had graduated to the big time. "That meant so much to the club," he said at the end of the season. "To go from playing teams like Oxford to playing Milan in such a short time is a wonderful thing. And we competed with them, we could have beaten them. It was a big step for Chelsea to make and we made it successfully."

According to Vialli though, the first phase highlight was the final match of Group H at home to Hertha Berlin with both teams needing a point to go through. "No-one was expecting us to play a real match, everybody was expecting the two teams to be happy with one point, a boring draw, but it wasn't like that," said Vialli. "We played the match with the right attitude and we beat Berlin 2-0. We had proved we could play nice football, but in that game we also showed we had the right spirit to play in such an important competition."

Chelsea went from strength to strength to finish second in Group D after brushing aside Feyenoord and Marseille. Lazio proved a tougher test, but Vialli's charges still qualified for a mouth-watering quarter-final against the world's biggest club, Barcelona. Not that they were intimidated. By the time the Spanish giants arrived at Stamford Bridge, The Blues were brimming with confidence. "They are not on top of their game," noted Vialli. "We have a great chance to beat them."

And beat them they did. A free-kick from Zola and two goals from Flo gave Chelsea a 3-0 half-time lead which sent shockwaves around Europe. But Luis Figo's 54th-minute strike gave Barca hope and proved crucial in the second leg.

In the awesome Nou Camp, in front of 100,000 fans, Chelsea looked nervous for the first time in the campaign and Barcelona were in no mood for mercy. Inspired by Figo, the Catalans besieged Ed de Goey's goal. By half-time it was 2-0 and with Figo's away goal Barca had the advantage. But Chelsea dug deep. Flo capitalised on a goalkeeping error to pull one back and a semi-final place beckoned. Then, with seven minutes left, disaster. Dani made it 3-1 and a minute later, to the disbelief of Chelsea's players, Barcelona won a penalty. Amazingly, Rivaldo missed and the tie went into extra-time, but after Celestine Babayaro conceded a penalty, Rivaldo made up for his earlier miss from the spot and the game was over. Kluivert made it 5-1 and Chelsea were out.

GLORIOUS FAILURE MAY BE A VERY BRITISH THING, BUT even Chelsea's Italian manager was able to reflect with pride on what could only be seen as a successful Champions League campaign. "We took a lot of people by surprise and we surprised ourselves," confessed Vialli. "We realised we could play anybody and beat anybody. We had enough strength to be successful in such a difficult competition. To be in the Champions League quarter-final is part of the learning curve for Chelsea. It was a success for us. But perhaps in two years' time, only the final will be good enough. The aim now is to get to where I and Marcel Desailly have been."

For Dennis Wise, however, the feeling of accomplishment was tinged with disappointment. "At the start of the season, everyone thought, 'Chelsea won't be able to compete', but we were seven minutes from knocking out Barcelona. We blew it because we got sloppy, but it shows how far we've come. It was a good tournament for us, but we were disappointed to go out because we felt we could have gone all the way."

Chelsea returned to England with plenty to play for, not least a place in the next Champions League campaign. After coming so close to a place in the semi-finals, the idea of not qualifying for the next season's competition was unthinkable, but they needed to finish in the top three to make it.

It was by no means impossible. The mid-season break from European action had helped Chelsea regain their league form and a 16-match unbeaten run had lifted them to third. The return of the Champions League saw a slight dip in form, but they were fifth after the Barcelona defeat, so when Chelsea visited Old Trafford in late-April, the all-important Champions League berth was still up for grabs. Chelsea couldn't have wished for a better time to face Man. United. Although they had also lost in Europe, United had sealed their sixth Premiership title in eight years just two days before the sides met and were expecting a celebration. The scene was set for The Blues to spoil the party by taking all three points at a stadium where they were unbeaten in seven years.

One poor performance later, Chelsea's Champions League hopes lay in tatters and Vialli was furious. "We were too casual, too sloppy," he fumed after the 3-2 defeat. "It leaves us with no hope of playing in the Champions League next season. The future of this club depends on the right attitude from the players. Otherwise, in the end, I will be sacked."

Little did Vialli know how right he would be – or how quickly he would be proved right. But for the time being, the manager and his team had to concentrate on the FA Cup. A 6-1 win at Hull City had got The Blues' campaign off to a great start and the run had quickly taken on a feeling of inevitability. Nottingham Forest, Leicester and Gillingham were comfortably beaten and when, just nine days before the Nou Camp epic, Gus Poyet's brace overcame an impressive Newcastle to carry Chelsea to their third FA Cup Final in seven years, the old cliché about a team's name being on the Cup had never felt truer. Aston Villa didn't stand a chance.

WINNING THE FA CUP DID MORE FOR CHELSEA THAN earn them a European place. It allowed them, and forced critics, to see the season for what it was – a success, rather than talking about what might have been. Fifth place in the league may not have been what the club expected, but nor was a masterly run to the Champions League quarter-finals.

And even as he basked in the Wembley triumph over the close season, Vialli was planning to use Cup success as a springboard to greater glory. "Winning the FA Cup helps me a lot for next season in terms of credibility," said Vialli. "I'm a young, inexperienced manager and it helps to show that what I say and what I try to do is right. It helps the others to follow and support me. It means I can come back next year and try my best to make this club more successful."

Unfortunately, the manager had forgotten his chairman's comments from just before the Cup Final. By bringing the club success, he had fed Ken Bates' craving. As the 2000-01 season began, the chairman was demanding the Premiership title, but after three draws, one win and a defeat, the dream was already starting to fade. Those results, added to rumours of unrest among the players, proved too much for Bates. On September 12, 2000, in the week they would have started their Champions League campaign, he decided it was time for Vialli to go. The message was clear – Chelsea had come a long way in a short time, but they had no intention of standing still. ✪ ***HUGH SLEIGHT, deputy editor of MATCH***

"To be in the Champions League quarter-final was a success for us. But perhaps in two years' time only the final will be good enough."

GIANLUCA VIALLI

GAME-BY-GAME FORM GUIDE **1999-2000**

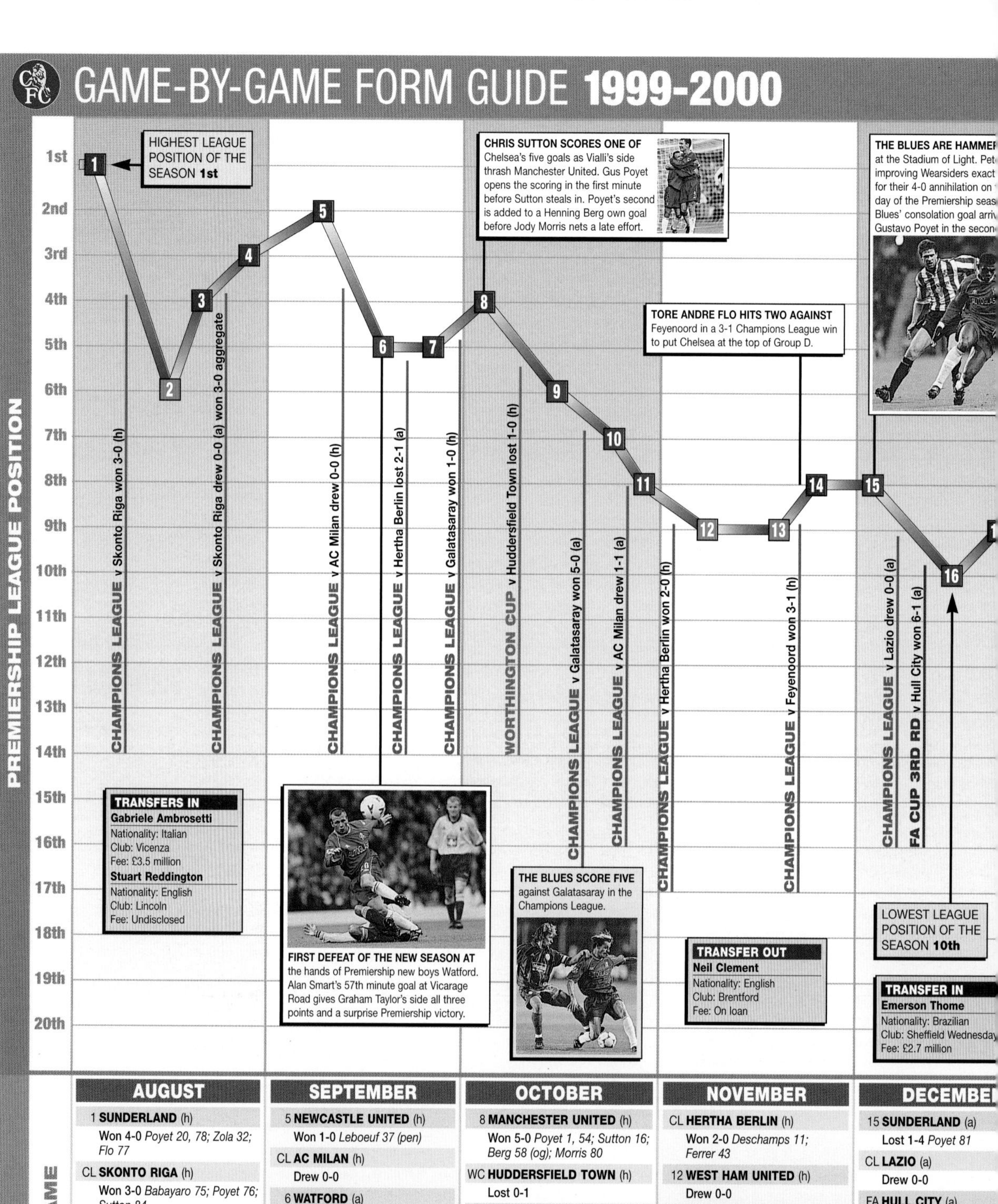

PREMIERSHIP LEAGUE POSITION
1st
2nd
3rd
4th
5th
6th
7th
8th
9th
10th
11th
12th
13th
14th
15th
16th
17th
18th
19th
20th
HIGHEST LEAGUE POSITION OF THE SEASON **1st**
CHAMPIONS LEAGUE v Skonto Riga won 3-0 (h)
CHAMPIONS LEAGUE v Skonto Riga drew 0-0 (a) won 3-0 aggregate
CHAMPIONS LEAGUE v AC Milan drew 0-0 (h)
CHAMPIONS LEAGUE v Hertha Berlin lost 2-1 (a)
CHAMPIONS LEAGUE v Galatasaray won 1-0 (h)
WORTHINGTON CUP v Huddersfield Town lost 1-0 (h)
CHAMPIONS LEAGUE v Galatasaray won 5-0 (a)
CHAMPIONS LEAGUE v AC Milan drew 1-1 (a)
CHAMPIONS LEAGUE v Hertha Berlin won 2-0 (h)
CHAMPIONS LEAGUE v Feyenoord won 3-1 (h)
CHAMPIONS LEAGUE v Lazio drew 0-0 (a)
FA CUP 3RD RD v Hull City won 6-1 (a)
CHRIS SUTTON SCORES ONE OF Chelsea's five goals as Vialli's side thrash Manchester United. Gus Poyet opens the scoring in the first minute before Sutton steals in. Poyet's second is added to a Henning Berg own goal before Jody Morris nets a late effort.
THE BLUES ARE HAMME at the Stadium of Light. Pet improving Wearsiders exact for their 4-0 annihilation on day of the Premiership seas Blues' consolation goal arriv Gustavo Poyet in the secon
TORE ANDRE FLO HITS TWO AGAINST Feyenoord in a 3-1 Champions League win to put Chelsea at the top of Group D.
TRANSFERS IN
Gabriele Ambrosetti
Nationality: Italian
Club: Vicenza
Fee: £3.5 million
Stuart Reddington
Nationality: English
Club: Lincoln
Fee: Undisclosed
FIRST DEFEAT OF THE NEW SEASON AT the hands of Premiership new boys Watford. Alan Smart's 57th minute goal at Vicarage Road gives Graham Taylor's side all three points and a surprise Premiership victory.
THE BLUES SCORE FIVE against Galatasaray in the Champions League.
TRANSFER OUT
Neil Clement
Nationality: English
Club: Brentford
Fee: On loan
LOWEST LEAGUE POSITION OF THE SEASON **10th**
TRANSFER IN
Emerson Thome
Nationality: Brazilian
Club: Sheffield Wednesday
Fee: £2.7 million

GAME-BY-GAME

AUGUST

1 **SUNDERLAND** (h)
Won 4-0 *Poyet 20, 78; Zola 32; Flo 77*

CL **SKONTO RIGA** (h)
Won 3-0 *Babayaro 75; Poyet 76; Sutton 84*

2 **LEICESTER CITY** (a)
Drew 2-2 *Wise 48; Sinclair 90 (og)*

3 **ASTON VILLA** (h)
Won 1-0 *Ehiogu 52 (og)*

CL **SKONTO RIGA** (a)
Drew 0-0

4 **WIMBLEDON** (a)
Won 1-0 *Petrescu 78*

SEPTEMBER

5 **NEWCASTLE UNITED** (h)
Won 1-0 *Leboeuf 37 (pen)*

CL **AC MILAN** (h)
Drew 0-0

6 **WATFORD** (a)
Lost 0-1

CL **HERTHA BERLIN** (a)
Lost 1-2 *Leboeuf 86 (pen)*

7 **MIDDLESBROUGH** (a)
Won 1-0 *Lambourde 55*

CL **GALATASARAY** (h)
Won 1-0 *Petrescu 55*

OCTOBER

8 **MANCHESTER UNITED** (h)
Won 5-0 *Poyet 1, 54; Sutton 16; Berg 58 (og); Morris 80*

WC **HUDDERSFIELD TOWN** (h)
Lost 0-1

9 **LIVERPOOL** (a)
Lost 0-1

CL **GALATASARAY** (a)
Won 5-0 *Flo 31, 48; Zola 54; Wise 79; Ambrosetti 88*

10 **ARSENAL** (h)
Lost 2-3 *Flo 39; Petrescu 51*

CL **AC MILAN** (a)
Drew 1-1 *Wise 77*

11 **DERBY COUNTY** (a)
Lost 1-3 *Leboeuf 10*

NOVEMBER

CL **HERTHA BERLIN** (h)
Won 2-0 *Deschamps 11; Ferrer 43*

12 **WEST HAM UNITED** (h)
Drew 0-0

13 **EVERTON** (a)
Drew 1-1 *Flo 90*

CL **FEYENOORD** (h)
Won 3-1 *Babayaro 45; Flo 67, 86*

14 **BRADFORD CITY** (h)
Won 1-0 *Flo 15*

DECEMBE

15 **SUNDERLAND** (a)
Lost 1-4 *Poyet 81*

CL **LAZIO** (a)
Drew 0-0

FA **HULL CITY** (a)
Won 6-1 *Poyet 8, 48, 5 Sutton 30, Di Matteo 4*

16 **LEEDS UNITED** (h)
Lost 0-2

17 **SOUTHAMPTON** (a)
Won 2-1 *Flo 18, 43*

18 **SHEFFIELD WEDNES**
Won 3-0 *Wise 32; Flo 3 Morris 84*

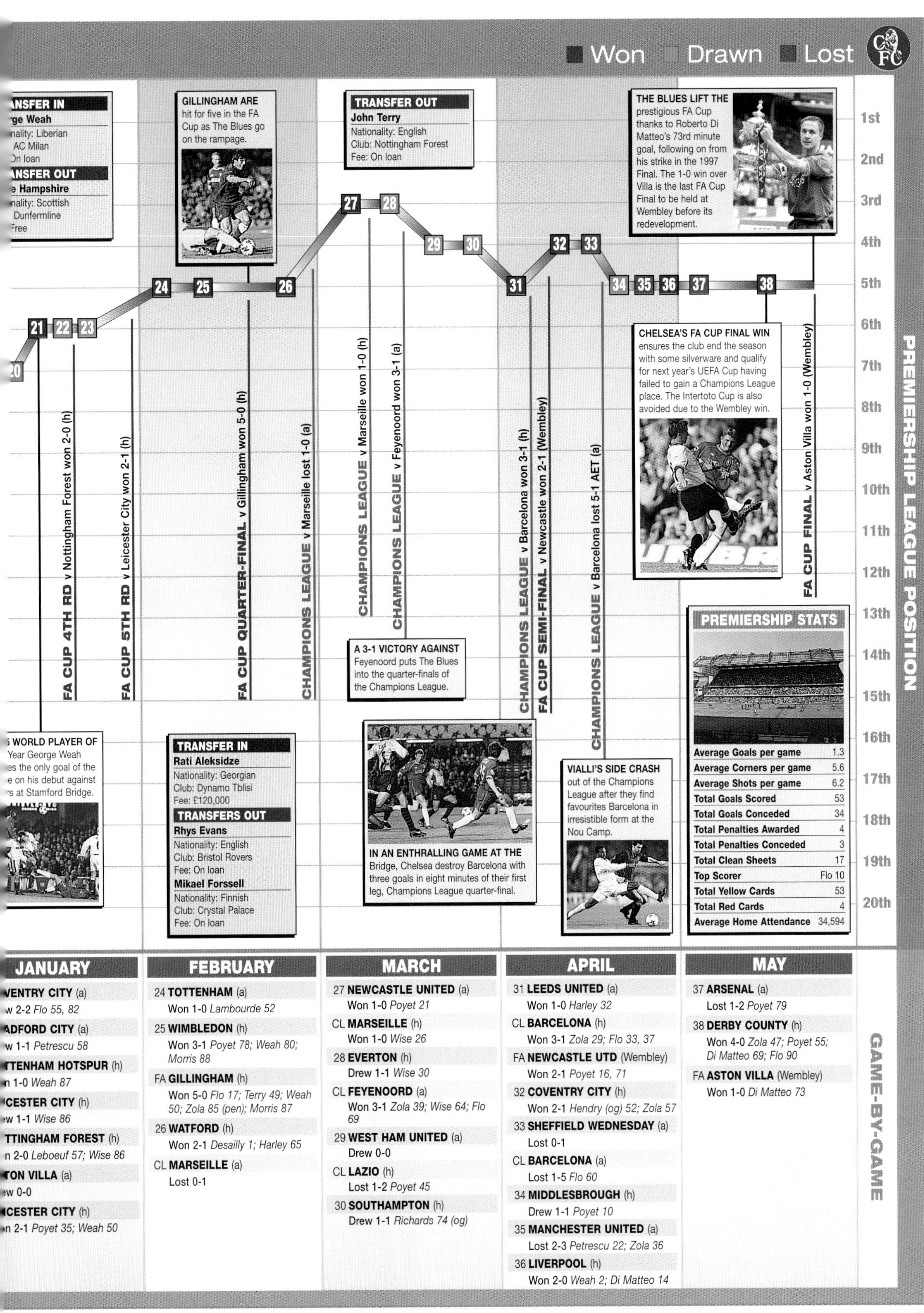
Won Drawn Lost
CFC
…NSFER IN
…ge Weah
…nality: Liberian
… AC Milan
…On loan
…NSFER OUT
…e Hampshire
…nality: Scottish
… Dunfermline
…Free
GILLINGHAM ARE hit for five in the FA Cup as The Blues go on the rampage.
TRANSFER OUT
John Terry
Nationality: English
Club: Nottingham Forest
Fee: On loan
THE BLUES LIFT THE prestigious FA Cup thanks to Roberto Di Matteo's 73rd minute goal, following on from his strike in the 1997 Final. The 1-0 win over Villa is the last FA Cup Final to be held at Wembley before its redevelopment.
1st
2nd
3rd
4th
5th
6th
7th
8th
9th
10th
11th
12th
13th
14th
15th
16th
17th
18th
19th
20th
20 21 22 23 24 25 26 27 28 29 30 31 32 33 34 35 36 37 38
FA CUP 4TH RD v Nottingham Forest won 2-0 (h)
FA CUP 5TH RD v Leicester City won 2-1 (h)
FA CUP QUARTER-FINAL v Gillingham won 5-0 (h)
CHAMPIONS LEAGUE v Marseille lost 1-0 (a)
CHAMPIONS LEAGUE v Marseille won 1-0 (h)
CHAMPIONS LEAGUE v Feyenoord won 3-1 (a)
CHAMPIONS LEAGUE v Barcelona won 3-1 (h)
FA CUP SEMI-FINAL v Newcastle won 2-1 (Wembley)
CHAMPIONS LEAGUE v Barcelona lost 5-1 AET (a)
FA CUP FINAL v Aston Villa won 1-0 (Wembley)
CHELSEA'S FA CUP FINAL WIN ensures the club end the season with some silverware and qualify for next year's UEFA Cup having failed to gain a Champions League place. The Intertoto Cup is also avoided due to the Wembley win.
PREMIERSHIP LEAGUE POSITION
A 3-1 VICTORY AGAINST Feyenoord puts The Blues into the quarter-finals of the Champions League.
…S WORLD PLAYER OF … Year George Weah …es the only goal of the …e on his debut against …s at Stamford Bridge.
TRANSFER IN
Rati Aleksidze
Nationality: Georgian
Club: Dynamo Tblisi
Fee: £120,000
TRANSFERS OUT
Rhys Evans
Nationality: English
Club: Bristol Rovers
Fee: On loan
Mikael Forssell
Nationality: Finnish
Club: Crystal Palace
Fee: On loan
IN AN ENTHRALLING GAME AT THE Bridge, Chelsea destroy Barcelona with three goals in eight minutes of their first leg, Champions League quarter-final.
VIALLI'S SIDE CRASH out of the Champions League after they find favourites Barcelona in irresistible form at the Nou Camp.
PREMIERSHIP STATS
Average Goals per game 1.3
Average Corners per game 5.6
Average Shots per game 6.2
Total Goals Scored 53
Total Goals Conceded 34
Total Penalties Awarded 4
Total Penalties Conceded 3
Total Clean Sheets 17
Top Scorer Flo 10
Total Yellow Cards 53
Total Red Cards 4
Average Home Attendance 34,594
JANUARY
…VENTRY CITY (a)
…w 2-2 Flo 55, 82
…ADFORD CITY (a)
…w 1-1 Petrescu 58
…TTENHAM HOTSPUR (h)
…n 1-0 Weah 87
…CESTER CITY (h)
…w 1-1 Wise 86
…TTINGHAM FOREST (h)
…n 2-0 Leboeuf 57; Wise 86
…TON VILLA (a)
…w 0-0
…CESTER CITY (h)
…n 2-1 Poyet 35; Weah 50
FEBRUARY
24 TOTTENHAM (a)
Won 1-0 Lambourde 52
25 WIMBLEDON (h)
Won 3-1 Poyet 78; Weah 80; Morris 88
FA GILLINGHAM (h)
Won 5-0 Flo 17; Terry 49; Weah 50; Zola 85 (pen); Morris 87
26 WATFORD (h)
Won 2-1 Desailly 1; Harley 65
CL MARSEILLE (a)
Lost 0-1
MARCH
27 NEWCASTLE UNITED (a)
Won 1-0 Poyet 21
CL MARSEILLE (h)
Won 1-0 Wise 26
28 EVERTON (h)
Drew 1-1 Wise 30
CL FEYENOORD (a)
Won 3-1 Zola 39; Wise 64; Flo 69
29 WEST HAM UNITED (a)
Drew 0-0
CL LAZIO (h)
Lost 1-2 Poyet 45
30 SOUTHAMPTON (h)
Drew 1-1 Richards 74 (og)
APRIL
31 LEEDS UNITED (a)
Won 1-0 Harley 32
CL BARCELONA (h)
Won 3-1 Zola 29; Flo 33, 37
FA NEWCASTLE UTD (Wembley)
Won 2-1 Poyet 16, 71
32 COVENTRY CITY (h)
Won 2-1 Hendry (og) 52; Zola 57
33 SHEFFIELD WEDNESDAY (a)
Lost 0-1
CL BARCELONA (a)
Lost 1-5 Flo 60
34 MIDDLESBROUGH (h)
Drew 1-1 Poyet 10
35 MANCHESTER UNITED (a)
Lost 2-3 Petrescu 22; Zola 36
36 LIVERPOOL (h)
Won 2-0 Weah 2; Di Matteo 14
MAY
37 ARSENAL (a)
Lost 1-2 Poyet 79
38 DERBY COUNTY (h)
Won 4-0 Zola 47; Poyet 55; Di Matteo 69; Flo 90
FA ASTON VILLA (Wembley)
Won 1-0 Di Matteo 73
GAME-BY-GAME

AUGUST

START OF MONTH **1st** END OF MONTH **3rd**

"We know how well we have to play, and with the players Gianluca has brought into the club we're optimistic that we can challenge for the title this season." Gianfranco Zola

CHELSEA BEGAN THE 1999-2000 CAMPAIGN FULL OF CONFIDENCE. The club had finished the previous season in third place in the Premiership, having lost only three out of their 38 league games – an impressive record which only champions Manchester United could equal. Gianluca Vialli had added to his squad in the summer by capturing sought-after forward Chris Sutton, who had been tempted away from relegated Blackburn Rovers by the prospect of silverware. Many observers saw him as the missing piece in the Chelsea jigsaw. There was an abundance of skilful attacking players at the club, but not a natural goalscorer. Sutton, who had been a prolific striker throughout his career, seemed to fit the bill and Blues fans hoped he would bring the championship to Stamford Bridge for the first time in 45 years.

The new season began with a baptism of fire for promoted Sunderland as Chelsea recorded a convincing 4-0 win. In this kind of form The Blues were expected to demolish Latvian minnows Skonta Riga in the qualifying round of the Champions League. It was a tougher tie than expected, with Gianluca Vialli's side struggling to a 3-0 aggregate win which flattered the Londoners, but at least Chelsea had qualified for the group stages of the competition.

The Blues knew they had to remain focused on their league form if they wanted to win the Premiership title, and the first month of the new season went almost exactly to plan with two 1-0 victories against Aston Villa and Wimbledon and a hard-fought 2-2 draw against Leicester City. The draw at Filbert Street was the only game in August where Chelsea dropped any points, representing a highly encouraging start to the new campaign for the highly-fancied London side. But Gianluca Vialli refused to rest on his laurels, bringing the talented Vicenza winger Gabriele Ambrosetti to Stamford Bridge for £3.5 million to provide more options on the left-hand side of midfield.

THE GAMES

Aug. 7 v **Sunderland** (h)

Aug. 11 v **Skonto Riga** (h)

Aug. 14 v **Leicester** (a)

Aug. 21 v **Aston Villa** (h)

Aug. 25 v **Skonto Riga** (a)

Aug. 28 v **Wimbledon** (a)

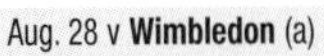

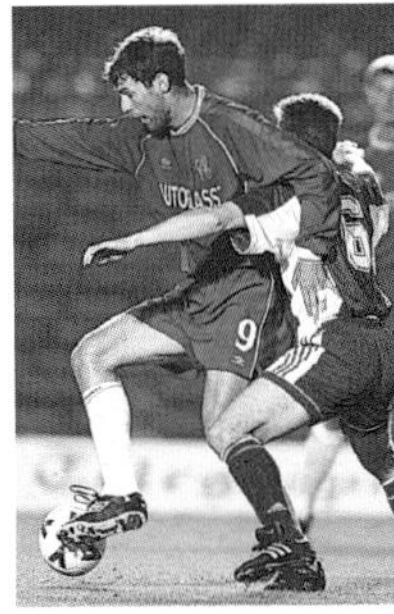

TRANSFERS IN

Gabriele Ambrosetti
Position: **Midfield**
Fee: **£3.5 million**
From: **Vicenza**

Stuart Reddington
Position: **Defender**
Fee: **Undisclosed**
From: **Lincoln**

TRANSFERS OUT

None

MATCH facts

Matchman Of The Month

DAN PETRESCU
Average Rating: 7.50

Chelsea	(2) **4**
Sunderland	(0) **0**

Competition: **FA Carling Premiership**

Date: **Saturday August 7, 1999**

Attendance: **34,831**

Referee: **M Riley** (Leeds) 7

THE GAME: Chelsea ran out convincing 4-0 winners against promoted Sunderland on the first day of the new season, but it could and perhaps should have reached double figures at Stamford Bridge. Only some wayward finishing – in contrast to their fluent, decisive attacking play – spared Peter Reid's side from a much heavier defeat. Record signing Chris Sutton was the main culprit, spurning two gilt-edged chances either side of half-time, but his strike partner Gianfranco Zola was in inspired form. The diminutive Italian scored Chelsea's second goal and set up Gus Poyet brilliantly for the fourth, which even at this stage was a serious contender for Goal Of The Season. Chelsea's title challenge had started with a bang, and judging by this performance, they certainly had the credentials.

CHELSEA GOALS: Poyet *(20 mins):* A corner from Wise was headed in emphatically by Poyet; **Zola** *(32 mins):* Struck home neatly following Poyet's throughball; **Flo** *(77 mins):* A clever interchange between Zola and Petrescu left Flo to finish with a fine header; **Poyet** *(78 mins):* Zola flicked a pass over the defence for Poyet to hammer in a jumping scissor-kick.

MATCH RATING: ★★★★ **LEAGUE POSITION: 1st**

CHELSEA	
de Goey	6
Ferrer	6
Desailly	8
Leboeuf	8
Le Saux (booked)	7
Booked: 6 mins (foul)	
Petrescu	7
Subbed: 89 mins (Di Matteo)	
Wise	7
Deschamps	6
Poyet (goal) (goal)	8
Goals: 20, 78 mins; Subbed: 79 mins (Babayaro)	
Sutton	5
Subbed: 69 mins (Flo)	
Zola (goal)	☆ 9
Goal: 32 mins	
sub: *Flo* (goal)	8
Goal: 77 mins	
sub: *Babayaro*	
sub: *Di Matteo*	

Subs not used: *Hogh, Hitchcock.*

SUNDERLAND	
Sorensen	☆ 8
Makin (booked)	6
Booked: 26 mins (foul)	
Bould	6
Subbed: 67 mins (Fredgaard)	
Butler, P	5
Gray	8
Summerbee	7
Ball	6
Rae (booked)	5
Booked: 8 mins (foul)	
Lumsden	5
Subbed: 46 mins (McCann)	
Quinn (booked)	6
Booked: 50 mins (foul)	
Phillips	6
sub: *McCann*	5
sub: *Fredgaard*	7

Subs not used: *Helmer, Dichio, Marriott.*

MATCH FACTS		
Shots On Target		
Chelsea	8-5	Sunderland
Shots Off Target		
Chelsea	5-6	Sunderland
Hit Woodwork		
Chelsea	1-0	Sunderland
Corners		
Chelsea	5-5	Sunderland

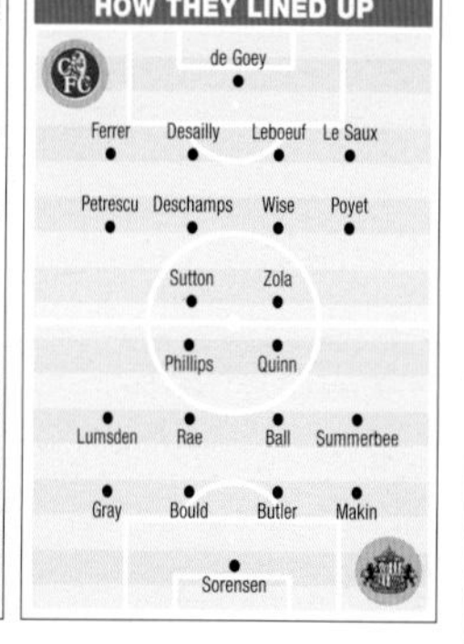

HOW THEY LINED UP

de Goey
Ferrer, Desailly, Leboeuf, Le Saux
Petrescu, Deschamps, Wise, Poyet
Sutton, Zola

Phillips, Quinn
Lumsden, Rae, Ball, Summerbee
Gray, Bould, Butler, Makin
Sorensen

Sealed with a kiss – Poyet celebrates with Zola after scoring a memorable goal.

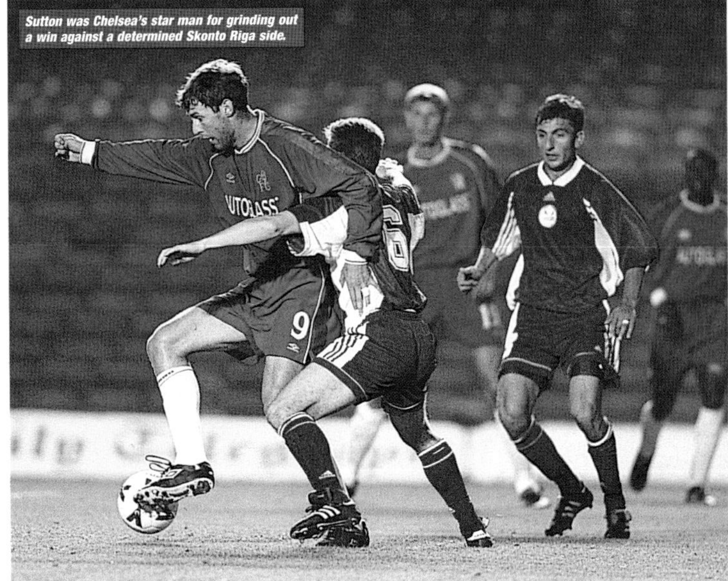

Sutton was Chelsea's star man for grinding out a win against a determined Skonto Riga side.

Chelsea (0) 3
Skonto Riga (0) 0

Competition: **Champs Lge Qual 1st Leg**

Date: **Wednesday August 11, 1999**

Attendance: **22,043**

Referee: **U Meier** (Switzerland) 7

Game 2

THE GAME: Chris Sutton got off the mark for his new club, scoring the 100th goal of his career as Chelsea moved a step closer to the Champions League group stages. The Latvian side were reduced to ten men on 34 minutes and decided to hold on for a draw. The Riga 'keeper thwarted everything the home side could throw at him until Celestine Babayaro broke the deadlock in the 75th minute. The game suddenly opened up after this, with Chelsea adding two further goals before the end to give them a crucial 3-0 lead for the second leg.

CHELSEA GOALS: Babayaro *(75 mins):* Flo chested down for Babayaro to sweep in a low drive; **Poyet** *(76 mins):* Curled home a sweet 20-yard effort; **Sutton** *(84 mins):* Turned sharply and scored from just inside the box following Leboeuf's cross.

MATCH RATING: ★★★ **LEAGUE POSITION: 5th**

"This is one of the most important games in Chelsea's history. Now we have the opportunity to join in with the really big boys of European football." GIANLUCA VIALLI

MATCH FACTS

Shots On Target		
Chelsea	14-1	Skonto Riga
Shots Off Target		
Chelsea	9-5	Skonto Riga
Hit Woodwork		
Chelsea	0-0	Skonto Riga
Corners		
Chelsea	10-0	Skonto Riga

HOW THEY LINED UP

Chelsea: de Goey; Ferrer, Desailly, Leboeuf, Le Saux; Petrescu, Deschamps, Wise, Poyet; Zola, Sutton

Skonto Riga: Miholaps, Chaladze; Rubins, Astafjevs, Bleidelis, Rekhviashvili; Tereskinas, Silagadze, Zemlinskis, Laizans; Kolinko

CHELSEA

Player	Rating
de Goey	6
Petrescu *Subbed: 76 mins (Goldbaek)*	6
Leboeuf	7
Desailly	7
Deschamps *Subbed: 65 mins (Babayaro)*	7
Poyet ⚽ *Goal: 76 mins*	7
Zola *Subbed: 65 mins (Flo)*	6
Sutton ⚽ ▯ *Goal: 84 mins; Booked: 90 mins (unsporting behaviour)*	☆8
Wise	7
Le Saux	6
Ferrer	6
sub: Babayaro ⚽ *Goal: 75 mins*	7
sub: Flo	7
sub: Goldbaek	

Subs not used: *Hogh, Hitchcock, Morris, Forssell.*

SKONTO RIGA

Player	Rating
Kolinko	☆8
Silagadze	7
Zemlinskis	7
Rekhviashvili	7
Bleidelis	6
Rubins	7
Miholaps ▯ *Subbed: 77 mins (Menteshashbili)*	6
Laizans	6
Tereskinas ■ *Sent-off: 34 mins (serious foul play)*	4
Astafjevs	6
Chaladze *Subbed: 40 mins (Blagonadezdins)*	6
sub: Blagonadezdins	6
sub: Menteshashbili	

Subs not used: *Stepamous, Babicevs, Piedels, Kolesnicenko, Olsanskis.*

THIS WEEK...

IN THE NEWS

CHELSEA: The Blues' opening day performance against Sunderland is so impressive that media experts are already tipping them for the title... Gianluca Villa admits that Chris Sutton came to ask him for help with his finishing after the £10 million man missed a number of chances on his debut.

PREMIERSHIP: Frank Lampard and **Rio Ferdinand** sign new deals at West Ham that will keep them at the club until 2005... Arsenal sign Croatian star striker **Davor Suker** for £2.5 million... Spurs manager George Graham brings Liverpool's **Oyvind Leonhardsen** to White Hart Lane for £2.75 million... Magpies boss Ruud Gullit is considering playing again after Newcastle lose their first two league games... Gary Lineker is lined up as the new presenter of 'Match Of The Day' after Des Lynam is tempted by a big-money offer from ITV.

THE FINAL SCORE!

AUGUST 7		
Arsenal	2-1	Leicester
Chelsea	4-0	Sunderland
Coventry	0-1	**Southampton**
Leeds	0-0	Derby
Middlesbrough	0-1	**Bradford**
Newcastle	0-1	**Aston Villa**
Sheff. Wed.	1-2	**Liverpool**
Watford	2-3	**Wimbledon**
West Ham	1-0	Tottenham
AUGUST 8		
Everton	1-1	Man. United
AUGUST 9		
Tottenham	3-1	Newcastle
AUGUST 10		
Derby	1-2	**Arsenal**
Sunderland	2-0	Watford
Wimbledon	2-3	**Middlesbrough**
AUGUST 11		
Aston Villa	3-0	Everton
Leicester	1-0	Coventry
Man. United	4-0	Sheff. Wed.
Southampton	0-3	**Leeds**

TOP OF THE PREMIERSHIP

	P	W	D	L	Pts
1. Arsenal	2	2	0	0	6
2. Aston Villa	2	2	0	0	6
3. Leeds	2	1	1	0	4
5. Chelsea	1	1	0	0	3

Wise grabbed the first equaliser, but Sinclair's own goal decided it.

Leicester City	(1)	**2**
Chelsea	(0)	**2**

Competition: **FA Carling Premiership**

Date: **Saturday August 14, 1999**

Attendance: **21,068**

Referee: **S Lodge** (Barnsley) 7

THE GAME: Chelsea dramatically snatched a draw from the jaws of defeat in this thrilling game at Filbert Street. Leicester thought the three points were safe when Muzzy Izzet scored a last-minute penalty, but Gianluca Vialli's side refused to be beaten and forced an injury-time equaliser courtesy of an own goal from ex-Chelsea defender Frank Sinclair – his second in a week. The Blues, who left out Chris Sutton, Marcel Desailly and Didier Deschamps, went behind after only ten minutes and had to wait until early in the second half before Dennis Wise restored parity. Chelsea took control of the game after that but were denied by Tim Flowers in the Leicester goal. Izzet's penalty looked to have won it, but The Blues came away with a point after Sinclair's timely intervention.

LEICESTER GOALS: Heskey *(10 mins):* Heskey crashed a half-volley beyond de Goey from just inside Chelsea's box; **Izzet** *(penalty 90 mins):* Ferrer was adjudged to have brought down Heskey and Izzet stepped up to score from the spot.

CHELSEA GOALS: Wise *(48 mins):* Ferrer crossed for Wise, who timed his run superbly to send a firm header into the net; **Sinclair** *(own goal 90 mins):* Poyet's dangerous cross into the crowded penalty area was headed into his own net by Sinclair.

MATCH RATING: ★★★★ **LEAGUE POSITION: 6th**

> **"Chris came to ask me for help with his finishing. I didn't think he did that badly against Sunderland, but of course he now has that £10 million price tag hanging over him."**
> **GIANLUCA VIALLI**

MATCH FACTS

Shots On Target		
Leicester	8-8	Chelsea
Shots Off Target		
Leicester	8-11	Chelsea
Hit Woodwork		
Leicester	1-2	Chelsea
Corners		
Leicester	4-10	Chelsea

HOW THEY LINED UP

Flowers
Sinclair, Elliott, Taggart
Impey, Savage, Lennon, Izzet, Guppy
Cottee, Heskey

Zola, Flo
Babayaro, Poyet, Wise, Petrescu
Le Saux, Leboeuf, Hogh, Ferrer
de Goey

LEICESTER CITY

Player	Rating
Flowers ☆	8
Sinclair ⚽ *Own Goal: 90 mins*	6
Taggart *Subbed: 85 mins (Gilchrist)*	6
Izzet ⚽ *Goal: 90 mins*	7
Lennon ▯ *Booked: 47 mins (foul)*	7
Heskey ⚽ *Goal: 10 mins*	7
Guppy	7
Savage	6
Elliott ▯ *Booked: 50 mins (foul)*	7
Impey	7
Cottee *Subbed: 72 mins (Marshall)*	6
sub: Gilchrist	6
sub: Marshall	6

Subs not used: Arphexad, Oakes, Zagorakis.

CHELSEA

Player	Rating
de Goey	7
Petrescu ▯ *Booked: 47 mins (foul)*	7
Babayaro ▯ *Booked: 85 mins (foul)*	7
Hogh	6
Leboeuf	7
Poyet ▯ ☆ *Booked: 65 mins (foul)*	8
Wise ▯ ⚽ *Booked: 2 mins (foul); Goal: 48 mins*	7
Le Saux *Subbed: 23 mins (Goldbaek)*	6
Ferrer ▯ *Booked: 90 mins (foul)*	6
Flo	6
Zola *Subbed: 69 mins (Sutton)*	6
sub: Goldbaek	7
sub: Sutton	6

Subs not used: Nicholls, Cudicini, Percassi.

Luckily for Chelsea, it was Ugo Ehiogu's turn to score past his own 'keeper.

Chelsea (0) 1

Aston Villa (0) 0

Competition: **FA Carling Premiership**

Date: **Saturday August 21, 1999**

Attendance: **35,071**

Referee: **N Barry** (Scunthorpe) 7

THE GAME: Chelsea extended their hoodoo over Aston Villa with victory at Stamford Bridge, but The Blues were made to work hard for their three points in an exciting encounter. The battle in midfield was particularly competitive, with five yellow cards issued in the first half alone. In the 27th minute Chelsea had a penalty appeal turned down by the referee when Villa's Ugo Ehiogu felled Gianfranco Zola with an awkward challenge from behind. The spot-kick wasn't given and Poyet and Sutton were booked for their protests, but the home fans felt justice was done in the 51st minute when Ehiogu got the last touch on Dan Petrescu's drive to give Chelsea a deserved win.

CHELSEA GOAL: **Ehiogu** *(own goal 51 mins):* The Villa man edged Petrescu's low, right foot drive past his own 'keeper.

MATCH RATING: ★★★ **LEAGUE POSITION: 4th**

"We know how well we have to play to win the title, and with the players Gianluca has brought into the club this year, we are optimistic that we can challenge for the title without falling away this season." GIANFRANCO ZOLA

CHELSEA	
de Goey	6
Petrescu	8
Subbed: 76 mins (Goldbaek)	
Babayaro	7
Leboeuf	6
Booked: 34 mins (foul)	
Desailly	6
Poyet	5
Booked: 16 mins (foul)	
Sutton	6
Booked: 21 mins (foul); Subbed: 76 mins (Flo)	
Wise	6
Ferrer	7
Morris	7
Zola	7
Subbed: 86 mins (Ambrosetti)	
sub: *Goldbaek*	
sub: *Flo*	
sub: *Ambrosetti*	
Subs not used: *Hogh, Cudicini.*	

ASTON VILLA	
James	6
Wright	7
Southgate	6
Ehiogu ⚽	7
Own goal: 51 mins	
Taylor	6
Booked: 17 mins (foul)	
Dublin	6
Thompson	6
Booked: 59 mins (foul); Subbed: 70 mins (Merson)	
Joachim	6
Hendrie	☆8
Booked: 28 mins (foul)	
Delaney	6
Calderwood	6
Subbed: 76 mins (Stone)	
sub: *Merson*	6
sub: *Stone*	
Subbed: 88 mins (Draper)	
sub: *Draper*	
Subs not used: *Oakes, Barry.*	

MATCH FACTS

	Chelsea	Aston Villa
Shots On Target	4	1
Shots Off Target	9	3
Hit Woodwork	0	0
Corners	1	3

HOW THEY LINED UP

de Goey

Ferrer, Leboeuf, Desailly, Babayaro

Petrescu, Wise, Morris, Poyet

Sutton, Zola

Dublin, Joachim

Hendrie, Taylor, Thompson

Wright, Calderwood, Ehiogu, Southgate, Delaney

James

THIS WEEK...

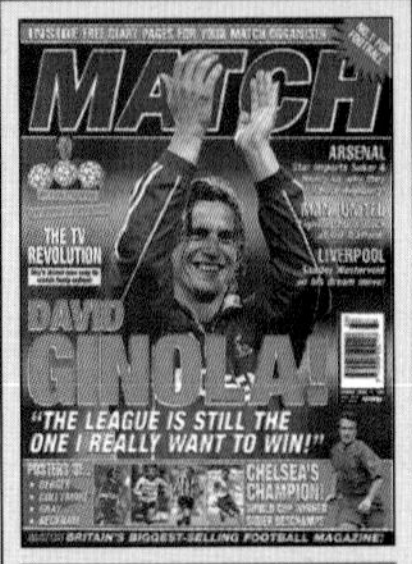

IN THE NEWS

CHELSEA: Chris Sutton may have scored his first Blues goal against Skonto Riga in the Champions League qualifier, but the press still prefer to focus on the chances he missed in the game... Gianluca Vialli adds to his squad by signing midfielder **Gabriele Ambrosetti** for £3.5 million from Vicenza, adding pace to an attack full of skill but criticised for a lack of speed.

PREMIERSHIP: Liverpool midfield ace **Dietmar Hamann** is out for two months after picking up an injury on the opening day... Aston Villa are heading the race for the Wolves and Republic Of Ireland striker **Robbie Keane**... Everton's **Francis Jeffers** withdraws his transfer request at Everton after making up with Goodison manager Walter Smith... Sunderland striker **Kevin Phillips** has set himself a target of 20 goals for the season after a brace against Watford.

THE FINAL SCORE!

AUGUST 14		
Bradford	1-1	Sheff. Wed
Derby	1-3	**Middlesbrough**
Leicester	2-2	Chelsea
Liverpool	0-1	**Watford**
Man. United	2-0	Leeds
Sunderland	0-0	Arsenal
Tottenham	3-2	Everton
Wimbledon	1-1	Coventry
AUGUST 15		
Southampton	4-2	Newcastle
AUGUST 16		
Aston Villa	2-2	West Ham
AUGUST 21		
Chelsea	1-0	Aston Villa
Coventry	2-0	Derby
Everton	4-1	Southampton
Leeds	2-1	Sunderland
Middlesbrough	1-0	Liverpool
Newcastle	3-3	Wimbledon
Sheff. Wed.	1-2	**Tottenham**
Watford	1-0	Bradford
West Ham	2-1	Leicester

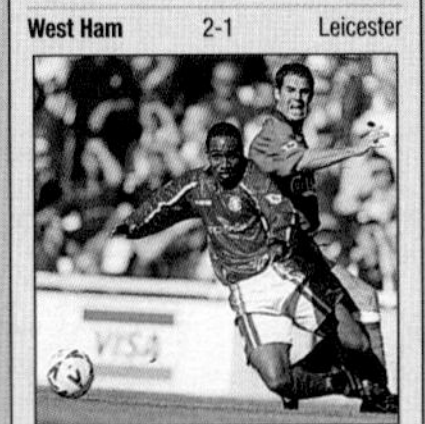

TOP OF THE PREMIERSHIP

	P	W	D	L	Pts
1. Tottenham	4	3	0	1	9
2. Middlesbro	4	3	0	1	9
3. Man. United	3	2	1	0	7
4. Chelsea	**3**	**2**	**1**	**0**	**7**

Bjarne Goldbaek made a rare start in the 0-0 draw in Latvia.

Skonto Riga	(0) **0**
Chelsea	(0) **0**

Chelsea win 3-0 on aggregate.

Competition: **Champs Lge Qual 2nd Leg**

Date: **Wednesday August 25, 1999**

Attendance: **5,600**

Referee: **G Veissiere** (France) 6

THE GAME: Chelsea successfully negotiated a tricky fixture in Latvia to ensure a lucrative place in the group stages of the Champions League, which was potentially worth £20 million to the club. In a professional performance, Gianluca Vialli's side dominated the entire first half and were only denied a goal by a combination of inspired goalkeeping and wayward finishing. The second half was a different story. Riga threw everything at The Blues in an attempt to get back into the tie, but a defence that was marshalled outstandingly by Marcel Desailly held firm under pressure and Ed de Goey was in commanding form in the Chelsea goal. As the Latvians realised the tie was beyond them, the pace of the game slowed, allowing Gianluca Vialli to give Nicholls, Cudicini and Harley a taste of European football. A new chapter in Chelsea's history awaited as they embarked on the first ever Champions League campaign, with the club's status in European football about to change dramatically.

MATCH RATING: ★★ **LEAGUE POSITION: 4th**

"I am proud that we have made history, but it will be tough in the Champions League. We have some exciting times to look forward to and though we won't be the favourites, we have a good chance." GIANLUCA VIALLI

MATCH FACTS

Shots On Target		
Skonto Riga	3-4	Chelsea
Shots Off Target		
Skonto Riga	5-7	Chelsea
Hit Woodwork		
Skonto Riga	0-1	Chelsea
Corners		
Skonto Riga	5-3	Chelsea

HOW THEY LINED UP

Kolinko

Laizans, Zemlinskis, Silagadze, Blagonadezdins

Bleidelis, Rekhviashvili, Astafjevs, Rubins

Chaladze, Miholaps

Forssell, Flo

Poyet, Wise, Morris, Goldbaek

Babayaro, Hogh, Desailly, Petrescu

de Goey

SKONTO RIGA

Player	Rating
Kolinko	6
Zemlinskis	6
Silagadze	6
Blagonadezdins	6
Laizans ▯	6
Booked: 57 mins (foul); Subbed: 87 mins (Kolesnicenko)	
Bleidelis	7
Subbed: 74 mins (Menteshashbili)	
Rekhviashvili	7
Astafjevs	7
Rubins	☆8
Chaladze	6
Subbed: 62 mins (Babicevs)	
Miholaps	6
sub: Kolesnicenko	
sub: Menteshashbili	
sub: Babicevs	

Subs not used: *Stepamous, Piedels, Olsanskis, Korgalidze.*

CHELSEA

Player	Rating
de Goey	7
Subbed: 79 mins (Cudicini)	
Petrescu	6
Hogh	6
Babayaro	6
Desailly	☆8
Morris	7
Poyet	6
Subbed: 64 mins (Nicholls)	
Wise	6
Goldbaek	7
Subbed: 83 mins (Harley)	
Forssell	6
Flo	6
sub: Nicholls	6
sub: Cudicini	
sub: Harley	

Subs not used: *Leboeuf, Sutton, Zola, Clement.*

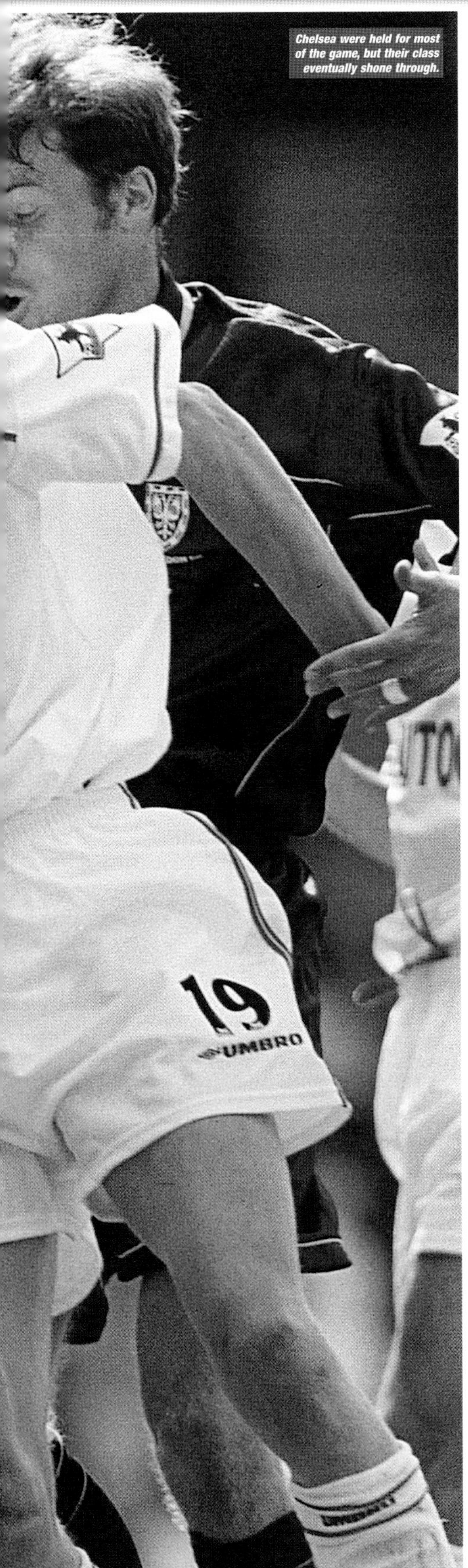

Chelsea were held for most of the game, but their class eventually shone through.

Wimbledon (0) 0

Chelsea (0) 1

Competition: **FA Carling Premiership**

Date: **Saturday August 28, 1999**

Attendance: **22,167**

Referee: **S Dunn** (Bristol) 7

THE GAME: In a match they dominated from start to finish, Chelsea were repeatedly frustrated by a resolute Wimbledon side at Selhurst Park. The three points were vital, but the 1-0 victory didn't reflect their superiority. After having three goals disallowed it looked as if the game would finish goalless, but Dan Petrescu's strike from just outside Wimbledon area's with 12 minutes to go made sure of the victory. Although The Dons rarely tested Ed de Goey in the Chelsea goal, the 'keeper had to save twice from England U-21 striker Carl Cort, who looked dangerous on the rare occasions that Wimbledon threatened.

CHELSEA GOAL: Petrescu *(78 mins):* Controlled Poyet's throughball before firing his shot emphatically past Sullivan and into the net from outside the area.

MATCH RATING: ★★★ **LEAGUE POSITION: 3rd**

> **"Sometimes we are a little bit too nice, too precise on the edge of the box. We want to score great goals all the time instead of concentrating on putting the ball in the back of the net." GIANLUCA VIALLI**

WIMBLEDON	
Sullivan	7
Cunningham	☆ 8
Roberts ▯	6
Booked: 90 mins (violent conduct)	
Thatcher ▯	7
Booked: 90 mins (violent conduct)	
Cort	6
Earle	6
Subbed: 74 mins (Leaburn)	
Gayle	6
Pedersen	5
Subbed: 46 mins (Kimble)	
Hughes	7
Badir	6
Subbed: 65 mins (Euell)	
Andersen	6
sub: Kimble	6
sub: Euell ▯	6
Booked: 82 mins (foul)	
sub: Leaburn	

Subs not used: *Davis, Ainsworth.*

CHELSEA	
de Goey	7
Petrescu ⚽	☆ 8
Goal: 78 mins; Subbed: 80 mins (Ambrosetti)	
Babayaro	7
Leboeuf ▯	7
Booked: 13 mins (foul)	
Desailly	7
Deschamps	8
Subbed: 88 mins (Morris)	
Poyet	8
Wise ▯	8
Booked: 90 mins (violent conduct)	
Ferrer	6
Flo	7
Subbed: 67 mins (Sutton)	
Zola	8
sub: Sutton	6
sub: Ambrosetti	
sub: Morris	

Subs not used: *Hogh, Cudicini.*

MATCH FACTS

Shots On Target		
Wimbledon	3-5	Chelsea

Shots Off Target		
Wimbledon	3-6	Chelsea

Hit Woodwork		
Wimbledon	0-0	Chelsea

Corners		
Wimbledon	1-10	Chelsea

HOW THEY LINED UP

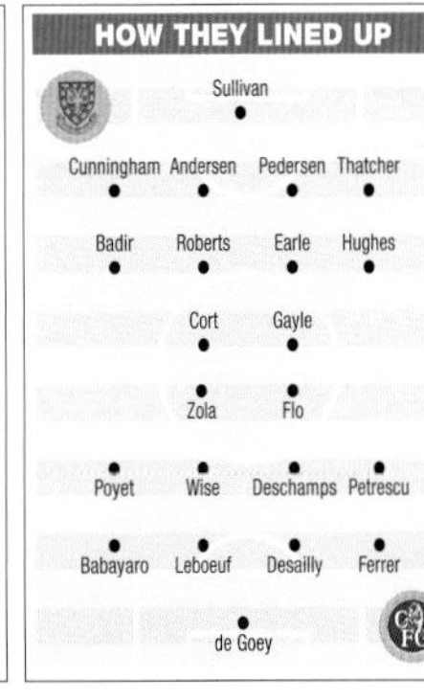

THIS WEEK...

IN THE NEWS

CHELSEA: The 0-0 draw with Skonto Riga means Chelsea will play in the Champions League for the first time ever. The Blues were eligible to play in the tournament in 1956 as English champions, but were advised not to take part by the Football League... The draw for the first group stage puts The Blues in the same pool as Hertha Berlin, Galatasaray and AC Milan.

PREMIERSHIP: Coventry manager Gordon Strachan pips his Midlands rival John Gregory at Aston Villa to sign highly-rated Wolves frontman **Robbie Keane** for £6 million... Tottenham say they have turned down two £21 million offers for **Sol Campbell** from two unnamed Spanish and Italian clubs.

THE FINAL SCORE!

AUGUST 22		
Arsenal	1-2	**Man. United**
AUGUST 23		
Leeds	1-2	**Liverpool**
AUGUST 24		
Middlesbrough	0-3	**Leicester**
Watford	0-1	**Aston Villa**
AUGUST 25		
Arsenal	2-0	Bradford
Coventry	1-2	**Man.United**
Everton	4-0	Wimbledon
Newcastle	1-2	**Sunderland**
Sheff. Wed.	0-2	**Derby**
AUGUST 28		
Aston Villa	1-0	Middlesbrough
Bradford	0-3	**West Ham**
Derby	1-0	Everton
Liverpool	2-0	Arsenal
Southampton	2-0	Sheff.Wed.
Tottenham	1-2	**Leeds**
Wimbledon	0-1	**Chelsea**
AUGUST 29		
Sunderland	1-1	Coventry
AUGUST 30		
Leicester	1-0	Watford
Man. United	5-1	Newcastle

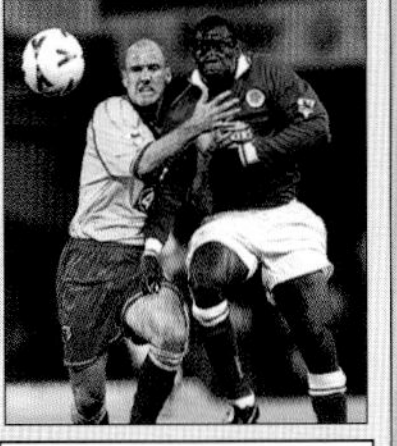

TOP OF THE PREMIERSHIP

	P	W	D	L	Pts
1. Man. United	6	5	1	0	16
2. Aston Villa	6	4	1	1	13
3. Chelsea	**4**	**3**	**1**	**0**	**10**
4. West Ham	4	3	1	0	10

SEPTEMBER

 START OF MONTH **3rd** END OF MONTH **5th** 

"We've done well in Europe before but there is no room for complacency. We need to be tested at the very top level. Doing well in Europe is important." Gianfranco Zola

IF AUGUST PROVED TO BE SOMETHING OF A HONEYMOON PERIOD for Chelsea, September brought home the harsh realities of a side expected to excel at home and abroad. In contrast to the previous month's impressive performances, they struggled to find any kind of consistency in September as the demands of the Champions League in midweek began to affect their Premiership displays at the weekend.

At the beginning of September The Blues faced a Newcastle side which had only won one point from six games and were anchored in 19th place in the Premiership. But The Magpies had been lifted by the arrival of their new manager Bobby Robson, so there was nothing to take for granted and the team gained a professional 1-0 victory thanks to Frank Leboeuf's penalty.

The Blues kicked off their Champions league campaign proper by taking on Italian champions AC Milan at Stamford Bridge. In a hard-fought game, Chelsea proved their European credentials and were unlucky not to grab all three points. The next game in Europe, against German side Hertha Berlin, was a different story, as The Blues were beaten 2-1 in a lacklustre display. It was a disappointing result for the fans, but their heroes soon redeemed themselves by beating Turkish side Galatasaray at the end of the month.

As Chelsea juggled their European and Premiership fixtures, something had to give way, but no one thought it would be at Watford, where a goal from Alan Smart condemned The Blues to their first Premiership defeat of the season. Gianluca Vialli's side soon bounced back though, overcoming Middlesbrough 1-0 despite squandering a number of chances. Two months into the season, niggling injuries to the likes of Gustavo Poyet and Bernard Lambourde were starting to affect the line-up, but there was better news from Roberto Di Matteo, who was back in training after his ankle injury.

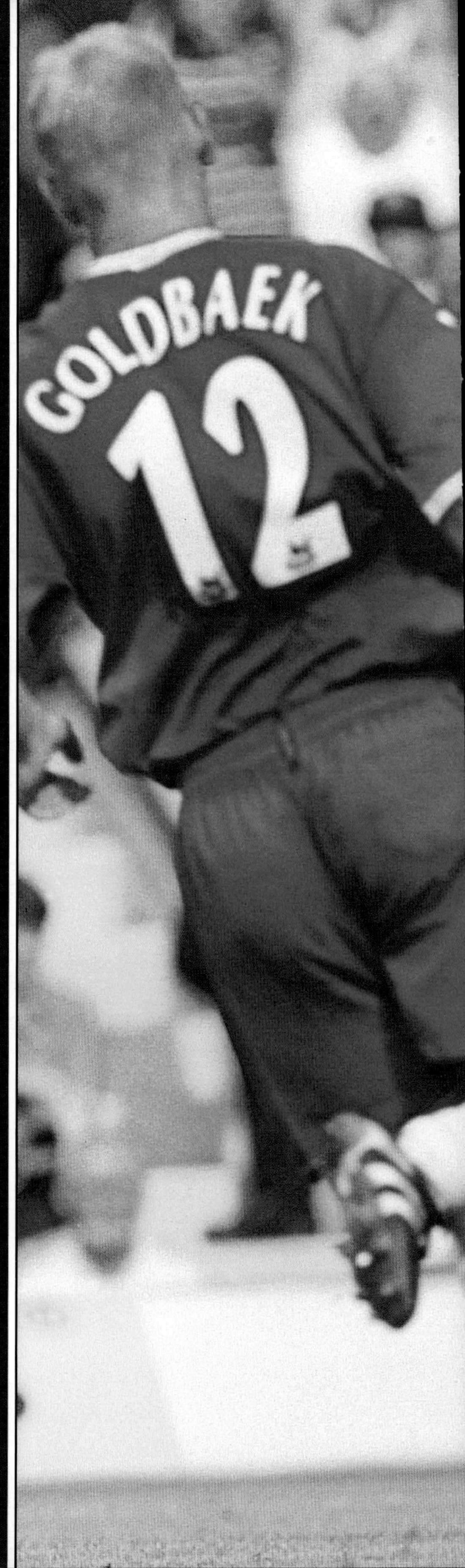

THE GAMES

Sept. 11 v **Newcastle** (h)

Sept. 15 v **AC Milan** (h)

Sept. 18 v **Watford** (a)

Sept. 21 v **Hertha Berlin** (a)

Sept. 25 v **Middlesbrough** (a)

Sept. 28 v **Galatasaray** (h)

TRANSFERS IN

None

TRANSFERS OUT

None

MATCH facts

Matchman Of The Month

MARCEL DESAILLY
Average Rating: 7.33

Morris tries to skip away from Dyer's challenge in Chelsea's 1-0 victory.

FROM THE PAGES OF MATCH

THE NEW RECRUIT

Name: **Chris Sutton**
Position: **Striker**
Signed: **July 5, 1999**
From: **Blackburn Rovers**
Fee: **£10 million**
Chelsea debut: **v Sunderland**

Do you think you're worth £10 million? *"It's not really a question of whether I'm worth it because it's all relative to the current marketplace. The transfer fee is big, but football has taken off in the past few years and the money that has come into the game in recent years was always bound to see prices escalate. No fee that sees a player move from one club to another is ever influenced by the player – they have absolutely no control over it. It's a deal struck by the selling club and the buyer."*

Why did you choose to sign for Chelsea? *"Well, because I wanted success. I wanted to be part of a quality side that I knew were going to fulfil my personal ambitions. I never considered any other options. As far as I was concerned, as soon as Chelsea came in with an offer for me I wanted to come here to Stamford Bridge. I'm no different to any other ambitious player – money is secondary, it's the success that I want most of all."*

What impressed you most about Chelsea? *"I can't think of anything that didn't impress me to be honest. The whole set-up here is geared towards achieving success. You could go on about the players at Chelsea all day – they're proven internationals and World Cup winners. I couldn't have come to a better club to fulfil my persional ambitions. I want to win medals, plenty of them, and I think Chelsea will give me the platform to do that."*

Will your England chances improve now you're playing at a big club like Chelsea? *"The more success you have at any club, the more likely you are of getting the opportunity to play at international level. I've never been the sort of player who takes things for granted, though. Success will hopefully bring me more success, but the most important thing for me is to settle as quickly as possible at the club and play well for the team. If I can get it right here, then fingers crossed it will lead to other things."*

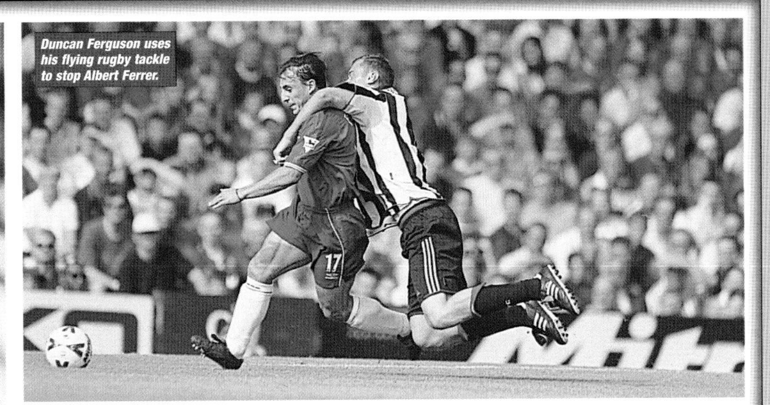
Duncan Ferguson uses his flying rugby tackle to stop Albert Ferrer.

Chelsea	(1) **1**
Newcastle United	(0) **0**

Competition: **FA Carling Premiership**

Date: **Saturday September 11, 1999**

Attendance: **35,092**

Referee: **G Poll** (Tring) 6

Game 7

THE GAME: In a largely disappointing encounter at Stamford Bridge, Chelsea made it six clean sheets from seven matches and took all three points against a struggling Newcastle side. In Bobby Robson's first game in charge of his hometown club, the first 45 minutes were instantly forgettable, with both teams struggling to produce their best football. The only excitement during the first half came when Chelsea took the lead through a Frank Leboeuf spot-kick after a push on Celestine Babayaro in the Newcastle area. The visitors thought they had a penalty of their own after Ed de Goey's challenge on Kieron Dyer, but the referee ignored their strong protests. Despite this scare, the home side had some good chances to extend their lead late on in the game through Zola and Tore Andre Flo, but both shots were well saved by veteran Newcastle 'keeper Tommy Wright. Chelsea's third consecutive 1-0 victory in the league meant they had already won 13 out of a possible 15 points in an impressive start to the new season, taking them to second place in the table behind Manchester United.

CHELSEA GOAL: **Leboeuf** *(penalty 37 mins)* Speed pushed Babayaro following a Zola free-kick from the left and Leboeuf took the penalty, putting it to the left of the Newcastle 'keeper.

MATCH RATING: ★★ **LEAGUE POSITION: 2nd**

"I'm not stupid. I know how football works. Chris Sutton is a high profile, expensive signing who Gianluca Vialli will be looking to play from the start. All that I can do is work hard on my own game." TORE ANDRE FLO

MATCH FACTS

Shots On Target		
Chelsea	5-1	Newcastle
Shots Off Target		
Chelsea	5-2	Newcastle
Hit Woodwork		
Chelsea	0-0	Newcastle
Corners		
Chelsea	9-3	Newcastle

HOW THEY LINED UP

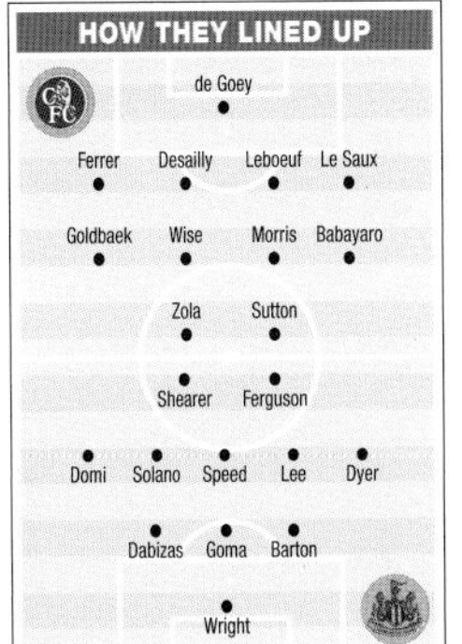

CHELSEA

de Goey	7
Babayaro	7
Leboeuf ⚽ ▯	7
Goal: 37 mins (pen); Booked: 59 mins (foul)	
Desailly	☆8
Sutton	5
Subbed: 68 mins (Flo)	
Wise ▯	7
Booked: 32 mins (foul)	
Goldbaek	6
Subbed: 46 mins (Petrescu)	
Le Saux	7
Subbed: 57 mins (Poyet)	
Ferrer ▯	7
Booked: 79 mins (dissent)	
Morris	6
Zola	7
sub: Flo	6
sub: Petrescu	7
sub: Poyet	7

Subs not used: *Hogh, Cudicini.*

NEWCASTLE UNITED

Wright	☆8
Barton ▯	7
Booked: 36 mins (foul)	
Domi	6
Goma	7
Dyer ▯	7
Booked: 60 mins (dissent)	
Shearer	5
Speed	6
Solano ▯	6
Booked: 12 mins (foul); Subbed: 86 mins (Hughes)	
Ferguson	6
Subbed: 73 mins (Robinson)	
Dabizas ▯	7
Booked: 37 mins (foul)	
Lee	7
Subbed: 77 mins (Maric)	
sub: Hughes	
sub: Maric	
sub: Robinson	

Subs not used: *Harper, McClen.*

THIS WEEK...

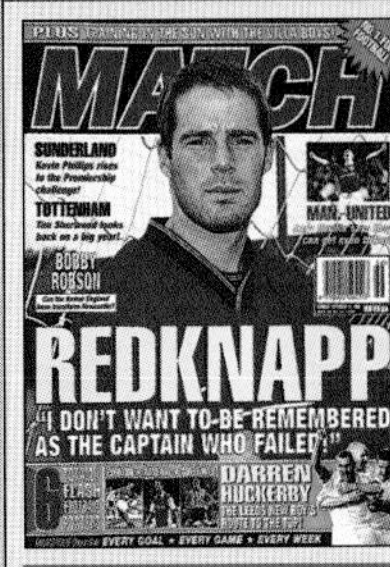

IN THE NEWS

CHELSEA: Former Chelsea striker **Mark Hughes**, now plying his trade at Southampton, is to take over as the national manager of Wales... Chairman Ken Bates is outraged and said to be suing a firm of accountancy consultants which claimed that Chelsea were not financially viable and on the verge of financial ruin.

PREMIERSHIP: Ruud Gullit leaves Newcastle after an awful start to the new season which... sees the Tyneside club at the bottom of the Premiership table... Leeds boss David O'Leary has been given all of the £13.8 million that BSkyB has invested into the club to bring some new faces to Elland Road... Twenty seven players and staff from Leicester City are charged by the Football Association in connection with an investigation into black market ticket sales at last season's Worthington Cup Final against Tottenham... Prime Minister Tony Blair intervenes to grant Brazilian midfielder **Juninho** a work permit which will allow the player to return to Middlesbrough on loan until the end of June... Manchester United's young central defender **Ronnie Wallwork** is hit with a lifetime ban by the Belgian FA after attacking a referee while playing on loan for Belgian side Royal Antwerp. United insist they will appeal against the decision.

THE FINAL SCORE!

SEPTEMBER 11		
Arsenal	3-1	Aston Villa
Chelsea	1-0	Newcastle
Coventry	3-4	**Leeds**
Liverpool	2-3	**Man. United**
Middlesbrough	3-2	Southampton
Sheff. Wed	0-2	**Everton**
Sunderland	2-0	Leicester
West Ham	1-0	Watford
Wimbledon	2-2	Derby

TOP OF THE PREMIERSHIP

	P	W	D	L	Pts
1. Man. United	7	6	1	0	19
2. Chelsea	**5**	**4**	**1**	**0**	**13**
3. West Ham	5	4	1	0	13
4. Leeds	7	4	1	2	13

Chelsea showed they were ready to challenge the best in Europe after their 0-0 draw with Milan.

FROM THE PAGES OF MATCH

When Gianluca Vialli spent £10 million on Chris Sutton, many people thought **TORE ANDRE FLO**'s days at Stamford Bridge were numbered. But the Norwegian had other ideas, as he told **MATCH**.

Was it a shock when Chris Sutton was signed? *"It was something I was prepared for, because a club like Chelsea is always going to add to their squad. I expected the club to buy more big-name players, so I don't think I was surprised when Chris came here."*

Did it make you want to leave? *"I've never felt like leaving here because I know that if I play well I'll get my chance in the team. If you're at a big club like Chelsea you know you can win something, and that's the most important thing for football players."*

Can Chelsea be really successful this season? *"I'm sure we can. The team is getting better every year. We now have three World Cup winners at Chelsea so we have the right experience to bring us the ultimate success in the league and Europe. They know what it is all about and we have a good side now."*

So what will be the key to success this season? *"Maybe it'll be Gianluca Vialli. He's a great motivator and is learning all the time because it takes a lot to be the manager of a big club in England. He's making the transition to a conventional boss, but at times he's still one of the boys. That could make the difference."*

 **Chelsea** (0) **0**

 **AC Milan** (0) **0**

Competition: **Champions Lge Group H**

Date: **Wednesday September 15, 1999**

Attendance: **33,873**

Referee: **A Frisk** (Sweden) 7

THE GAME: In their first ever game in the Champions League Chelsea proved they were capable of competing with Europe's best and were unlucky not to beat reigning Italian champions AC Milan. In a professional performance at Stamford Bridge, Gianluca Vialli's side controlled possession for large parts of the game but could not overcome a resilient and experienced Italian back line. The first half was a tense affair with few real openings, but it was a different story after the interval as The Blues began to find more space in the opposition's half. After 65 minutes Gianfranco Zola, who had a fine game against his compatriots, hit the inside of Milan's post with a low, rasping shot from 12 yards and forced a superb save from Abbiati two minutes later. The home side had a late scare when Leonardo rattled the bar from 25 yards, but they held on for a valuable first Champions League point on a memorable night.

MATCH RATING: ★★★★ **LEAGUE POSITION: 2nd**

"This game against Milan is not just about winning three points. It's about starting a new adventure well. It's about getting confidence and about getting known in Italy and across Europe." GIANLUCA VIALLI

CHELSEA	
de Goey	7
Petrescu	7
Babayaro	7
Leboeuf	7
Subbed: 80 mins (Hogh)	
Desailly	8
Deschamps	☆ 9
Poyet	7
Subbed: 79 mins (Le Saux)	
Wise	8
Ferrer	7
Flo	6
Subbed: 85 mins (Sutton)	
Zola	8
sub: *Hogh*	
sub: *Le Saux*	
sub: *Sutton*	

Subs not used: *Cudicini, Ambrosetti, Morris, Lambourde.*

AC MILAN	
Abbiati	☆ 8
Helveg ▯	7
Booked: 68 mins (foul)	
Maldini	7
Albertini	7
Costacurta	7
Shevchenko	6
Gattuso	7
Ayala	7
Leonardo	7
Subbed: 83 mins (Giunti)	
Bierhoff ▯	5
Booked: 25 mins (dissent)	
Guly	6
sub: *Giunti*	

Subs not used: *Rossi, Ganz, De Ascentis, N'Gotty, Serginho, Sala.*

MATCH FACTS

Shots On Target
Chelsea 4-3 AC Milan

Shots Off Target
Chelsea 7-1 AC Milan

Hit Woodwork
Chelsea 1-1 AC Milan

Corners
Chelsea 7-2 AC Milan

HOW THEY LINED UP

de Goey

Ferrer Desailly Leboeuf Babayaro

Petrescu Deschamps Wise Poyet

Flo Zola

Leonardo Bierhoff Shevchenko

Guly Gattuso Albertini Helveg

Maldini Ayala Costacurta

Abbiati

THIS WEEK...

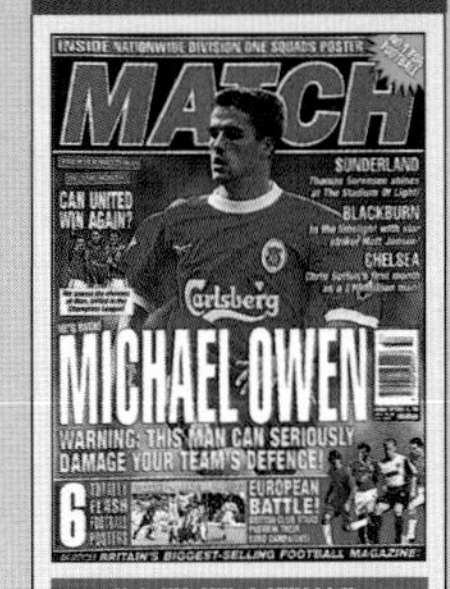

IN THE NEWS

CHELSEA: The Blues are believed to be monitoring the progress of Spanish star **Luis Enrique**, who was recently dropped by Spanish club Barcelona... Gianluca Vialli is expected to extend his Chelsea contract, ending the rumours of a move to the continent for The Blues chief... AC Milan prepare for their crucial European tie with Chelsea by recording an ominous 3-1 win over Reggiana, with the lethal strike partnership of Bierhoff and Shevchenko in top form for the Italian champions. AC Milan coach **Alberto Zaccheroni** says Chelsea may be an English team in name but they think and play like an like an Italian one... Gianluca Vialli shows he has got the hang of the English sense of humour when he tells the assembled English media that, as a former Sampdoria and Juventus player, he is expecting to receive a wonderful reception from the AC Milan fans in the San Siro.

PREMIERSHIP: Martin O'Neill's position as manager of Leicester City is in the balance as the power struggle in the club's boardroom continues to drag on. O'Neill's future depends on whether his allies, chairman John Elsom and Plc chief executive Sir Rodney Walker, emerge victorious from the battle... Only 250,000 viewers throughout Britain tune in to watch Manchester United and Arsenal open their Champions League campaigns which are screened on ONdigital... Watford manager Graham Taylor smashes the club's transfer record to sign striker **Nordin Wooter** for £975,000 from Spanish outfit Real Zaragoza.

THE FINAL SCORE!

SEPTEMBER 12

Bradford 1-1 Tottenham

TOP OF THE PREMIERSHIP

	P	W	D	L	Pts
1. Man. United	7	6	1	0	19
2. Chelsea	**5**	**4**	**1**	**0**	**13**
3. West Ham	5	4	1	0	13
4. Leeds	7	4	1	2	13

Watford (0) 1

Chelsea (0) 0

Competition: **FA Carling Premiership**

Date: **Saturday September 18, 1999**

Attendance: **21,244**

Referee: **M Reed** (Birmingham) 6

THE GAME: Chelsea were brought back down to earth with a bump following their midweek Champions League exertions, losing 1-0 to Premiership strugglers Watford at Vicarage Road. Alan Smart was the hero for The Hornets, scoring the winning goal from close range in the 57th minute. Chances were few and far between in the first half, with Ed de Goey having little to trouble him. Bjarne Goldbaek had the visitors' best chances of the half, but he struck one volley straight at the goalkeeper and wasted another opportunity moments later. After Smart's goal, only the third Chelsea have conceded so far this season, The Blues fought hard to equalise, but they will have to beat sides like this regularly if they want to challenge for honours.

WATFORD GOAL: Smart *(56 mins):* Stroked the ball past de Goey from close range after a sweeping Watford move.

MATCH RATING: ★★★ **LEAGUE POSITION: 5th**

"It's no good playing well in one match and then losing form in the next one. We went to Watford in the league and were rather naive in our approach. We can't afford to be throwing games away." GIANFRANCO ZOLA

WATFORD	
Chamberlain	7
Gibbs	☆9
Page	7
Booked: 54 mins (foul)	
Williams	6
Robinson	6
Hyde	7
Booked: 9 mins (foul)	
Easton	6
Palmer	8
Kennedy	4
Smart	7
Goal: 56 mins; Subbed: 80 mins (Mooney)	
Wooter	8
Subbed: 65 mins (Wright)	
sub: *Wright*	6
sub: *Mooney*	
Subbed: 86 mins (Ngonge)	
sub: *Ngonge*	

Subs not used: *Day, Bonnot.*

CHELSEA	
de Goey	6
Ferrer	6
Hogh	6
Desailly	7
Le Saux	7
Booked: 1 min (foul)	
Goldbaek	6
Subbed: 61 mins (Petrescu)	
Morris	7
Deschamps	☆8
Ambrosetti	7
Flo	6
Subbed: 61 mins (Zola)	
Sutton	
Booked: 76 mins (foul)	
sub: *Zola*	6
sub: *Petrescu*	6

Subs not used: *Lambourde, Cudicini, Wolleaston.*

MATCH FACTS

Shots On Target		
Watford	3-5	Chelsea
Shots Off Target		
Watford	7-6	Chelsea
Hit Woodwork		
Watford	0-0	Chelsea
Corners		
Watford	2-7	Chelsea

HOW THEY LINED UP

Chamberlain

Gibbs, Williams, Page, Robinson

Wooter, Palmer, Hyde, Kennedy

Smart, Easton

Sutton, Flo

Ambrosetti, Morris, Deschamps, Goldbaek

Le Saux, Hogh, Desailly, Ferrer

de Goey

Watford grabbed a surprise win over Chelsea with Alan Smart's second-half goal.

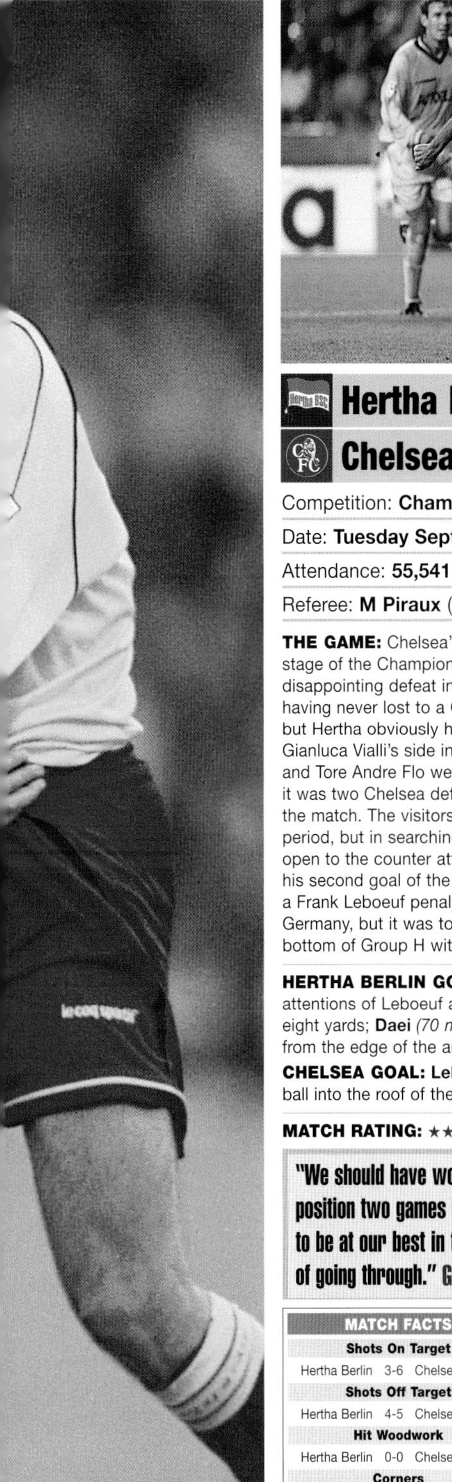

Leboeuf scored a consolation goal from the penalty spot – his second of the season.

Hertha Berlin (1) 2
Chelsea (0) 1

Competition: **Champions Lge Group H**
Date: **Tuesday September 21, 1999**
Attendance: **55,541**
Referee: **M Piraux** (Belgium) 7

Game 10

THE GAME: Chelsea's hopes of reaching the second group stage of the Champions League received a setback with this disappointing defeat in Berlin. The Blues went into the game having never lost to a German side in European competition, but Hertha obviously hadn't read the script as they outplayed Gianluca Vialli's side in the first half. Strikers Gianfranco Zola and Tore Andre Flo were kept quiet by the home defence and it was two Chelsea defensive errors that ultimately cost them the match. The visitors had plenty of chances in the second period, but in searching for an equaliser they left themselves open to the counter attack and Daei took advantage to claim his second goal of the game. The Blues pulled one back with a Frank Leboeuf penalty in the dying minutes of the match in Germany, but it was to no avail as the defeat left them at the bottom of Group H with one point from their first two games.

HERTHA BERLIN GOALS: Daei *(3 mins):* Escaped the close attentions of Leboeuf and Desailly to head past de Goey from eight yards; **Daei** *(70 mins):* Drilled an unstoppable low shot from the edge of the area which went in off the post.

CHELSEA GOAL: Leboeuf *(penalty 86 mins):* Powered the ball into the roof of the net giving the 'keeper no chance.

MATCH RATING: ★★★ LEAGUE POSITION: 5th

"We should have won. This result leaves us in a difficult position two games into our European campaign. We have to be at our best in the last four games to stand a chance of going through." GIANFRANCO ZOLA

MATCH FACTS

Shots On Target		
Hertha Berlin	3-6	Chelsea
Shots Off Target		
Hertha Berlin	4-5	Chelsea
Hit Woodwork		
Hertha Berlin	0-0	Chelsea
Corners		
Hertha Berlin	2-8	Chelsea

HOW THEY LINED UP

Hertha Berlin: Kiraly; Herzog, van Burik, Schmidt; Sanneh, Wosz, Tretschok, Dardai, Deisler; Daei, Preetz

Chelsea: Zola, Flo; Babayaro, Wise, Deschamps, Petrescu; Le Saux, Leboeuf, Desailly, Ferrer; de Goey

HERTHA BERLIN

Player	Rating
Kiraly	7
Herzog	7
van Burik (booked) *Booked: 86 mins (foul)*	7
Schmidt	7
Sanneh *Subbed: 66 mins (Veit)*	6
Dardai *Subbed: 80 mins (Helmer)*	7
Deisler	6
Tretschok *Subbed: 12 mins (Michalke)*	
Wosz	7
Daei ⚽⚽ *Goals: 3, 70 mins*	☆ 9
Preetz	7
sub: Michalke (booked) *Booked: 85 mins (foul)*	6
sub: Veit	6
sub: Helmer	

Subs not used: *Fiedler, Roy, Reiss, Aracic.*

CHELSEA

Player	Rating
de Goey	6
Ferrer *Subbed: 64 mins (Ambrosetti)*	6
Petrescu	7
Babayaro (booked) *Booked: 84 mins*	6
Le Saux *Subbed: 71 mins (Morris)*	6
Desailly (booked) *Booked: 61 mins (foul)*	5
Deschamps	6
Leboeuf ⚽ *Goal: 86 mins*	5
Wise (booked) *Booked: 76 mins (foul)*	7
Zola	☆ 8
Flo *Subbed: 64 mins (Sutton)*	6
sub: Ambrosetti	6
sub: Sutton	5
sub: Morris	

Subs not used: *Cudicini, Hogh, Lambourde, Forssell.*

THIS WEEK...

IN THE NEWS

CHELSEA: Leading up to the vital Champions League fixture against Hertha Berlin, there is much talk in the media about Chelsea's inability to score goals, with Chris Sutton and Tore Andre Flo being singled out for criticism... **Gustavo Poyet** is receiving treatment on his injury from the Indian physiotherapist he used during his time at former club Real Zaragoza... **Frank Leboeuf**'s late consolation spot-kick against Hertha Berlin is Chelsea's first goal in 318 minutes of football... The goalkeeping coach at Stamford Bridge, Eddie Niedswiecki, is told he can carry on as Mark Hughes' assistant with Wales despite his increasing workload.

PREMIERSHIP: David Batty is handed a two-game international ban after the Leeds midfielder was red-carded in England's European Championship qualifying game with Poland... Former Nottingham Forest manager Brian Clough says Man. United are wrong to pull out of the FA Cup to play in the World Club Championships in January, and says he hopes the team all get diarrhoea in Brazil.

THE FINAL SCORE!

SEPTEMBER 18		
Aston Villa	1-0	Bradford
Derby	0-5	**Sunderland**
Leicester	2-2	Liverpool
Man. United	1-1	Wimbledon
Southampton	0-1	**Arsenal**
Watford	1-0	Chelsea
SEPTEMBER 19		
Everton	1-0	West Ham
Leeds	2-0	Middlesbrough
Newcastle	8-0	Sheff. Wed
Tottenham	3-2	Coventry

TOP OF THE PREMIERSHIP

	P	W	D	L	Pts
1. Man. United	8	6	2	0	20
2. Leeds	8	5	1	2	16
3. Arsenal	8	5	1	2	16
5. Chelsea	**6**	**4**	**1**	**1**	**13**

Middlesbrough	(0) 0
Chelsea	(0) 1

Competition: **FA Carling Premiership**

Date: **Saturday September 25, 1999**

Attendance: **34,183**

Referee: **P Alcock** (Halstead) 6

THE GAME: By scoring their first ever goal at the Riverside Stadium, Chelsea claimed their first victory on Teesside since 1931. Gianluca Vialli will have been happy with the result, if not his team's performance, as they spent much of the first period defending against Middlesbrough's attacks. The game never reached its true potential, considering so many quality players were on display, but after the events of the previous week The Blues were more than happy to get back to winning ways. They dominated in the second half and were rewarded for their superior possession when Bernard Lambourde scored after Mark Schwarzer failed to clear Gianfranco Zola's cross. The home side suffered further agony when Paul Gascoigne was sent-off in the 90th minute, but that didn't concern the travelling Chelsea fans as they left Teesside victorious at last.

CHELSEA GOAL: Lambourde *(55 mins):* Zola's curled cross was punched clear by Schwarzer, but only as far as defender Lambourde, who was on hand to bundle the ball into the net.

MATCH RATING: ★★ **LEAGUE POSITION: 5th**

MIDDLESBROUGH	
Schwarzer	6
Fleming	7
Festa	7
Pallister	7
Cooper (Booked: 69 mins (foul))	7
Ziege (Booked: 20 mins (foul))	☆8
Juninho (Subbed: 89 mins (Armstrong))	6
Ince (Subbed: 35 mins (Mustoe))	6
O'Neill (Booked: 29 mins (foul))	6
Deane (Subbed: 70 mins (Gascoigne))	6
Ricard (Booked: 59 mins (foul))	6
sub: Gascoigne (Sent-off: 90 mins (foul and abusive language))	5
sub: Mustoe	6
sub: Armstrong	

Subs not used: *Vickers, Roberts.*

CHELSEA	
de Goey	6
Lambourde (Goal: 55 mins)	7
Leboeuf	7
Desailly (Booked: 59 mins (foul))	7
Le Saux	6
Petrescu (Booked: 87 mins (foul))	7
Deschamps (Booked: 89 mins (dissent); Subbed: 90 mins (Morris))	7
Wise	☆8
Ambrosetti (Subbed: 80 mins (Babayaro))	6
Sutton (Booked: 18 mins (foul))	6
Zola (Subbed: 70 mins (Flo))	6
sub: Flo	6
sub: Morris	
sub: Babayaro	

Subs not used: *Hogh, Cudicini.*

MATCH FACTS

Shots On Target		
Middlesbrough	1-6	Chelsea
Shots Off Target		
Middlesbrough	6-3	Chelsea
Hit Woodwork		
Middlesbrough	0-0	Chelsea
Corners		
Middlesbrough	2-8	Chelsea

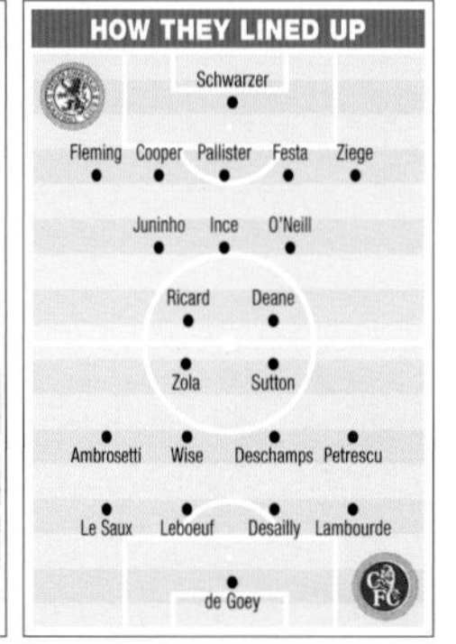

HOW THEY LINED UP

Middlesbrough: Schwarzer; Fleming, Cooper, Pallister, Festa, Ziege; Juninho, Ince, O'Neill; Ricard, Deane

Chelsea: Zola, Sutton; Ambrosetti, Wise, Deschamps, Petrescu; Le Saux, Leboeuf, Desailly, Lambourde; de Goey

The travelling Blues fans watched a dull game at The Riverside, but they still came away with a win.

Sutton gets sandwiched by the Galatasaray defence in Chelsea's vital 1-0 victory.

Chelsea	(0)	**1**
Galatasaray	(0)	**0**

Competition: **Champions Lge Group H**

Date: **Tuesday September 28, 1999**

Attendance: **33,462**

Referee: **D Jol** (Holland) 8

THE GAME: Chelsea secured their first Champions League win of the campaign with a 1-0 win over ten-man Galatasaray. Brazilian 'keeper Taffarel was sent-off in the 33rd minute for handling the ball outside his area while under pressure from Dan Petrescu, but The Blues failed to make their numerical advantage count until the second half. They started the game cautiously, with Gheorghe Hagi's dangerous balls into the box causing concern for Frank Leboeuf and Marcel Desailly. Dan Petrescu finally broke the deadlock for The Blues in the 55th minute, but they should have recorded a convincing victory after this point. Gianfranco Zola, Gus Poyet and Petrescu all went close before Zola hit the post with a free-kick. This was a crucial win, but Gianluca Vialli would have been concerned that his players only converted one of their many chances.

CHELSEA GOAL: Petrescu *(55 mins):* Drove the ball into the net with a low left-foot shot after the ball rebounded to him.

MATCH RATING: ★★★★ **LEAGUE POSITION: 5th**

"We're creating plenty of chances at the moment and it's a pity that we're scoring so few goals. I am not worried as long as we get three points, but it's something I'm not completely happy about." GIANFRANCO ZOLA

MATCH FACTS		
Shots On Target		
Chelsea	13-3	Galatasaray
Shots Off Target		
Chelsea	10-5	Galatasaray
Hit Woodwork		
Chelsea	1-0	Galatasaray
Corners		
Chelsea	10-5	Galatasaray

HOW THEY LINED UP

CHELSEA	
de Goey	7
Petrescu ⚽	☆8
Goal: 55 mins	
Babayaro	6
Leboeuf	6
Desailly	6
Subbed: 63 mins (Hogh)	
Sutton	7
Subbed: 84 mins (Flo)	
Wise	5
Ferrer	6
Ambrosetti	4
Subbed: 53 mins (Poyet)	
Morris	6
Zola	7
sub: Hogh	6
sub: Poyet	7
sub: Flo	

Subs not used: *Hitchcock, Le Saux, Forssell, Lambourde.*

GALATASARAY	
Taffarel ■	4
Sent-off: 32 mins (professional foul)	
Popescu	6
Arif	6
Subbed: 34 mins (Mehmet)	
Okan	6
Subbed: 72 mins (Emre)	
Sukur	7
Hagi	☆8
Subbed: 73 mins (Hasan)	
Fatih	6
Umit	6
Unsal	6
Capone	7
Ergun	7
sub: Mehmet	7
sub: Emre	
sub: Hasan	

Subs not used: *Bruno, Ahmet, Marcio.*

THIS WEEK...

SQUAD POSTERS LEICESTER & TOTTENHAM

MATCH

MICHAEL OWEN

SUPER ZOLA

"CHELSEA CAN'T AFFORD ANY MORE MISTAKES THIS SEASON!"

ROBERT LEE ROARS BACK!

BRITAIN'S BIGGEST-SELLING FOOTBALL MAGAZINE!

IN THE NEWS

CHELSEA: Italian international **Roberto Di Matteo** has returned to full training with The Blues after recovering from the ankle injury which has limited him to just one substitute appearance so far this season... Officials from Turkish club Galatasaray accuse Chelsea of rudeness, saying there were no Blues officials to meet them from the airport as they arrived for their Champions League encounter at Stamford Bridge. They are also unhappy about the distance they had to travel to their training facilities while in England.

PREMIERSHIP: The troubled Aston Villa striker **Stan Collymore** is linked with a move to Turkey to join either Besiktas or Galatasaray, both of whom are believed to be interested... Southampton agree to sell The Dell to Barrett Homes for £5 million. The money will now be used to fund a move to a 32,000 all-seater stadium... Bobby Robson's injury crisis at St James' Park sees him bring Scotland striker **Kevin Gallacher** to the club. **Kieron Dyer** offers **Rob Lee** his prized No. 7 shirt as the former Toon captain returns to training with the first team following the departure of Ruud Gullit from St James' Park.

THE FINAL SCORE!

SEPTEMBER 25		
Arsenal	1-0	Watford
Coventry	1-0	West Ham
Derby	0-1	**Bradford**
Leeds	3-2	Newcastle
Leicester	3-1	Aston Villa
Man. United	3-3	Southampton
Middlesbrough	0-1	**Chelsea**
Sunderland	1-0	Sheff. Wed.
SEPTEMBER 26		
Wimbledon	1-1	Tottenham
SEPTEMBER 27		
Liverpool	0-1	**Everton**

TOP OF THE PREMIERSHIP

	P	W	D	L	Pts
1. Man. United	9	6	3	0	21
2. Leeds	9	6	1	2	19
3. Arsenal	9	6	1	2	19
5. Chelsea	**7**	**5**	**1**	**1**	**16**

OCTOBER

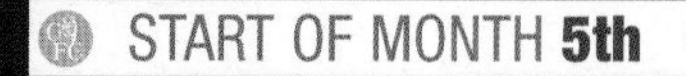

"Man. United have been the benchmark for many years. To maintain that level of success is fantastic. Now it's up to us to put an end to it with our own success." Graeme Le Saux

THE MONTH OPENED WITH A VISIT FROM REIGNING PREMIERSHIP champions Manchester United. The press had predicted a close encounter between the two title-chasers, but The Blues tore up the script to destroy the treble-winners 5-0. United weren't helped by Nicky Butt's dismissal with the score at 2-0, but it did little to affect the result in a fantastic performance from Gianluca Vialli's side. An away tie against First Division Huddersfield Town in the Worthington Cup was next for Chelsea, who were expected to win comfortably after their result against the champions. The Blues fielded a weakened team, though, and were knocked out of the competition after losing 1-0 to The Terriers. However, the positive side of this defeat was that it allowed the club to concentrate on winning other pieces of silverware.

After losing at Liverpool in the league, Vialli's charges responded superbly against Turkish champions Galatasaray in the Champions League, recording an outstanding 5-0 win in the intimidating atmosphere of the Ali Sami Yen Stadium. Chelsea's erratic form in the Premiership continued as they threw away a commanding 2-0 lead against close rivals Arsenal to lose the game 3-2 courtesy of a remarkable Kanu hat-trick. It wasn't the best preparation for a trip to Milan, but once again The Blues confounded their critics by coming away with a 1-1 draw from the San Siro.

The club ended a hectic month of mixed fortunes at Derby, losing 3-1 to a team that was struggling in the Premiership. The disappointing result at Pride Park made it three league defeats in a row and the Blues supporters who were tipping their team for the title at the start of the month were now forced to question their early prediction after seeing Chelsea's form go from irresistable in one game to ordinary in the next. Ending October in 8th place in the league, Vialli's team needed a winning run to get back on track.

THE GAMES

Oct. 3 v **Man. United** (h)
Oct. 13 v **Huddersfield** (h)
Oct. 16 v **Liverpool** (a)
Oct. 20 v **Galatasaray** (a)
Oct. 23 v **Arsenal** (h)
Oct. 26 v **AC Milan** (a)
Oct. 30 v **Derby** (a)

TRANSFERS IN

None

TRANSFERS OUT

None

MATCH facts

Matchman Of The Month

DAN PETRESCU
Average Rating: 7.33

FROM THE PAGES OF *MATCH*

THE NEW RECRUIT

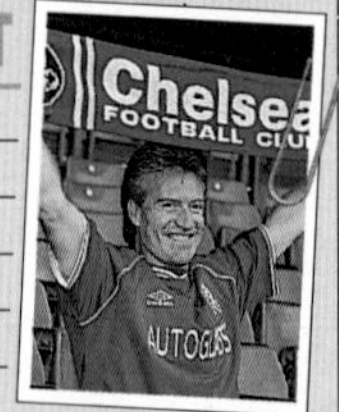

Name: **Didier Deschamps**

Position: **Midfielder**

From: **Juventus**

Signed: **June 21, 1999**

Fee: **£3 million**

Chelsea debut **v Sunderland**

How are you finding life at Chelsea? *"I haven't got a clear idea at the moment. I've only played a couple of games at Stamford Bridge and the rest of my time has been spent on the training ground. But it's a lively club with a lot of things going on and I'll see when the championship gets going."*

How much of Chelsea had you seen before you came? *"I've seen them quite a lot. For the last few years Chelsea have been one of the three main teams in England along with Arsenal and Manchester United, so I've seen a lot of them. When I was in Italy, they would show one English game live on a Sunday, so I would watch that."*

What key things do you bring to the side? *"I think my real quality is as a defensive midfielder but most of all, it's for my experience that Gianluca Vialli wanted to bring me here. I'm going to try to win the championship with Chelsea. Now that we have a lot of experience, we have a good chance."*

Are you aware of the debate in this country saying there are too many foreign players? *"Yes, but it's the same in Italy, Germany – everywhere has exactly the same argument. Everywhere it's controversial. But we are all internationals here. Every country is talking about reducing the number of foreign players in their game, but I think there's an equal number of foreigners in all of the big leagues in Europe."*

How long will you stay in England? *"For three years, the length of my contract with Chelsea. I want to play for three years and then finish. I won't go back to France and play club football there. I will retire from football."*

Can Chelsea win the Champions League during your time at Stamford Bridge? *"I think so, but I'd much rather win the Premier League. In England, the league title is the most important thing. That's the thing the fans follow all the way through the season and that's what's most important. The European Cup doesn't matter as much."*

Chris Sutton celebrates his first Premiership goal of the season in the 5-0 drubbing.

Chelsea	(2)	**5**
Manchester United	(0)	**0**

Competition: **FA Carling Premiership**

Date: **Sunday October 3, 1999**

Attendance: **34,909**

Referee: **D Gallagher** (Banbury) 7

THE GAME: Chelsea ended Manchester United's 29 game unbeaten run in spectacular fashion and installed themselves as real championship contenders with a fantastic performance at Stamford Bridge. After scoring with just 28 seconds on the clock through Gus Poyet, The Blues dominated proceedings and deserved their emphatic victory. United weren't helped by the first-half dismissal of Nicky Butt for a kick on Dennis Wise or the erratic goalkeeping of new signing Massimo Taibi, but they could do little to combat the power of Chelsea. United might still be the title favourites, but The Blues announced themselves as serious contenders with this superb display.

CHELSEA GOALS: Poyet *(1 min):* Taibi collided with Irwin as they went for the ball, leaving Poyet to head home Petrescu's cross; **Sutton** *(16 mins)*: A teasing ball from Ferrer was met by Sutton, who directed a looping header into the corner; **Poyet** *(54 mins):* Taibi parried Leboeuf's shot but Poyet was there to fire into the roof of the net from close range; **Berg** *(own goal 58 mins):* A cross from Zola was put into his own net by Berg; **Morris** *(80 mins):* Scored a bizarre goal through Taibi's legs.

MATCH RATING: ★★★★ **LEAGUE POSITION: 4th**

CHELSEA	
de Goey	6
Petrescu *Subbed: 76 mins (Le Saux)*	7
Hogh	7
Babayaro	8
Deschamps (booked) *Booked: 48 mins (foul)*	7
Leboeuf	7
Sutton ⚽ *Goal: 16 mins*	8
Wise (booked) *Booked: 24 mins (foul); Subbed: 65 mins (Morris)*	8
Ferrer	7
Zola *Subbed: 68 mins (Flo)*	8
Poyet ⚽⚽ *Goals: 1, 54 mins*	☆9
sub: Morris ⚽ *Goal: 80 mins*	7
sub: Flo	6
sub: Le Saux	7

Subs not used: *Lambourde, Cudicini.*

MANCHESTER UNITED	
Taibi	4
Irwin	6
Stam	7
Beckham *Subbed: 65 mins (Wilson)*	6
Butt (sent off) *Sent-off: 24 mins (violent conduct)*	5
Cole *Subbed: 65 mins (Solskjaer)*	5
Neville, P	5
Scholes (booked) *Booked: 54 mins (foul); Subbed: 65 mins (Sheringham)*	5
Yorke	6
Berg ⚽ *Own goal: 58 mins*	5
Silvestre	☆7
sub: Wilson	6
sub: Solskjaer	5
sub: Sheringham	5

Subs not used: *Clegg, van der Gouw.*

MATCH FACTS

Shots On Target		
Chelsea	6-1	Man. United
Shots Off Target		
Chelsea	6-2	Man. United
Hit Woodwork		
Chelsea	0-0	Man. United
Corners		
Chelsea	4-0	Man. United

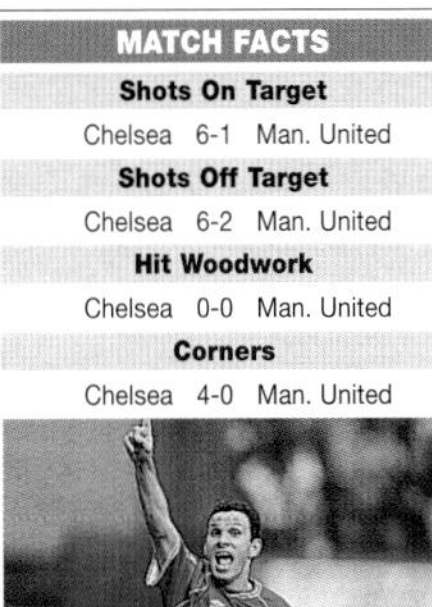

HOW THEY LINED UP

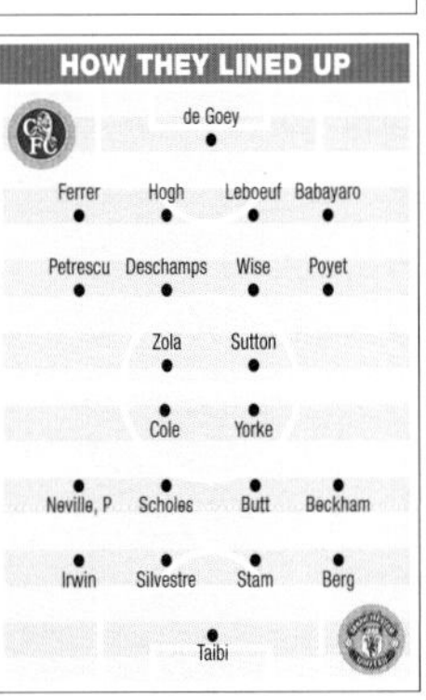

THIS WEEK...

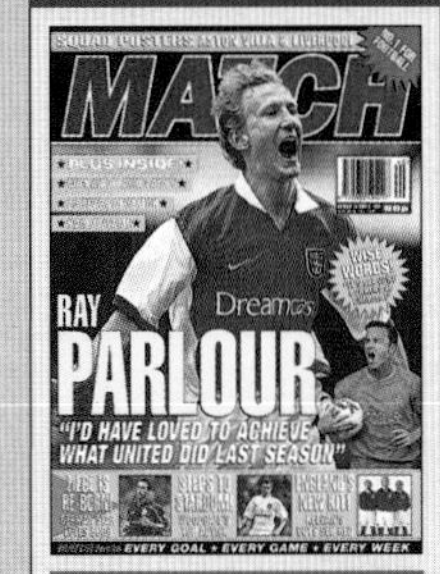

MATCH
RAY
PARLOUR
"I'D HAVE LOVED TO ACHIEVE WHAT UNITED DID LAST SEASON"
EVERY GOAL • EVERY GAME • EVERY WEEK

IN THE NEWS

CHELSEA: Dennis Wise is handed a recall to the full England squad after some fine performances for Chelsea, especially in Europe... The Press are suddenly hailing Chelsea as title favourites after their 5-0 slaying of champions Manchester United. The victory is a personal triumph for much maligned striker **Chris Sutton**, who scores his first league goal for Chelsea against the champions... Gianluca Vialli's latest transfer target is said to be ex-Juventus team-mate **Roberto Baggio**... Romanian star **Dan Petrescu** has warned that he will be looking for a new club in January unless he's offered a new contract.

PREMIERSHIP Manchester United midfielder **David Beckham** is fined two weeks' wages for attending a party at London Fashion Week just 48 hours before his club's vital Champions League encounter with Sturm Graz. Beckham has also been called by the FA to discuss his behaviour on the pitch... Huddersfield boss **Steve Bruce** has announced the end of his professional playing career after 737 games... **Benito Carbone** turns down a move to Derby, but Sheffield Wednesday are still keen to sell the striker before he is able to move on a free transfer.

THE FINAL SCORE!

OCTOBER 2		
Aston Villa	0-0	Liverpool
Bradford	0-4	**Sunderland**
Everton	1-1	Coventry
Sheff.Wed.	5-1	Wimbledon
OCTOBER 3		
Chelsea	5-0	Man. United
Newcastle	2-1	Middlesbrough
Tottenham	2-3	**Leicester**
Watford	1-2	**Leeds**
West Ham	2-1	Arsenal

TOP OF THE PREMIERSHIP

	P	W	D	L	Pts
1. Leeds	10	7	1	2	22
2. Man. United	10	6	3	1	21
3. Sunderland	10	6	2	2	20
4. Chelsea	8	6	1	1	19

The face of Jody Morris says it all as Chelsea go out of Worthington Cup.

Chelsea	(0)	**0**
Huddersfield Town	(0)	**1**

Competition: **Worthington Cup 3rd Rd**
Date: **Wednesday October 13, 1999**
Attendance: **21,008**
Referee: **R Styles** (Waterlooville) 6

THE GAME: After thrashing Manchester United in their last game, Chelsea made wholesale changes for the Worthington Cup tie against Huddersfield, but the plan backfired. Ten new faces were drafted in from the side that convincingly beat the treble-winners only ten days before, but Chelsea still played some excellent football early on. A one-two with Jody Morris left Bernard Lambourde with space in the Huddersfield area, but his magnificent first-time shot cannoned off the crossbar, while young Finnish striker Mikael Forssell squandered two good chances to put his side ahead. As the game went on, the First Division visitors became the stronger side and they settled the tie with an impressive strike from Kenny Irons to put Chelsea out of the competition at the first hurdle.

HUDDERSFIELD GOAL: Irons *(75 mins):* The midfielder hit a 25-yard drive into the left-hand corner of the net.

MATCH RATING: ★★★ **LEAGUE POSITION: 6th**

"This year, it seems we need to have a big match for us to play our best football. I suppose I can understand why that might happen, but at the end of the day it's just not good enough." GIANLUCA VIALLI

MATCH FACTS

Shots On Target		
Chelsea	9-7	Huddersfield
Shots Off Target		
Chelsea	6-5	Huddersfield
Hit Woodwork		
Chelsea	1-0	Huddersfield
Corners		
Chelsea	7-5	Huddersfield

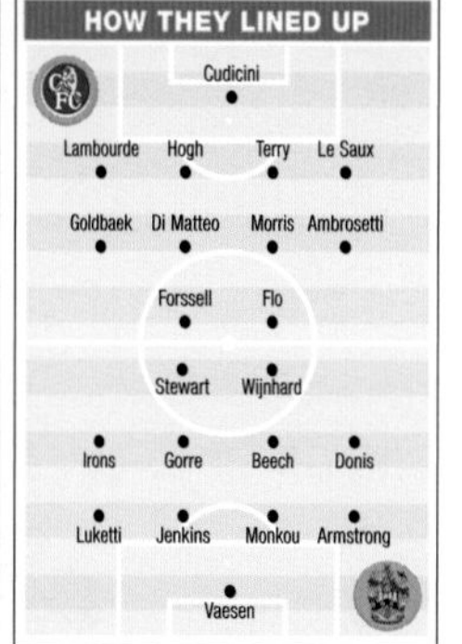

HOW THEY LINED UP

Cudicini
Lambourde, Hogh, Terry, Le Saux
Goldbaek, Di Matteo, Morris, Ambrosetti
Forssell, Flo
Stewart, Wijnhard
Irons, Gorre, Beech, Donis
Luketti, Jenkins, Monkou, Armstrong
Vaesen

CHELSEA	
Cudicini	6
Hogh (booked)	6
Booked: 55 mins (foul)	
Goldbaek	7
Le Saux	6
Di Matteo	7
Subbed: 84 mins (Wolleaston)	
Ambrosetti	☆ 8
Flo	6
Morris	7
Lambourde	6
Subbed: 80 mins (Nicholls)	
Terry	5
Forssell (booked)	7
Booked: 18 mins (dissent)	
sub: *Wolleaston*	
sub: *Nicholls*	

Subs not used: *Hitchcock, Dalla Bona, Harley.*

HUDDERSFIELD TOWN	
Vaesen	7
Jenkins	6
Armstrong	7
Lucketti	7
Donis (booked)	☆ 8
Booked: 61 mins (foul)	
Irons (goal)	7
Goal: 75 mins	
Stewart	7
Wijnhard (booked)	7
Booked: 58 mins (foul); Subbed: 90 mins (Vincent)	
Beech (booked)	7
Booked: 9 mins (foul)	
Monkou	7
Gorre	7
sub: *Vincent*	

Subs not used: *Sellars, Thornley, Margetson, Horne.*

The Blues just couldn't keep Liverpool at bay and ended the game with nine men.

Liverpool	(0) **1**
Chelsea	(0) **0**

Competition: **FA Carling Premiership**

Date: **Saturday October 16, 1999**

Attendance: **44,826**

Referee: **M Reed** (Birmingham) 6

THE GAME: Any wildly premature title aspirations Chelsea may have had after beating Manchester United earlier in the month were put back into perspective with this 1-0 defeat at Anfield. Liverpool produced a mature, spirited display to beat The Blues, who had Dennis Wise and Marcel Desailly sent-off and lost Frank Leboeuf through injury. In a highly competitive game that often stretched the rules of fair play, referee Mike Reed brandished eight yellow cards in addition to the two red cards. Desailly was the first to receive his marching orders for a second bookable offence when he fouled Danny Murphy in the penalty area in the 73rd minute, although Michael Owen missed the resulting spot-kick. Dennis Wise went for an early bath just before the end after striking out at Vladimir Smicer, ending an instantly forgettable match for Gianluca Vialli's side.

LIVERPOOL GOAL: Thompson *(47 mins):* After Owen was brought down near the Chelsea area, Staunton swung over a free-kick which Thompson lashed into the Chelsea net.

MATCH RATING: ★★★★ **LEAGUE POSITION: 6th**

LIVERPOOL	
Friedel	6
Henchoz	6
Song	7
Staunton (booked) *Booked: 53 mins (foul)*	6
Smicer	7
Owen *Subbed: 86 mins (Meijer)*	5
Redknapp (booked) *Booked: 54 mins (foul)*	7
Hyypia	7
Carragher	7
Murphy (booked) *Booked: 67 mins (foul); Subbed 80 mins (Heggem)*	☆ 8
Thompson (goal) (booked) *Goal: 47 mins; Booked: 90 mins (foul)*	6
sub: *Meijer*	
sub: *Heggem*	

Subs not used: *Nielsen, Matteo, Camara.*

CHELSEA	
de Goey	6
Petrescu *Subbed: 74 mins (Lambourde)*	☆ 7
Babayaro	5
Leboeuf (booked) *Booked: 47 mins (foul); Subbed: 64 mins (Le Saux)*	5
Desailly (booked) (sent-off) *Booked: 37 mins (foul); Sent-off: 73 mins (second bookable offence: foul)*	6
Deschamps	6
Poyet	5
Sutton (booked) *Booked: 41 mins (foul)*	5
Wise (sent-off) *Sent-off: 87 mins (violent conduct)*	6
Ferrer	6
Zola *Subbed: 68 mins (Flo)*	6
sub: *Le Saux*	6
sub: *Flo*	6
sub: *Lambourde* (booked) *Booked: 82 mins (foul)*	

Subs not used: *Morris, Cudicini.*

MATCH FACTS

Shots On Target		
Liverpool	2-2	Chelsea
Shots Off Target		
Liverpool	6-5	Chelsea
Hit Woodwork		
Liverpool	0-0	Chelsea
Corners		
Liverpool	2-1	Chelsea

HOW THEY LINED UP

Liverpool: Friedel; Song, Henchoz, Hyypia, Staunton; Thompson, Redknapp, Murphy, Carragher; Smicer, Owen

Chelsea: Sutton, Zola; Poyet, Wise, Deschamps, Petrescu; Babayaro, Leboeuf, Desailly, Ferrer; de Goey

THIS WEEK...

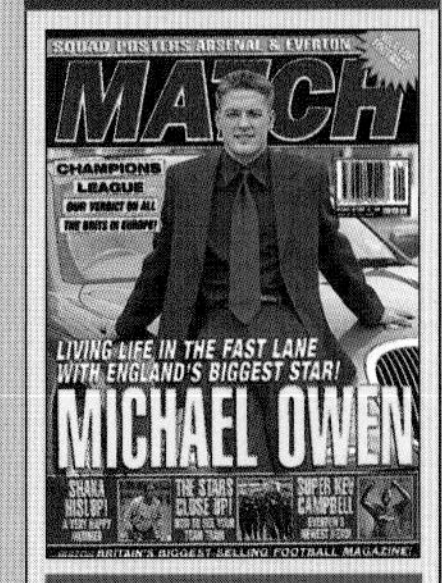

MATCH
LIVING LIFE IN THE FAST LANE WITH ENGLAND'S BIGGEST STAR!
MICHAEL OWEN
BRITAIN'S BIGGEST-SELLING FOOTBALL MAGAZINE!

IN THE NEWS

CHELSEA: Frank Leboeuf says the ideal of English fair play is a myth and that he fears getting injured in most of the games he plays. The defender says he has become a target because he is French and a World Cup winner... **Jes Hogh** backs his new side to succeed in the forthcoming away tie against Galatasaray, despite the fear factor involved in playing an away match at the home of the Turkish champions... Chelsea's defeat at Liverpool, their third of the season, leaves certain sections of the media already ruling them out of the title race.

PREMIERSHIP: Peter Reid is said to be considering a £2 million bid for Bolton's prolific Icelandic striker **Eidur Gudjohnsen**, but Wanderers are keen to hold on to their prized asset... Kenny Dalglish comes to a settlement with Newcastle, who agree to pay their former manager £1.5 million for the two and a half years of this contract he didn't see out due to his early dismissal... Manchester United midfield ace **David Beckham** escapes a fine from the Football Association for his recent on-field conduct due to the amount of abuse he receives from opposing supporters.

THE FINAL SCORE!

OCTOBER 4		
Southampton	3-3	Derby
OCTOBER 16		
Arsenal	4-1	Everton
Coventry	4-1	Newcastle
Derby	0-1	**Tottenham**
Leeds	2-0	Sheff.Wed
Leicester	2-1	Southampton
Liverpool	1-0	Chelsea
Man. United	4-1	Watford
Wimbledon	3-2	Bradford

TOP OF THE PREMIERSHIP

	P	W	D	L	Pts
1. Leeds	11	8	1	2	25
2. Man. United	11	7	3	1	24
3. Arsenal	11	7	1	3	22
6. Chelsea	**9**	**6**	**1**	**2**	**19**

Dennis Wise added the fourth goal in the 5-0 rout of Galatasaray.

FROM THE PAGES OF *MATCH*

Star Italian striker **GIANFRANCO ZOLA** told **MATCH** how he thought **CHELSEA** would fare as they entered the European Champions League for the first time in the club's history.

How do you rate your chances in Europe? *"Our chances are good, but there's no room for any complacency. We're in a tough group but Chelsea need to be tested at the top level and doing well in Europe is very important to the club."*

What do you think of your group? *"It could've been much worse. Trips to Turkey, Germany and Italy will be a big test of our determination to do well but we have the advantage at home. Milan are strong and play with patience to break sides down, but if we play to our strengths, we'll do well."*

What are the strengths and weaknesses in the Chelsea squad? *"We've strengthened the squad and our experience in European tournaments will be invaluable. We have a big Italian influence and other than what Man. United achieved last season, the greater threat normally comes from Italian sides. There's no room for error. Injuries and suspensions happen, so it's how we overcome them that counts."*

What other teams do you see as the biggest threats? *"Fiorentina, Milan and Lazio are the biggest threats. Their tactical awareness, experience and ability gives them an edge. Man. United have gone to Italy and won, and they'll be the team the Italians fear most. Chelsea have a good chance, as do Arsenal. There are lots of good teams."*

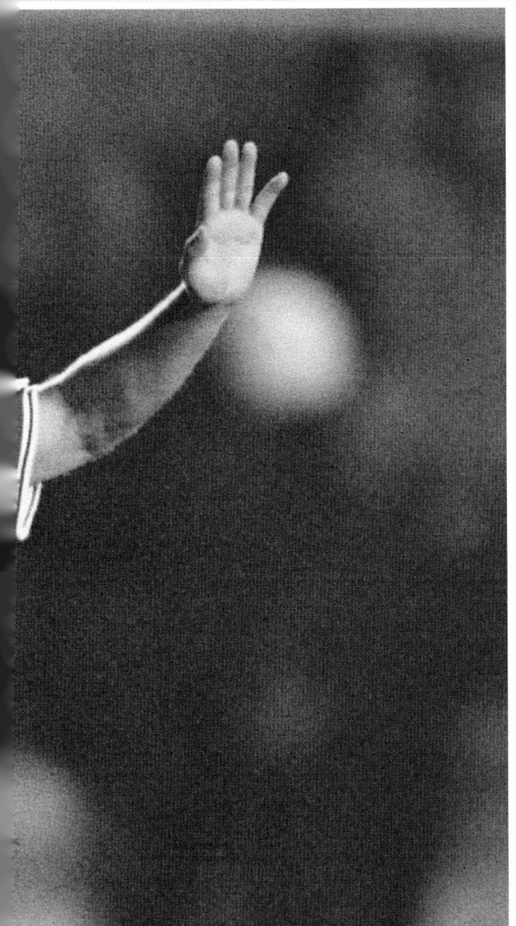

Galatasaray (0) 0
Chelsea (1) 5

Competition: **Champs League Group H**

Date: **Wednesday October 20, 1999**

Attendance: **25,500**

Referee: **V Melo Pereira** (Portugal) 8

THE GAME: Chelsea moved up into second place in their Champions League group by smashing Galatasaray 5-0 with with a superb performance in Turkey. The Blues comfortably dealt with the intimidating atmosphere of the Ali Sami Yen Stadium to produce a display of discipline, skill and clinical finishing. But the game was actually closer than the scoreline suggests, and it was Chelsea's superior finishing on the night which proved the decisive factor. With the half-time score at 1-0 the game was finely balanced, but Tore Andre Flo scored a second goal early in the second half before Gianfranco Zola added a third to kill the game off, leaving Dennis Wise and Gabriel Ambrosetti to complete a memorable victory.

CHELSEA GOALS: **Flo** *(31 mins):* Scored from eight yards with a low, right-foot shot past Mehmet; **Flo** *(48 mins):* Took the ball on his chest and grabbed his second from six yards; **Zola** *(54 mins):* Dummied the 'keeper and passed a tame shot into the empty net; **Wise** *(79 mins):* Flo pulled the ball back for Wise, who blasted a shot past Mehmet; **Ambrosetti** *(88 mins):* Made it 5-0 with a drive from the edge of the penalty area.

MATCH RATING: ★★★★ **LEAGUE POSITION: 6th**

GALATASARAY	
Mehmet	5
Popescu	6
Emre	6
Arif	5
Okan	5
Sukur (booked)	6
Booked: 61 mins (unsporting behaviour); Subbed: 62 mins (Saffet)	
Hagi	6
Subbed: 46 mins (Hasan)	
Fatih	6
Subbed: 46 mins (Umit)	
Tugay	☆7
Unsal (booked)	5
Booked: 90 mins (foul)	
Capone	5
***sub:** Umit* (booked)	5
Booked: 75 mins (foul)	
***sub:** Saffet*	5
***sub:** Hasan*	6

Subs not used: *Inan, Ahmet, Ergun, Marcio.*

CHELSEA	
de Goey	7
Babayaro	7
Leboeuf (booked)	8
Booked: 9 mins (foul)	
Desailly	8
Deschamps	6
Subbed: 66 mins (Wise)	
Poyet	7
Subbed: 66 mins (Petrescu)	
Le Saux	6
Ferrer	7
Flo ⚽⚽	☆9
Goals: 31, 48 mins	
Morris	7
Zola ⚽	8
Goal: 54 mins; Subbed: 76 mins (Ambrosetti)	
***sub:** Wise* ⚽	6
Goal: 79 mins	
***sub:** Petrescu*	6
***sub:** Ambrosetti* ⚽	
Goal: 88 mins	

Subs not used: *Cudicini, Hogh, Sutton, Lambourde.*

MATCH FACTS

Shots On Target		
Galatasaray	3-7	Chelsea
Shots Off Target		
Galatasaray	6-2	Chelsea
Hit Woodwork		
Galatasaray	2-0	Chelsea
Corners		
Galatasaray	1-2	Chelsea

HOW THEY LINED UP

THIS WEEK...

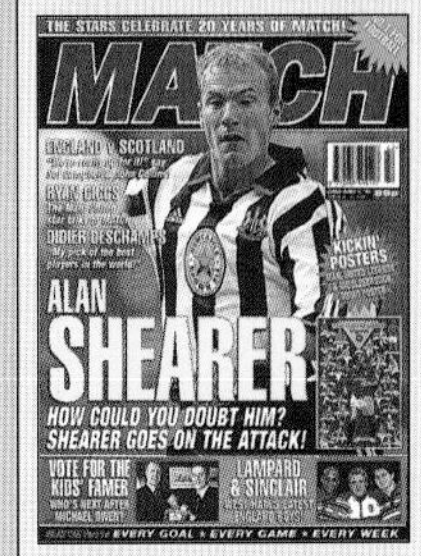

IN THE NEWS

CHELSEA: The Blues touch down in Istanbul to a hostile reception ahead of their Champions League clash with Galatasaray. Rocks and coins are hurled at the Chelsea team coach by supporters of the Turkish champions as it transfers the players from the airport to their hotel... The much talked about goalscoring 'crisis' at Chelsea is forgotten at least for one evening as The Blues thrash Galatasaray 5-0 in Turkey. For once, Chelsea's winning margin flattered them and the main difference between the two sides was, according to the press, the superior finishing of Vialli's outfit. Inside the stadium, the Galatasaray crowd, usually so vocal and intimidating, is stunned into silence as the home team are thrashed by The Blues.

PREMIERSHIP: Patrick Vieira is charged with misconduct after an alleged incident in the players' tunnel involving a policeman after he is sent-off against West Ham... **Steve Coppell** admits that Crystal Palace cannot afford to pay his existing players' wages and are £12 million in debt... Man. United goalkeeper **Massimo Taibi** has pleaded with Sir Alex Ferguson for more time to prove himself after his costly errors in recent weeks... A number of Premiership clubs, including Sheffield Wednesday, Coventry and West Ham, are all said to be chasing out-of-contract centre-back **Colin Hendry**, who is no longer guaranteed a first-team place at Scottish giants Rangers.

THE FINAL SCORE!

OCTOBER 17

Middlesbrough	2-0	West Ham

OCTOBER 18

Sunderland	2-1	Aston Villa

TOP OF THE PREMIERSHIP

	P	W	D	L	Pts
1. Leeds	11	8	1	2	25
2. Man. United	11	7	3	1	24
3. Sunderland	11	7	2	2	23
6. Chelsea	**9**	**6**	**1**	**2**	**19**

Flo put The Blues in front, but Arsenal staged an incredible comeback to win 3-2.

FROM THE PAGES OF *MATCH*

Two years into his second spell at **CHELSEA**, England defender **GRAEME LE SAUX** talked to **MATCH** about how life had changed at Stamford Bridge since he first arrived at the club.

There aren't many English players at Chelsea are there? *"No, there aren't. There's myself, Wisey and Jody Morris, obviously, and some of the younger players too. We are in a minority, but fortunately a lot of the backroom staff are English so they add weight to our numbers."*

Do you understand all of the other players? *"I noticed when I came back that they've all put in a massive effort to speak and learn English. If you're in the right frame of mind to learn a language, it's no problem. They feel they work in England and want to be like English people."*

Does speaking French help when you play with French defenders? *"It's nice to know what they're saying. If they're criticising you in French, you know what they're on about."*

Why do foreign players in their prime still choose to go to Italy or Spain? *"I think a lot of that's probably because of personal circumstances. There's still a certain amount of mystique about playing in Italy or Spain, but the value of playing here has also increased in recent years."*

How much has Chelsea changed over the years? *"Well, it's got better beyond belief and developed into a club that has become very successful. You expect a certain amount of change but it was like joining a completely new club. It felt so different coming back."*

Chelsea (1) 2
Arsenal (0) 3

Competition: **FA Carling Premiership**

Date: **Saturday October 23, 1999**

Attendance: **34,958**

Referee: **A Wilkie** (Chester-le-Street) 7

Game 17

THE GAME: Chelsea blew a comfortable 2-0 lead to London rivals and title challengers Arsenal to hand the visitors all three points at a rain-soaked Stamford Bridge. The Gunners looked beaten after goals from Tore Andre Flo and Dan Petrescu gave The Blues a good lead after 50 minutes, but Nwankwo Kanu conjured up a late hat-trick to leave Chelsea reeling. Gianluca Vialli knew his side would have to protect their leads better if they wanted to be serious challengers for the Premiership title.

CHELSEA GOALS: Flo *(39 mins):* Petrescu crossed from the right and Flo rose to head emphatically past Seaman into the corner of Arsenal's net; **Petrescu** *(51 mins):* Le Saux crossed from the right and Petrescu scored with a powerful header.

ARSENAL GOALS: Kanu *(73 mins):* Squeezed the ball home with a right-foot shot into de Goey's left-hand corner; **Kanu** *(81 mins):* Overmars provided the cross and Kanu applied the simple finish; **Kanu** *(90 mins):* Pounced on a de Goey blunder by the touchline and rounded the 'keeper before slotting the ball home from an unbelievable angle to the left of the goal.

MATCH RATING: ★★★★★ **LEAGUE POSITION: 7th**

CHELSEA	
de Goey	6
Petrescu ⚽	☆8
Goal: 51 mins	
Babayaro	6
Leboeuf	7
Desailly	7
Deschamps	7
Booked: 58 mins (foul)	
Sutton	6
Booked: 85 mins (foul)	
Wise	6
Booked: 40 mins (foul)	
Le Saux	7
Booked: 33 mins (unsporting behaviour); Subbed: 53 mins (Poyet)	
Ferrer	6
Flo ⚽	7
Goal: 39 mins; Subbed: 69 mins (Zola)	
sub: *Poyet*	6
sub: *Zola*	6

Subs not used: *Hogh, Morris, Cudicini.*

ARSENAL	
Seaman	6
Dixon	6
Booked: 2 mins (violent conduct)	
Keown	6
Adams	6
Ljungberg	7
Subbed: 61 mins (Henry)	
Suker	7
Booked: 29 mins (foul)	
Overmars	7
Subbed: 90 mins (Vernazza)	
Parlour	6
Silvinho	6
Petit	6
Booked: 50 mins (foul); Subbed: 64 mins (Vivas)	
Kanu ⚽⚽⚽	☆9
Goals: 73, 81, 90 mins	
sub: *Henry*	7
sub: *Vivas*	6
Booked: 87 mins (foul)	
sub: *Vernazza*	

Subs not used: *Manninger, Upson.*

MATCH FACTS

Shots On Target		
Chelsea	5-8	Arsenal
Shots Off Target		
Chelsea	2-6	Arsenal
Hit Woodwork		
Chelsea	0-0	Arsenal
Corners		
Chelsea	7-5	Arsenal

HOW THEY LINED UP

de Goey

Ferrer · Desailly · Leboeuf · Le Saux

Petrescu · Deschamps · Wise · Babayaro

Flo · Sutton

Suker · Kanu

Overmars · Petit · Ljungberg · Parlour

Silvinho · Keown · Adams · Dixon

Seaman

THIS WEEK...

IN THE NEWS

CHELSEA: Gianluca Vialli admits that he is perplexed by Chelsea's inconsistency this season... Some media critics are blaming the use of the rotation system and the lack of a settled Chelsea first team for the problems... Vialli takes some comfort from the league form of many of the other teams in the Champions League, which has been indifferent so far this season – Man. United apart, that is... Barcelona midfielder **Luis Enrique** is once again linked with a move to Stamford Bridge. The Spaniard believes that he has no future at the Nou Camp since the arrival of Finland winger Jari Litmanen... Chelsea announce that midfielder **Paul Hughes** is available on the transfer market for £150,000... **Roberto Di Matteo** is ready to battle his way back into the first team after recovering from a long lay-off with a serious ankle injury. "I hated having to sit and watch games," he said. "It's the longest I've been injured for some time."

PREMIERSHIP: Arsenal may have to smash their wage structure to keep hold of **Dennis Bergkamp** and **Marc Overmars**. Both players are said to be stalling on new contract talks... **Benito Carbone** joins Aston Villa until the end of the season, after which the Italian will become a free agent... Veteran Southampton striker **Mark Hughes** faces an FA charge after playing in Sir Alex Ferguson's testimonial while he should have been serving a suspension... Leeds boss David O'Leary is said to be closing in on Leicester striker **Emile Heskey**. The Irish manager has plenty of money to spend and has made no secret of his plans to replace the departed Jimmy Floyd Hasselbaink with another big name striker... **David Beckham** has insisted he is happy at Manchester United after his wife's admission in a new book that she was hoping he'd move to a London club instead of agreeing to sign a new deal at Old Trafford.

THE FINAL SCORE!

OCTOBER 23		
Aston Villa	1-1	Wimbledon
Bradford	3-1	Leicester
Chelsea	2-3	**Arsenal**
Sheff. Wed.	0-0	Coventry
Southampton	1-1	Liverpool
Tottenham	3-1	Man. United

TOP OF THE PREMIERSHIP

	P	W	D	L	Pts
1. Leeds	11	8	1	2	25
2. Arsenal	12	8	1	3	25
3. Man. United	12	7	3	2	24
7. Chelsea	**10**	**6**	**1**	**3**	**19**

AC Milan	(0) 1
Chelsea	(0) 1

Competition: **Champs League Group H**

Date: **Tuesday October 26, 1999**

Attendance: **74,855**

Referee: **N Levnikov** (Russia) 6

Game 18

THE GAME: Chelsea moved a step closer to qualifying from their Champions League group with a well-deserved point in the famous San Siro. During a tight first half, The Blues looked composed and assured, with Tore Andre Flo leading the line superbly for Gianluca Vialli's side. It was the Norwegian who came nearest to getting the visitors off the mark, but he could only watch in dismay as his header from Dennis Wise's cross was saved by Abbiati with an outstanding block from close range. The speed of Milan's counter-attacks allowed them to take the lead through Oliver Bierhoff in the 74th minute, but their advantage lasted for only three minutes. Dennis Wise scored a dramatic equaliser to leave The Blues needing only a point against Hertha Berlin to qualify for the next round.

AC MILAN GOAL: Bierhoff *(74 mins):* A quick counter-attack by Milan led to a surging run from full-back Serginho, whose near post cross was met by the head of Bierhoff.

CHELSEA GOAL: Wise *(77mins):* Di Matteo, back in the side after injury, played a sweeping 30-yard pass up to Wise. The Chelsea captain controlled the ball instantly, then ran on to slot the ball under the on-rushing Milan 'keeper Abbiati.

MATCH RATING: ★★★ **LEAGUE POSITION: 7th**

AC MILAN	
Abbiati	7
Maldini	8
Costacurta	7
Booked: 63 mins (foul)	
Shevchenko	☆ 9
Gattuso	8
Ayala	7
Booked: 43 mins (foul)	
Leonardo	7
Booked: 45 mins (foul); Subbed: 57 mins (Boban)	
Bierhoff	8
Goal: 74 mins	
Ambrosini	7
Booked: 13 mins (foul)	
Guly	8
Serginho	6
Subbed: 86 mins (Orlandini)	
sub: *Boban*	7
sub: *Orlandini*	

Subs not used: *Rossi, Helveg, Sala, De Ascentis, N'Gotty.*

CHELSEA	
de Goey	6
Petrescu	7
Subbed: 46 mins (Morris)	
Babayaro	7
Leboeuf	8
Desailly	7
Deschamps	☆ 9
Poyet	5
Subbed: 75 mins (Di Matteo)	
Wise	8
Goal: 77 mins	
Ferrer	8
Booked: 68 mins (foul)	
Flo	7
Zola	8
Booked: 39 mins (foul); Subbed: 80 mins (Ambrosetti)	
sub: *Morris*	6
sub: *Di Matteo*	
sub: *Ambrosetti*	

Subs not used: *Cudicini, Hogh, Sutton, Lambourde.*

MATCH FACTS

Shots On Target	
AC Milan 4-5 Chelsea	
Shots Off Target	
AC Milan 8-4 Chelsea	
Hit Woodwork	
AC Milan 0-0 Chelsea	
Corners	
AC Milan 7-4 Chelsea	

HOW THEY LINED UP

Abbiati

Costacurta Ayala Maldini

Guly Ambrosini Gattuso Serginho

Shevchenko Bierhoff Leonardo

Zola Flo

Poyet Wise Deschamps Petrescu

Babayaro Leboeuf Desailly Ferrer

de Goey

Captain Fantastic was the hero in the San Siro after his well-taken equaliser.

Leboeuf goes into hiding after his goal, but it wasn't enough to seal the points at Derby.

Derby County	(1)	**3**
Chelsea	(1)	**1**

Competition: **FA Carling Premiership**

Date: **Saturday October 30, 1999**

Attendance: **28,614**

Referee: **R Harris** (Oxford) 7

THE GAME: Gianluca Vialli's side suffered another hangover following their midweek heroics in the Champions League by losing to a Derby side which hadn't won any of their previous six Premiership matches. That was Chelsea's third successive league defeat since thrashing Manchester United 5-0, and the result seriously questioned their title aspirations. Deon Burton gave Jim Smith's side the lead with only seven minutes gone, but Frank Leboeuf levelled the score just three minutes later. At this stage of the game it looked like The Blues would take control, but they couldn't score a second goal and the home side regained the advantage with only ten minutes left on the clock through Rory Delap. The Derby midfielder doubled his tally two minutes from time with a long range effort to make it 3-1 to The Rams. It didn't help that the visitors lost both of their centre-backs, with Jes Hogh replaced after 33 minutes and Leboeuf substituted early in the second period for Didier Deschamps. Chelsea's fourth defeat of the season saw them drop to eighth place in the league – a disappointing position considering their impressive results in Europe.

DERBY GOALS: Burton *(7 mins):* A pass from Fuertes was met by Burton, who calmly placed his shot past the 'keeper; **Delap** *(80 mins):* Dispossessed Morris 30 yards out before curling a shot into the corner of the net; **Delap** *(88 minutes):* A long ball from Johnson was miscued by Morris and fell to Delap, who blasted his shot into the net via a deflection.
CHELSEA GOAL: Leboeuf *(10 minutes)*: Ferrer's cross was taken down by Leboeuf, who scooped his shot over Hoult.

MATCH RATING: ★★★★ **LEAGUE POSITION: 8th**

MATCH FACTS

Shots On Target		
Derby	4-3	Chelsea
Shots Off Target		
Derby	4-5	Chelsea
Hit Woodwork		
Derby	1-0	Chelsea
Corners		
Derby	4-2	Chelsea

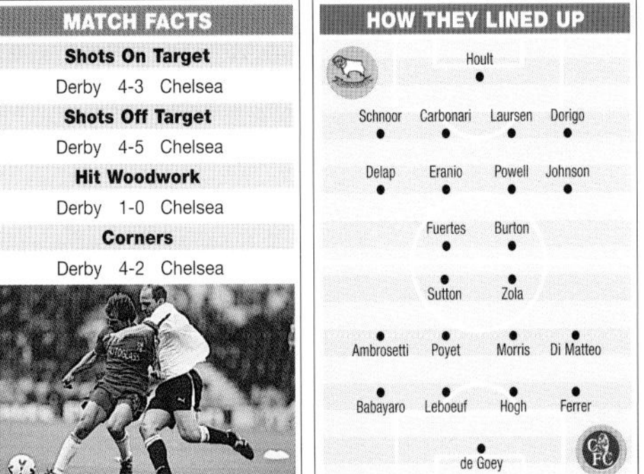

HOW THEY LINED UP

Derby: Hoult; Schnoor, Carbonari, Laursen, Dorigo; Delap, Eranio, Powell, Johnson; Fuertes, Burton

Chelsea: Sutton, Zola; Ambrosetti, Poyet, Morris, Di Matteo; Babayaro, Leboeuf, Hogh, Ferrer; de Goey

DERBY COUNTY

Player	Rating
Hoult	7
Carbonari	6
Schnoor (booked)	8
Booked: 25 mins (foul)	
Powell	7
Dorigo	7
Johnson	7
Burton (goal, booked)	7
Goal: 7 mins; Booked: 45 mins (foul)	
Delap (2 goals)	☆ 9
Goals: 80, 88 mins	
Laursen	6
Subbed: 53 mins (Prior)	
Fuertes	7
Subbed: 82 mins (Morris)	
Eranio	8
Subbed: 75 mins (Borbokis)	
sub: *Prior*	6
sub: *Morris*	
sub: *Borbokis*	

Subs not used: *Christie, Knight.*

CHELSEA

Player	Rating
de Goey	6
Babayaro	7
Hogh	6
Subbed: 33 mins (Lambourde)	
Leboeuf (goal)	6
Goal: 10 mins; Subbed: 53 mins (Deschamps)	
Poyet	7
Sutton	7
Di Matteo	7
Ferrer	7
Ambrosetti	☆ 8
Subbed: 63 mins (Harley)	
Morris	7
Zola	7
sub: *Lambourde* (booked)	6
Booked: 62 mins (foul)	
sub: *Harley*	6
sub: *Deschamps*	6

Subs not used: *Flo, Cudicini,.*

THIS WEEK...

IN THE NEWS

CHELSEA: Despite losing more Premiership games so far this term than they did in the whole of last season, Gianluca Vialli says he still believes his side can go on to lift the title... Chelsea's erratic form continues to confound the critics, management and fans alike, as a superb 1-1 draw away against Italian giants AC Milan is followed by a disappointing defeat against Jim Smith's modest Derby side.

PREMIERSHIP: Newcastle season ticket holders stage a protest at plans to either move their seating positions for next season or face paying three times the old price to retain their seats... England striker **Michael Owen** limps off only eight minutes after coming on the field as a substitute for Danny Murphy in Liverpool's 1-1 stalemate with Southampton at The Dell... Arsenal legend **Ian Wright** joins Celtic on loan from West Ham in an attempt to solve the Glasgow side's recent goalscoring problems and fill the void left by Henrik Larsson's injury.

THE FINAL SCORE!

OCTOBER 24		
Everton	4-4	Leeds
Watford	1-2	**Middlesbrough**
West Ham	1-1	Sunderland
OCTOBER 25		
Newcastle	2-0	Derby
OCTOBER 27		
Liverpool	1-0	West Ham
OCTOBER 30		
Arsenal	0-0	Newcastle
Derby	3-1	Chelsea
Leeds	1-0	West Ham
Leicester	3-0	Sheff.Wed.
Man. United	3-0	Aston Villa
Middlesbrough	2-1	Everton
Wimbledon	1-1	Southampton
OCTOBER 31		
Coventry	4-0	Watford
Sunderland	2-1	Tottenham

TOP OF THE PREMIERSHIP

	P	W	D	L	Pts
1. Leeds	13	9	2	2	29
2. Arsenal	13	8	3	2	27
3. Man. United	13	8	2	3	26
8. Chelsea	**11**	**6**	**1**	**4**	**19**

NOVEMBER

START OF MONTH **8th** END OF MONTH **8th**

"The Champions League is a huge challenge. We're in it for the first time but we've got experienced players and a manager who has won it as a player." Chris Sutton

THE CHAMPIONS LEAGUE CAMPAIGN CONTINUED IN EARNEST FOR Chelsea in November, with Gianluca Vialli's side needing a good result at home to Hertha Berlin to qualify for the second stage of the competition. After playing 19 games in three months, Chelsea were pleased to see they only had five games in November, four of which were at Stamford Bridge. They had a good league record at home, winning four of their five games since the start of the season, so the stage was set for a successful month.

Chelsea were level on points with Hertha Berlin at the top of Group H, but still needed to beat the Germans to stop AC Milan from qualifying instead of them – assuming the Italians could beat Galatasaray in Istanbul. Fortunately, the result in Turkey was irrelevant as The Blues beat Hertha 2-0 with goals from Albert Ferrer and Didier Deschamps to finish top of the group.

In the Premiership, a goalless stalemate with West Ham left Chelsea ten points behind leaders Manchester United but with two games in hand over the treble-winners. Gianluca Vialli believed these matches were crucial and said his side still had a good chance of lifting the title – but dropping two points in a 1-1 draw with Everton didn't help their championship hopes.

At least The Blues were succeeding in Europe. In the second round of the Champions League they were drawn with Lazio, Feyenoord and Marseille in Group D and immediately set about qualifying for the quarter-finals with an emphatic 3-1 win over Feyenoord in an awesome performance at Stamford Bridge. Success in Europe was alerting chairmen from all over the continent who were searching for a dynamic young coach. Real Madrid were the latest club said to be courting Gianluca Vialli following the dismissal of coach John Toshack. A 1-0 win over Bradford City completed the month and The Blues went into the festive period in a strong position.

THE GAMES

Nov. 3 v **Hertha Berlin** (h)

Nov. 7 v **West Ham** (h)

Nov. 20 v **Everton** (a)

Nov. 24 v **Feyenoord** (h)

Nov. 28 v **Bradford City** (h)

TRANSFERS IN

None

TRANSFERS OUT

Neil Clement

Position: **Defender**

Fee: **Loan**

To: **Brentford**

MATCH facts

Matchman Of The Month

JODY MORRIS
Average Rating: 7.33

Didier Deschamps hits a cracking long-range effort from 25 yards to send The Blues into the lead.

Chelsea	(2) **2**
Hertha Berlin	(0) **0**

Competition: **Champs League Group H**

Date: **Wednesday November 3, 1999**

Attendance: **33,623**

Referee: **K Nilsson** (Sweden) 6

Game 20

THE GAME: Didier Deschamps and Albert Ferrer scored their first ever goals for Chelsea to enhance the club's Champions League aspirations. The victory meant The Blues finished top of the competitive Group H and were seeded for the second round of the competition. Deschamps opened the scoring for Chelsea with a fantastic individual effort after 11 minutes, his first goal in 73 European matches. Defender Ferrer also got off the mark in the 44th minute to give Gianluca Vialli's side a 2-0 lead at the interval. The second half was less eventful as the home side tightened up their play in an effort to protect their two-goal lead. The only downside to the evening came when striker Chris Sutton, in an attacking trio with Gianfranco Zola and Tore Andre Flo, was given his marching orders for a heavy challenge on Hertha's Norwegian defender Kjetil Rekdal.

CHELSEA GOALS: Deschamps *(11 mins):* A slip by Daei allowed Deschamps to round the Hertha defence and unleash a ferocious 25-yard, right-foot strike from outside the area; **Ferrer** *(43 mins):* Wise whipped the ball in, allowing Ferrer to strike a powerful shot which went over the top of the 'keeper.

MATCH RATING: ★★★ **LEAGUE POSITION: 9th**

"When we play against a team in Europe we know a lot about them, we watch videos of how they play and how they work as a team. We know what they can do, that's why we do well against them." DAN PETRESCU

MATCH FACTS

Shots On Target		
Chelsea	6-2	Hertha Berlin
Shots Off Target		
Chelsea	7-5	Hertha Berlin
Hit Woodwork		
Chelsea	0-0	Hertha Berlin
Corners		
Chelsea	7-3	Hertha Berlin

HOW THEY LINED UP

CHELSEA	
de Goey	7
Petrescu	7
Babayaro	7
Hogh	8
Subbed: 66 mins (Leboeuf)	
Desailly	9
Subbed: 86 mins (Lambourde)	
Deschamps ⚽	☆ 9
Goal: 11 mins	
Sutton	6
Booked: 80 mins (foul); Sent-off: 90 mins (second bookable offence: foul)	
Wise	8
Ferrer ⚽	8
Goal: 43 mins	
Flo	7
Zola	7
Subbed: 64 mins (Poyet)	
sub: *Leboeuf*	7
sub: *Poyet*	7
sub: *Lambourde*	

Subs not used: *Cudicini, Ambrosetti, Morris, Forssell.*

HERTHA BERLIN	
Kiraly	6
van Burik	6
Sverrisson	6
Wosz	6
Subbed: 46 mins (Konstantinidis)	
Daei	7
Rekdal	6
Preetz	6
Subbed: 46 mins (Aracic)	
Sanneh	6
Michalke	6
Deisler	6
Helmer	☆ 7
Subbed: 58 mins (Schmidt)	
sub: *Konstantinidis*	6
sub: *Aracic*	6
sub: *Schmidt*	6

Subs not used: *Fiedler, Herzog, Neuendorf, Thom.*

CHAMPIONS LEAGUE

FINAL STANDINGS GROUP H

	P	W	D	L	Pts
1. Chelsea	6	3	2	1	11
2. Hertha Berlin	6	2	2	2	8
3. Galatasaray	6	2	1	3	7
4. AC Milan	6	1	3	2	6

The Blues had to be at their best in defence to keep out a strong West Ham side.

 **Chelsea** (0) 0

 **West Ham United** (0) 0

Competition: **FA Carling Premiership**

Date: **Sunday November 7, 1999**

Attendance: **34,935**

Referee: **M Riley** (Leeds) 5

THE GAME: After some poor displays in the league following their midweek Champions League games, Chelsea put on an improved showing against West Ham. But the home fans left disappointed with a point in this bad-tempered encounter at Stamford Bridge. The fluent passing game of Gianluca Vialli's side was restricted by a physical West Ham side which denied The Blues any space. There were more yellow cards than clear opportunities and Chelsea's first scoring chance didn't arrive until just before half time, when a Jody Morris piledriver forced a fine save from Hammers 'keeper Craig Forrest. The Blues raised their game after the break, with headed chances falling to Tore Andre Flo and Celestine Babayaro, but they failed to break the deadlock and West Ham seemed happy to hang on for an away point. Javier Margas was sent-off after receiving his second yellow card for a foul on Didier Deschamps, but it was too late for the home side to take advantage.

MATCH RATING: ★★★ **LEAGUE POSITION:** 9th

> **"A lot of teams have defended differently against us this year because we were ripping teams apart with our passing and getting behind them last year. Teams have started putting everyone behind the ball."** JODY MORRIS

CHELSEA	
de Goey	6
Petrescu	6
Babayaro	6
Leboeuf ▯ *Booked: 52 mins (foul)*	6
Desailly	6
Deschamps	6
Poyet ▯ *Booked: 37 mins (foul)*	7
Ferrer ▯ *Booked: 47 mins (foul)*	7
Flo	5
Morris	☆8
Zola *Subbed: 68 mins Ambrosetti*	5
sub: Ambrosetti	5

Subs not used: Di Matteo, Lambourde, Cudicini, Forssell.

WEST HAM	
Forrest	6
Stimac ▯ *Booked: 68 mins (foul)*	7
Keller	7
Sinclair	7
Lomas ▯ *Booked: 37 mins (foul)*	7
Wanchope	6
Foe	7
Ferdinand	8
Lampard	6
Cole ▯ *Booked 70 mins (unsporting behaviour); Subbed: 87 mins (Ruddock)*	☆9
Margas ▯▮ *Booked: 25 mins (foul); Sent-off: 85 mins (second bookable offence: foul)*	7
sub: Ruddock	

Subs not used: Charles, Kitson, Moncur, Bywater.

MATCH FACTS

Shots On Target		
Chelsea	5-2	West Ham
Shots Off Target		
Chelsea	8-5	West Ham
Hit Woodwork		
Chelsea	0-0	West Ham
Corners		
Chelsea	5-4	West Ham

HOW THEY LINED UP

THIS WEEK...

IN THE NEWS

CHELSEA: Despite the fact that The Blues are already ten points adrift of leaders Man. United, coach Gianluca Vialli points to his side's two games in hand and says they still have a chance of lifting the title... Arsenal boss Arsene Wenger names Chelsea as one of the teams he believes can lift the Champions League trophy, along with Man. United, Barcelona and Lazio... In the big Scotland versus England Euro 2000 play-off tie, Chelsea don't have a single player involved – England's first-choice left-back **Graeme Le Saux** is ruled out with an injury.

PREMIERSHIP: Sir Alex Ferguson hints that Man. United captain **Roy Keane** could sign a new contract at Old Trafford after several months of intense speculation regarding the Irishman's future... Leicester's **Matt Elliott** is given a one-match ban for his controversial challenge on Liverpool star striker **Michael Owen,** which went unpunished by referee Uriah Rennie...Former England boss Graham Taylor signs a three-year deal with Watford.

THE FINAL SCORE!

NOVEMBER 1		
Liverpool	3-1	Bradford
NOVEMBER 6		
Aston Villa	0-1	**Southampton**
Bradford	1-1	Coventry
Liverpool	2-0	Derby
Man. United	2-0	Leicester
Middlesbrough	1-1	Sunderland
Sheff. Wed.	2-2	Watford
NOVEMBER 7		
Chelsea	0-0	West Ham
Newcastle	1-1	Everton
Tottenham	2-1	Arsenal
Wimbledon	2-0	Leeds

TOP OF THE PREMIERSHIP

	P	W	D	L	Pts
1. Man. United	14	9	3	2	30
2. Leeds	14	9	2	3	29
3. Sunderland	14	8	4	2	28
9. Chelsea	**12**	**6**	**2**	**4**	**20**

Everton's solid defence proved hard to beat for Chelsea's star strikers.

Tore-Andre Flo was at his poaching best to see off Dutch side Feyenoord.

Everton (1) 1
Chelsea (0) 1

Competition: **FA Carling Premiership**

Date: **Saturday November 20, 1999**

Attendance: **38,225**

Referee: **M Halsey** (Welwyn) 7

THE GAME: A last-gasp strike from Tore Andre Flo earned ten-man Chelsea a much needed point at Goodison Park to deny Everton the victory they probably deserved. The Blues were strangely out of sorts, seeming to sacrifice their normal stylish build-up play in favour of hitting long hopeful balls in the direction of the two strikers. The Blues certainly seemed to be missing the midfield influence of the suspended Dennis Wise, giving Everton the upper hand. The game was played at a furious pace and, after a flurry of bookings, Frank Leboeuf received his second yellow card for a tackle from behind on Nick Barmby. The visitors looked doomed before Flo scored a dramatic injury-time equaliser to earn a share of the points.

EVERTON GOAL: **Campbell** *(15 mins):* Jeffers collected the ball in the Chelsea area before slipping a pass to Campbell, who tapped his shot past de Goey from five yards.

CHELSEA GOAL: **Flo** *(90 mins):* Indecision in the Everton area led to Dunne giving the ball straight to Flo, who calmly beat goalkeeper Gerrard with a shot to the 'keeper's right.

MATCH RATING: ★★★★ **LEAGUE POSITION: 9th**

"We have enough players in the squad to be able to cope with both competitions. It would be very foolish for us to concentrate on one of our objectives at the expense of the other one." GIANLUCA VIALLI

MATCH FACTS

Shots On Target		
Everton	1-6	Chelsea
Shots Off Target		
Everton	6-4	Chelsea
Hit Woodwork		
Everton	0-0	Chelsea
Corners		
Everton	6-5	Chelsea

HOW THEY LINED UP

Everton: Gerrard; Xavier, Cleland, Gough, Unsworth, Dunne; Barmby, Hutchison, Pembridge; Jeffers, Campbell

Chelsea: Sutton, Flo; Ambrosetti, Morris, Deschamps, Petrescu; Babayaro, Leboeuf, Desailly, Ferrer; de Goey

EVERTON

Player	Rating
Gerrard	8
Cleland	8
Dunne	8
Gough	☆8
Unsworth	8
Xavier	7
Pembridge (booked) *Booked: 68 mins (foul)*	7
Hutchison (booked) *Booked: 29 mins (foul)*	7
Barmby	8
Campbell (goal) *Goal: 15 mins*	7
Jeffers	6

Subs not used: *Ball, Collins, Gemmill, Simonsen, Grant.*

CHELSEA

Player	Rating
de Goey	6
Ferrer (booked) *Booked: 78 mins (foul); Subbed: 81 mins (Hogh)*	5
Leboeuf (booked, sent off) *Booked: 44 mins (foul); Sent-off: 56 mins (second bookable offence: foul)*	6
Desailly	7
Babayaro	6
Petrescu *Subbed: 51 mins (Zola)*	6
Deschamps	☆8
Morris	7
Ambrosetti *Subbed: 2 mins (Di Matteo)*	
Flo (booked, goal) *Booked: 81 mins (foul); Goal: 90 mins*	7
Sutton (booked) *Booked: 27 mins (foul)*	6
sub: *Zola*	6
sub: *Di Matteo*	6
sub: *Hogh*	

Subs not used: *Cudicini, Harley.*

Chelsea (1) 3
Feyenoord (0) 1

Competition: **Champs League Group D**

Date: **Wednesday November 24, 1999**

Attendance: **29,704**

Referee: **J-M Garcia Aranda** (Spain) 8

THE GAME: A brace from Tore-Andre Flo handed The Blues another memorable Champions League victory as Feyenoord were swept aside at Stamford Bridge. The Norwegian struck after 67 and 86 minutes to add to Celestine Babayaro's strike on the stroke of half time. Chelsea enjoyed 62 per cent of the possession in this one-sided encounter – a surprising statistic at this level of football. Only resolute defending by the Dutch visitors limited The Blues to a one-goal lead at half time – the home side could have reached double figures if their finishing had been more decisive. A last-minute error by Marcel Desailly allowed Cruz to score a consolation goal, but it was more than Feyenoord deserved after their poor contribution.

CHELSEA GOALS: **Babayaro** *(45 mins):* Headed home from Petrescu's right-wing cross; **Flo** *(67 mins):* A Babayaro header crashed off the underside of the bar and Flo pounced on the rebound to score; **Flo** *(86 mins):* Flo's backheel was parried by the 'keeper and the Norwegian fired in at the second attempt.

FEYENOORD GOAL: ***Cruz*** *(90 mins):* Desailly's slip left Cruz in against de Goey and the striker drove the ball into the net.

MATCH RATING: ★★★★ **LEAGUE POSITION: 9th**

"On our day we can beat anyone. I'd say we've played one or two good games in the Champions league this year. If we really start playing well, who knows what will happen? It'll be unbelievable for us." JODY MORRIS

Chelsea (1) 1
Bradford City (0) 0

Competition: **FA Carling Premiership**

Date: **Sunday November 28, 1999**

Attendance: **31,591**

Referee: **A Wiley** (Burntwood) 7

Game 24

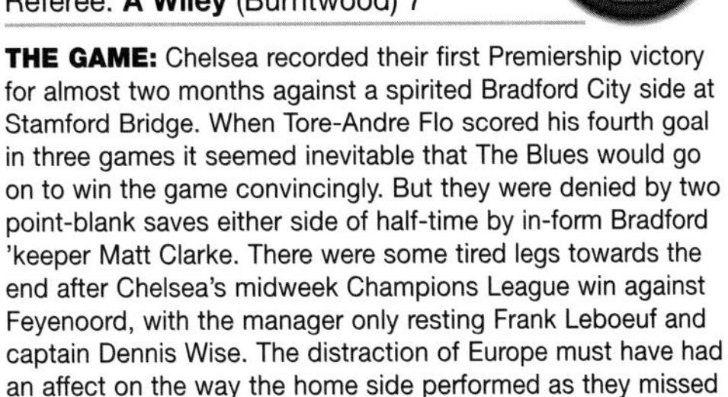

THE GAME: Chelsea recorded their first Premiership victory for almost two months against a spirited Bradford City side at Stamford Bridge. When Tore-Andre Flo scored his fourth goal in three games it seemed inevitable that The Blues would go on to win the game convincingly. But they were denied by two point-blank saves either side of half-time by in-form Bradford 'keeper Matt Clarke. There were some tired legs towards the end after Chelsea's midweek Champions League win against Feyenoord, with the manager only resting Frank Leboeuf and captain Dennis Wise. The distraction of Europe must have had an affect on the way the home side performed as they missed a host of chances. Gianfranco Zola, who hadn't scored in the league since the first game of the season against Sunderland, was unlucky not to get the goal his performance deserved.

CHELSEA GOAL: **Flo** *(15 mins):* A corner by Zola was swung in from the right and Flo held off the challenge of the Bradford defenders to drive a right-foot volley into the back of the net.

MATCH RATING: ★★★ **LEAGUE POSITION:** **8th**

"Bradford must have spent the whole week learning how to stop us from playing football. They gave a very brave defensive performance out there today but they hardly had a shot on goal." GIANLUCA VIALLI

CHELSEA		FEYENOORD	
de Goey	7	Dudek	☆8
Petrescu	8	van Gastel	7
Babayaro ⚽ *Goal: 45 mins*	8	Bosvelt	7
Leboeuf	6	Kalou	7
Desailly	7	van Wonderen	6
Deschamps *Subbed: 88 mins (Dalla Bona)*	8	Tomasson *Subbed: 58 mins (Cruz)*	6
Poyet *Subbed: 88 mins (Di Matteo)*	7	van Vossen *Subbed: 60 mins (Samardzic)*	7
Wise	7	Konterman	6
Ferrer	8	de Visser	6
Flo ⚽⚽ *Goals: 67, 86 mins*	8	van Gobbel	6
Zola	☆9	Somalia	6
sub: *Dalla Bona*		***sub:*** *Cruz* ⚽ *Goal: 90 mins*	7
sub: *Di Matteo*		***sub:*** *Samardzic*	6

Subs not used: *Cudicini, Hogh, Goldbaek, Morris, Harley.*

Subs not used: *Graafland, Rzasa, Paauwe, Korneev, de Haan.*

CHELSEA		BRADFORD CITY	
de Goey	6	Clarke	☆8
Petrescu *Subbed: 29 mins (Goldbaek)*	6	Myers	6
Babayaro	7	Wetherall	7
Hogh	7	Lawrence	7
Desailly	7	Mills *Subbed: 89 mins (Rankin)*	6
Deschamps ▯ *Booked: 88 mins (foul)*	8	Whalley *Subbed: 69 mins (Blake)*	6
Poyet	6	Beagrie	7
Ferrer	6	O'Brien	6
Flo ⚽ *Goal: 15 mins*	☆9	Windass	6
Morris	7	Halle	6
Zola	8	Redfearn	7
sub: *Goldbaek*	7	***sub:*** *Blake*	7
		sub: *Rankin*	

Subs not used: *Di Matteo, Lambourde, Cudicini, Dalla Bona.*

Subs not used: *Westwood, Dreyer, Taylor.*

MATCH FACTS

Shots On Target		
Chelsea	19-3	Feyenoord
Shots Off Target		
Chelsea	18-1	Feyenoord
Hit Woodwork		
Chelsea	1-0	Feyenoord
Corners		
Chelsea	18-2	Feyenoord

HOW THEY LINED UP

de Goey

Ferrer, Desailly, Leboeuf, Babayaro

Petrescu, Deschamps, Wise, Poyet

Flo, Zola

Somalia, Tomasson, Kalou

van Vossen, van Gastel, Bosvelt

de Visser, van Gobbel, van Wonderen, Konterman

Dudek

MATCH FACTS

Shots On Target		
Chelsea	6-8	Bradford
Shots Off Target		
Chelsea	12-8	Bradford
Hit Woodwork		
Chelsea	1-1	Bradford
Corners		
Chelsea	8-8	Bradford

HOW THEY LINED UP

de Goey

Ferrer, Desailly, Hogh, Babayaro

Petrescu, Deschamps, Morris, Poyet

Flo, Zola

Mills, Windass

Beagrie, Whalley, Redfearn, Lawrence

Myers, Wetherall, O'Brien, Halle

Clarke

THIS WEEK...

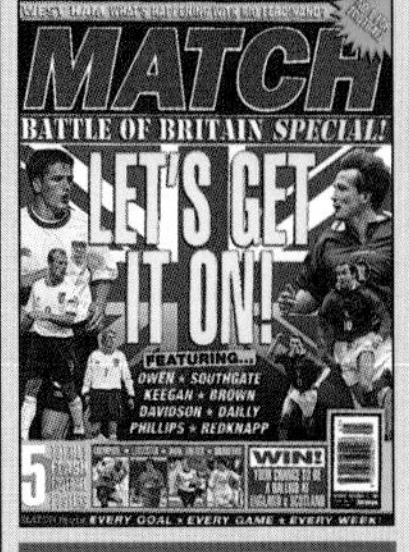

IN THE NEWS

CHELSEA: Responding to criticism about their league form, Gianluca Vialli says Chelsea are only two points behind where they were at the same time last season... Spanish side Real Madrid confirm **Gianluca Vialli** is one of several names on their managerial 'wish list' as they seek a replacement for former boss John Toshack.

PREMIERSHIP: Aston Villa skipper **Gareth Southgate** finds himself on a misconduct charge after his first ever sending-off away against Leicester... Derby's Argentinian striker **Esteban Fuertes** is banned from re-entering England after his passport is declared to be fake... Arsenal are looking at three sites in London on which to build a new £100 million, 60,000 stadium.

THE FINAL SCORE!

NOVEMBER 20		
Arsenal	5-1	Middlesbrough
Derby	1-2	**Man. United**
Everton	1-1	Chelsea
Leeds	2-1	Bradford
Leicester	2-1	Wimbledon
Southampton	0-1	**Tottenham**
Sunderland	0-2	**Liverpool**
Watford	1-1	Newcastle
NOVEMBER 21		
West Ham	4-3	Sheff. Wed.
NOVEMBER 22		
Coventry	2-1	Aston Villa
NOVEMBER 27		
Coventry	0-1	**Leicester**
Everton	0-0	Aston Villa
Middlesbrough	0-0	Wimbledon
Watford	2-3	**Sunderland**
West Ham	1-0	Liverpool
NOVEMBER 28		
Arsenal	2-1	Derby
Chelsea	1-0	Bradford
Leeds	1-0	Southampton
Newcastle	2-1	Tottenham

TOP OF THE PREMIERSHIP

	P	W	D	L	Pts
1. Leeds	16	11	2	3	35
2. Man. United	15	10	3	2	33
3. Arsenal	16	10	2	4	32
8. Chelsea	**14**	**7**	**3**	**4**	**24**

DECEMBER

START OF MONTH **8th**  END OF MONTH **7th**

"I want to win the title – it's the most important thing in England. The fans want their team to be the champions of their country more than anything." Didier Deschamps

WITH A BREAK IN THE CHAMPIONS LEAGUE COMING UP, CHELSEA knew that their December fixture against Lazio in Rome would be a crucial point in their European campaign. Some pundits said Gianluca Vialli's team had a better chance of succeeding in Europe than they did in the league as The Blues had another inconsistent month in the Premiership. Their form in Europe was winning admirers all over the continent, but their four domestic fixtures over the festive period didn't exactly go to plan.

Sunderland, thrashed 4-0 on the opening day of the season at Stamford Bridge, were the first opponents of the month. Peter Reid's determined side was eager to gain revenge for that early humiliation and were 1-0 up inside the first minute. Things didn't get any better for shell-shocked Chelsea and they were comprehensively beaten 4-1 by the Wearsiders.

The defeat at the Stadium Of Light didn't bode well for the daunting away trip to Lazio but The Blues defied their critics to earn a creditable 0-0 draw in the Italian capital to go top of Group D after two games. After impressing opponents Lazio with a solid performance in defence, Marcel Desailly was linked with a move back to Italy, but thankfully a deal never materialised.

The Blues also started their 2000 FA Cup campaign in December, which began with a comfortable 6-1 win over Third Division Hull City, with Vialli fielding a strong side to show how seriously he was taking the competition, in contrast to his tactics for the Worthington Cup. Chelsea's Premiership duties resumed with a 2-0 home defeat to pace-setters Leeds who, despite being second-best for most of the match, emerged from Stamford Bridge with three points. The year ended on a bright note, though, with The Blues beating Southampton 2-1 on Boxing Day and recording a commanding 3-0 victory over Sheffield Wednesday in their last fixture of the millennium.

THE GAMES

Dec. 4 v **Sunderland** (a)

Dec. 7 v **Lazio** (a)

Dec. 11 v **Hull City** (a)

Dec. 19 v **Leeds** (h)

Dec. 26 v **Southampton** (a)

Dec. 29 v **Sheff. Wed.** (h)

TRANSFERS IN

Emerson Thome

Position: **Defender**

Fee: **£2.7 million**

From: **Sheffield Wednesday**

TRANSFERS OUT

Paul Hughes

Position: **Midfielder**

Fee: **Loan**

To: **Crewe**

MATCH facts

Matchman Of The Month

GUSTAVO POYET
Average Rating: 7.50

Sunderland (4) 4
Chelsea (0) 1

Competition: **FA Carling Premiership**

Date: **Saturday December 4, 1999**

Attendance: **41,377**

Referee: **S Dunn** (Bristol) 8

THE GAME: Peter Reid's Sunderland gained sweet revenge for their 4-0 thrashing at Stamford Bridge on the opening day of the season with an awesome display in the first-half which left Chelsea completely stunned. After conceding an incredible goal in the first minute, The Blues struggled against a rampant Sunderland side and found themselves four goals down – and out of the game – by the interval. Chelsea tried to come back into it in the second half, but they failed to create any scoring chances and the best opportunities still seemed to fall to The Black Cats. The Blues grabbed a late goal through midfielder Gus Poyet, but it was nothing more than a consolation.

SUNDERLAND GOALS: **Quinn** *(1 min):* Roy beat two men in a surging forward run before crossing for Quinn to head home; **Phillips** *(23 mins):* Struck a powerful volley from 25 yards into the roof of the Chelsea net; **Phillips** *(35 mins):* de Goey could only palm away a Quinn shot and Phillips reacted first to drive the ball into the net; **Quinn** *(38 mins):* Poor defending let the big Irishman in to score and make it 4-0 within 40 minutes.

CHELSEA GOAL: **Poyet** *(81 mins):* Persistence paid off as Poyet surged into the penalty area to score from Zola's cross.

MATCH RATING: ★★★★★ **LEAGUE POSITION:** 8th

SUNDERLAND	
Sorensen	7
Makin	8
Gray	6
Thirlwell	7
Craddock	8
Williams	8
Summerbee *Subbed: 84 mins (Holloway)*	4
Quinn ⚽⚽ *Goals: 1, 38 mins*	9
Phillips ⚽⚽ *Goals: 23, 35 mins*	☆ 10
Schwarz	8
Roy	9
sub: *Holloway*	

Subs not used: *Oster, Marriott, Reddy, Butler, T.*

CHELSEA	
de Goey	7
Babayaro ▯ *Booked: 17 mins (foul)*	6
Hogh	7
Desailly *Subbed: 46 mins (Goldbaek)*	4
Poyet ⚽ *Goal: 81 mins*	☆ 8
Wise *Subbed: 77 mins (Wolleaston)*	5
Flo	4
Morris	4
Lambourde	4
Zola	4
Harley ▯ *Booked: 37 mins (foul); Subbed: 46 mins (Terry)*	4
sub: *Goldbaek*	5
sub: *Terry*	6
sub: *Wolleaston*	

Subs not used: *Petrescu, Cudicini.*

MATCH FACTS		
Shots On Target		
Sunderland	10-4	Chelsea
Shots Off Target		
Sunderland	1-7	Chelsea
Hit Woodwork		
Sunderland	0-0	Chelsea
Corners		
Sunderland	7-6	Chelsea

HOW THEY LINED UP

Sunderland: Sorensen; Thirlwell, Craddock, Makin, Gray; Summerbee, Schwarz, Williams, Roy; Phillips, Quinn

Chelsea: Zola, Flo; Babayaro, Poyet, Wise, Morris; Harley, Hogh, Desailly, Lambourde; de Goey

Ed de Goey stares in utter disbelief as Sunderland roar into a 4-0 lead.

Tore Andre encourages his opponent to get up and go with the Flo.

Lazio	(0) **0**
Chelsea	(0) **0**

Competition: **Champions Lge Group D**

Date: **Tuesday December 7, 1999**

Attendance: **64,500**

Referee: **H Krug** (Germany)

THE GAME: In a committed and professional performance in Rome, The Blues withstood pressure from the most expensive club side in the world to keep their Champions League dream alive. Lazio boasted the goalscoring power of Simone Inzaghi and Roberto Mancini, with Marcelo Salas and Alen Boksic on the bench, but none of these world-class strikers could break down Chelsea's towering defence which was unrecognisable from the back line that crumbled so badly against Sunderland three days earlier. It would have been even better for Chelsea if Gianfranco Zola's nonchalant chip, which followed a superb, flowing move, hadn't been hooked off Lazio's line by Guerino Gottardi. Gianluca Vialli had to watch most of the second half of the game on television after being sent-off for remonstrating too vigorously with the fourth official, but not even that could detract from another hugely encouraging night in Europe.

MATCH RATING: ★★★★ **LEAGUE POSITION: 8th**

> **"Lazio belong in the elite of European football. They are well organised and have great individual talent. You can stop them playing but there's always one player who can do something special." GIANLUCA VIALLI**

MATCH FACTS

Shots On Target		
Lazio	5-3	Chelsea
Shots Off Target		
Lazio	7-3	Chelsea
Hit Woodwork		
Lazio	0-0	Chelsea
Corners		
Lazio	8-1	Chelsea

HOW THEY LINED UP

Lazio: Marchegiani; Gottardi, Nesta, Couto, Favalli; Lombardo, Veron, Simeone, Nedved; Inzaghi, Mancini

Chelsea: Zola, Flo; Poyet, Wise, Deschamps, Petrescu; Babayaro, Leboeuf, Desailly, Ferrer; de Goey

LAZIO

Marchegiani	7
Favalli	7
Mancini	7
Subbed: 79 mins (Conceicao)	
Nesta	7
Simeone	☆9
Lombardo	7
Subbed: 69 mins (Boksic)	
Gottardi	8
Nedved	8
Inzaghi	7
Subbed: 46 mins (Salas)	
Veron	8
Couto	8
sub: *Salas*	8
sub: *Boksic*	7
sub: *Conceicao*	

Subs not used: *Ballotta, Marcolin, Sensini, Pinzi.*

CHELSEA

de Goey	8
Petrescu	8
Babayaro	7
Leboeuf	8
Desailly	☆9
Deschamps	8
Subbed: 75 mins (Di Matteo)	
Poyet	7
Wise	8
Ferrer ▯	7
Booked: 72 mins (foul)	
Flo	8
Zola	8
sub: *Di Matteo*	

Subs not used: *Cudicini, Hogh, Sutton, Goldbaek, Morris, Lambourde.*

THIS WEEK...

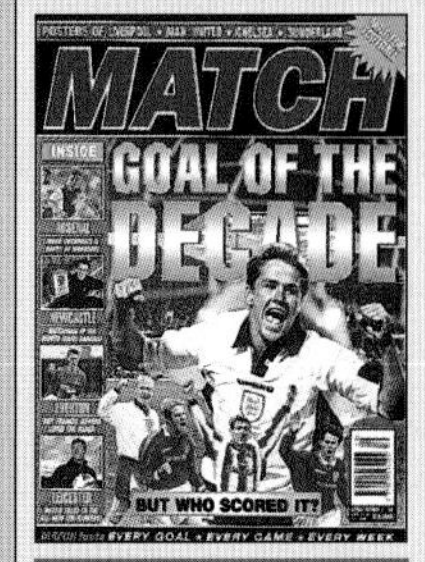

IN THE NEWS

CHELSEA: Hull City get a lucrative FA Cup third round draw against Chelsea after beating Conference side Hayes... Former Stamford Bridge favourite **Craig Burley** returns to the Premiership with Derby County, costing £3 million... Ken Bates accuses the chairman of the British Olympic Committee of provoking arguments between football and other sports' bodies over the designs for the improved Wembley stadium... Chelsea boss Gianluca Vialli expresses his relief at having a break from Champions League action. The coach says he is grateful for the chance to revive The Blues' ailing title aspirations.

PREMIERSHIP: Manchester United announce that skipper **Roy Keane** has signed a new contract which will earn him £52,000 a week at Old Trafford... Liverpool manager Gerard Houllier insists that striker **Michael Owen** is not available, despite a reported £35 million bid from Italian giants Lazio... Leicester City break their transfer record to sign Norwich City winger **Darren Eadie** for £3 million... Everton boss Walter Smith wants to open contract talks with veteran **Richard Gough** in an attempt to keep the centre-back at Goodison Park beyond the end of the season.

THE FINAL SCORE!

DECEMBER 4		
Aston Villa	0-1	**Newcastle**
Bradford	1-1	Middlesbrough
Leicester	0-3	**Arsenal**
Man. United	5-1	Everton
Southampton	0-0	Coventry
Sunderland	4-1	Chelsea
Wimbledon	5-0	Watford
DECEMBER 5		
Derby	0-1	**Leeds**
Liverpool	4-1	Sheff. Wed.
DECEMBER 6		
Tottenham	0-0	West Ham

TOP OF THE PREMIERSHIP

	P	W	D	L	Pts
1. Leeds	17	12	2	3	38
2. Man. United	16	11	3	2	36
3. Arsenal	17	11	2	4	35
8. Chelsea	**15**	**7**	**3**	**5**	**24**

It was a glamorous tie for Hull, but they went behind after just eight minutes.

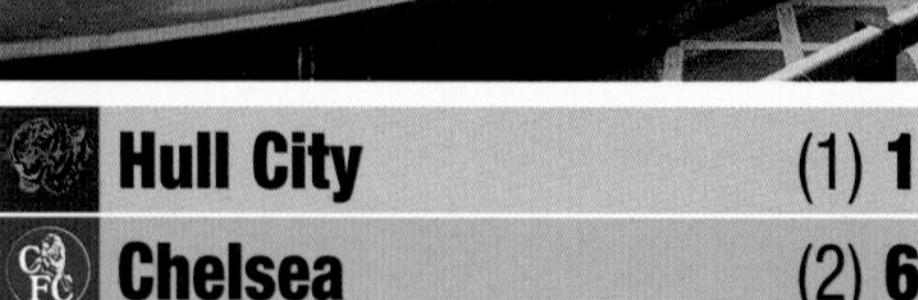

Hull City	(1) 1
Chelsea	(2) 6

Competition: **FA Cup 3rd Rd**
Date: **Saturday December 11, 1999**
Attendance: **10,279**
Referee: **P Jones** (Loughborough) 6

THE GAME: Following their fine Champions League display in Rome in midweek, Chelsea travelled to the less spectacular surroundings of Hull for their first FA Cup tie of the campaign. The Blues made light work of their Division Three opponents, but the fixture could have provided an upset after Chelsea's exertions against Lazio. Uruguayan midfielder Gustavo Poyet was the hero with an impressive hat-trick at Boothferry Park, but The Blues couldn't afford to underestimate the home side, having already been beaten by lower league opposition in the Worthington Cup. Although they were only one goal up at half time, the Premiership visitors quickly stamped their authority on the game in the second period with Chris Sutton, Roberto Di Matteo and Dennis Wise adding to Poyet's hat-trick to take The Blues into the next round of the competition.

HULL GOAL: Brown *(38 mins):* Ran on to Whitmore's pass, rounded the 'keeper and then scored from an acute angle.
CHELSEA GOALS: Poyet *(8 mins):* Struck a superb curling shot into the top left-hand corner from the edge of the area; **Sutton** *(30 mins):* Harley's pinpoint cross was met by Sutton's diving header which flew into City's net; **Di Matteo** *(47 mins):* Curled the loose ball past the helpless 'keeper from the edge of the area; **Poyet** *(48 mins):* Harley was once again involved as his left-footed cross was headed in powerfully by Poyet from close range; **Poyet** *(58 mins)*: Wise slid the ball across City's six-yard box and Poyet tapped in to claim his hat-trick; **Wise** *(90 mins):* Fired in a shot from an acute angle which squirmed under the luckless City 'keeper.

MATCH RATING: ★★★★ **LEAGUE POSITION:** 8th

MATCH FACTS

Shots On Target		
Hull City	6-9	Chelsea
Shots Off Target		
Hull City	3-2	Chelsea
Hit Woodwork		
Hull City	1-0	Chelsea
Corners		
Hull City	5-4	Chelsea

HOW THEY LINED UP

Bracey
Harper Goodison Edwards Whittle Whitney
Whitmore Schofield Joyce
Wood Brown
Sutton Zola
Poyet Wise Deschamps Di Matteo
Harley Leboeuf Hogh Ferrer
de Goey

HULL CITY	
Bracey	7
Goodison	7
Harper	7
Edwards	6
Whittle (booked)	7
Booked: 19 mins (foul)	
Whitney (booked)	6
Booked: 54 mins (foul)	
Whitmore	☆ 8
Schofield (booked)	6
Booked: 81 mins; Subbed: 81 mins (Morgan)	
Joyce (booked)	7
Booked: 80 mins (foul)	
Wood	7
Brown, D (goal)	7
Goal: 38 mins; Subbed: 59 mins (Eyre)	
sub: *Eyre*	6
sub: *Morgan*	

Subs not used: *Baker, Harris, Greaves.*

CHELSEA	
de Goey	6
Hogh	7
Subbed: 59 mins (Terry)	
Leboeuf	7
Deschamps	8
Subbed: 55 mins (Morris)	
Poyet (goal)(goal)(goal)	☆ 9
Goals: 8, 48, 58 mins	
Sutton (goal)	7
Goal: 30 mins	
Wise (goal)	8
Goal: 90 mins	
Di Matteo (goal)	7
Goal: 47 mins	
Ferrer	7
Zola	6
Subbed: 46 mins (Flo)	
Harley	8
sub: *Terry*	7
sub: *Morris*	6
sub: *Flo*	7

Subs not used: *Petrescu, Cudicini.*

Jon Harley didn't take long to make a big impression on the Chelsea faithful.

Chelsea	(0)	0
Leeds United	(0)	2

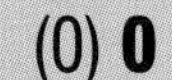

Competition: **FA Carling Premiership**

Date: **Sunday December 19, 1999**

Attendance: **35,106**

Referee: **J Winter** (Stockton) 6

THE GAME: There was little Christmas cheer for The Blues as Leeds returned to the top of the table and Frank Leboeuf was sent-off. Stephen McPhail scored his first goal for Leeds in the second half, but it was against the run of play following a period of unrelenting Chelsea pressure. Gianluca Vialli's side hit back and looked dangerous until Leboeuf was dismissed for tripping Harry Kewell and confronting the Australian. After conceding a late second goal, The Blues realised the contest was over and were left 17 points behind David O'Leary's side.

LEEDS GOALS: McPhail *(66 mins):* Tapped home from close range after Bowyer's cross; **McPhail** *(88 mins):* The Irishman's free-kick evaded everyone and crept into the Chelsea net.

MATCH RATING: ★★★★ **LEAGUE POSITION: 10th**

"After Leeds scored with practically their first shot on target of the whole game, the players got a little bit frustrated. They could feel the game was slipping away from them after that." GIANLUCA VIALLI

CHELSEA	
de Goey	6
Leboeuf	4
Booked: 62 mins (foul); Sent-off: 69 mins (second bookable offence: foul)	
Desailly	6
Subbed: 46 mins (Hogh)	
Deschamps	6
Poyet	7
Sutton	5
Wise	7
Booked: 69 mins (foul)	
Di Matteo	5
Booked: 90 mins (foul)	
Ferrer	7
Flo	6
Subbed: 58 mins (Zola)	
Harley	☆ 8
sub: Hogh	6
Subbed: 65 mins (Petrescu)	
sub: Petrescu	6
sub: Zola	6

Subs not used: *Morris, Cudicini.*

LEEDS	
Martyn	7
Kelly	7
Booked: 69 mins (foul)	
Harte	7
Booked: 52 mins (foul)	
Radebe	7
Woodgate	7
Bridges	6
Subbed: 49 mins (Wilcox)	
Kewell	6
Bowyer	7
Booked: 2 mins (foul); Subbed: 85 mins (Jones)	
Huckerby	7
McPhail	☆ 8
Goals: 66, 88 mins	
Bakke	7
sub: Wilcox	6
sub: Jones	

Subs not used: *Robinson, Mills, Duberry.*

MATCH FACTS

Shots On Target		
Chelsea	13-4	Leeds
Shots Off Target		
Chelsea	9-3	Leeds
Hit Woodwork		
Chelsea	0-1	Leeds
Corners		
Chelsea	10-6	Leeds

HOW THEY LINED UP

THIS WEEK...

IN THE NEWS

CHELSEA: Mick McGiven, who runs the Chelsea Youth Academy, calls for Premier League sides to be allowed to have nursery clubs in the Nationwide league, claiming it's the only way clubs of Chelsea's stature can complete the education of their young players... The press once again write off Chelsea's title chances after they lose to Leeds... The Blues have joined Derby and Coventry in watching Port Vale defender **Anthony Gardner**... Midfielder **Paul Hughes** has gone on trial at Crewe... Lazio are keen on bringing **Marcel Desailly** back to Italy, according to media reports.

PREMIERSHIP: Both Arsenal and Man. United are said to be leading the chase to sign Japanese star **Shinji Ono**, the most highly rated player in Asia... Everton have made a final contract offer to **Don Hutchison**, whose agent says that AC Milan are one of a number of clubs interested in the Scottish international's signature... West Ham value **Rio Ferdinand** at £15 million after Gerard Houllier shows an interest in taking the England defender to Anfield... After speculation about **Matthew Le Tissier**'s future, Saints manager Dave Jones says he's only received one bid for the player – a cheeky offer from Conference side Woking.

THE FINAL SCORE!

DECEMBER 18		
Arsenal	1-1	Wimbledon
Aston Villa	2-1	Sheff. Wed.
Bradford	2-0	Newcastle
Leicester	0-1	**Derby**
Liverpool	2-0	Coventry
Middlesbrough	2-1	Tottenham
Sunderland	2-0	Southampton
Watford	1-3	**Everton**
West Ham	2-4	**Man. United**
DECEMBER 19		
Chelsea	0-2	**Leeds**

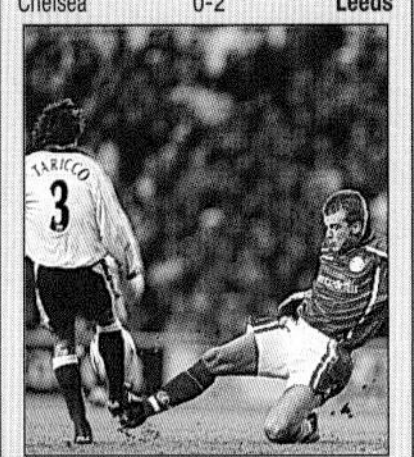

TOP OF THE PREMIERSHIP

	P	W	D	L	Pts
1. Leeds	18	13	2	3	41
2. Man. United	17	12	3	2	39
3. Sunderland	18	11	4	3	37
10. Chelsea	**16**	**7**	**3**	**6**	**24**

Flo scores Chelsea's second, despite a last-minute lunge from defender Richards.

Southampton	(0)	**1**
Chelsea	(2)	**2**

Competition: **FA Carling Premiership**

Date: **Sunday December 26, 1999**

Attendance: **15,232**

Referee: **P Alcock** (Halstead) 7

THE GAME: Chelsea made history on this Boxing Day fixture when they became the first team in English football to name a starting line-up which didn't contain any players from the Home Nations. Chelsea's young English hopefuls, Jon Harley and Jody Morris, came on as second-half substitutes, but the nationalities of the personnel were unimportant to the Chelsea faithful as their side picked up three crucial points away from home against a disappointing Saints side. Two first-half strikes from Tore Andre Flo helped The Blues to their first away win in the league since September and condemned Southampton to their fourth home defeat of the season. Kevin Davies gave The Saints hope with a late goal, but the home side didn't deserve a share of the spoils and Chelsea held firm to clinch victory.

SOUTHAMPTON GOAL: Davies *(80 mins):* The ball bounced around a crowd of players following Le Tissier's free-kick and eventually fell for Davies to prod home from close range.

CHELSEA GOALS: Flo *(18 mins):* Poyet found Flo clear in space and the Norwegian's low shot sneaked inside the far post; **Flo** *(43 mins):* Deschamps played a throughball to Flo, who sent a low drive past Jones which trickled over the line.

MATCH RATING: ★★★ **LEAGUE POSITION: 9th**

"I have 22 players. Sometimes the team will pick itself because of injury. We're an English team made of English and foreign players. It doesn't really matter, because we speak the same language on the field." GIANLUCA VIALLI

MATCH FACTS

Shots On Target		
Southampton	5-2	Chelsea
Shots Off Target		
Southampton	3-7	Chelsea
Hit Woodwork		
Southampton	2-2	Chelsea
Corners		
Southampton	4-5	Chelsea

HOW THEY LINED UP

Southampton: Jones; Dodd, Lundekvam, Richards, Benali; Oakley, Le Tissier, Soltvedt, Kachloul; Beattie, Pahars

Chelsea: Poyet, Flo; Ambrosetti, Deschamps, Di Matteo, Petrescu; Babayaro, Leboeuf, Thome, Ferrer; de Goey

SOUTHAMPTON	
Jones	6
Lundekvam	6
Dodd	5
Richards	☆7
Le Tissier (booked) *Booked: 89 mins (foul)*	6
Oakley (booked) *Booked: 34 mins (foul); Subbed: 74 mins (Tessem)*	7
Benali	6
Soltvedt	5
Pahars	5
Kachloul *Subbed: 52 mins (Boa Morte)*	5
Beattie *Subbed: 52 mins (Davies)*	5
sub: *Boa Morte*	6
sub: *Davies* ⚽ *Goal: 80 mins*	6
sub: *Tessem*	

Subs not used: *Moss, Hughes, M.*

CHELSEA	
de Goey	6
Petrescu *Subbed: 87 mins (Morris)*	6
Babayaro (booked) *Booked: 76 mins (foul)*	7
Thome	7
Leboeuf (booked) *Booked: 11 mins (foul)*	7
Deschamps (booked) *Booked: 57 mins (foul)*	7
Poyet	6
Di Matteo	6
Flo ⚽⚽ *Goals: 18, 43 mins*	☆8
Ferrer (booked) *Booked: 35 mins (foul)*	6
Ambrosetti *Subbed: 74 mins (Harley)*	6
sub: *Morris*	
sub: *Harley*	

Subs not used: *Terry, Nicholls, Cudicini.*

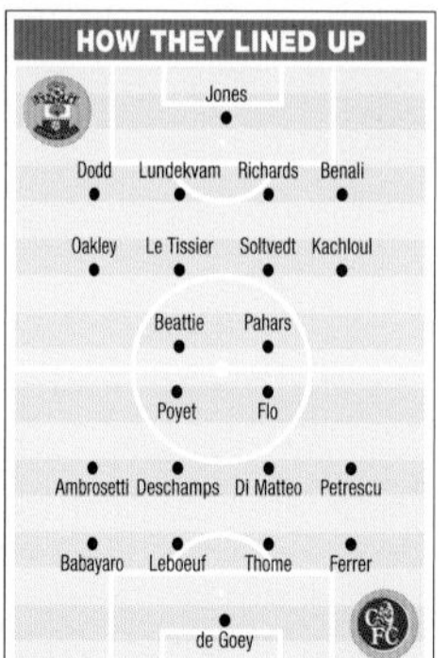

OWLS PROVE EASY PREY FOR VIALLI'S CHARGES

Morris and Poyet celebrate the third goal in a fine win for Gianluca Vialli's side.

Chelsea	(2)	**3**
Sheffield Wednesday	(0)	**0**

Competition: **FA Carling Premiership**

Date: **Wednesday December 29, 1999**

Attendance: **32,938**

Referee: **A D'Urso** (Billericay) 7

THE GAME: In Chelsea's final game of the century – and the 100th meeting between The Blues and Sheffield Wednesday – Dennis Wise scored the 100th goal of Gianluca Vialli's reign in a convincing 3-0 victory. Gustavo Poyet captained the side for the third time and made it three wins out of three as Chelsea skipper – causing the fans to wonder if Vialli should give him the armband for every match. The midfielder had a hand in all of Chelsea's goals, and with Dennis Wise also in top form, The Blues soon outclassed Wednesday. The Yorkshire side started well, but they couldn't match the home team for quality when they got into their stride. Goals from Wise, Tore Andre Flo and Jody Morris made it a Happy New Year for the Bridge faithful, and only heroics from Owls 'keeper Pavel Srnicek – the only shining light for Wednesday – denied The Blues a bigger win.

CHELSEA GOALS: Wise *(32 mins):* Petrescu's cross from the right was knocked down by Poyet for Wise, who rifled in a shot through Srnicek's legs; **Flo** *(35 mins):* Poyet played an inch-perfect pass to Flo, whose volley went over the 'keeper; **Morris** *(84 mins):* Poyet's flying header was forced out by Srnicek but only on to the chest of Morris and into the net.

MATCH RATING: ★★★★ **LEAGUE POSITION:**

CHELSEA	
de Goey	7
Petrescu	7
Babayaro	7
Leboeuf (booked) *Booked: 27 mins (foul)*	5
Deschamps *Subbed: 23 mins (Wise)*	7
Poyet ☆	9
Di Matteo	7
Ambrosetti *Subbed: 81 mins (Morris)*	5
Flo (goal) *Goal: 35 mins; Subbed: 81 mins (Zola)*	7
Lambourde	7
Thome	7
sub: Wise (goal) *Goal: 32 mins*	8
sub: Morris (goal) *Goal: 84 mins*	
sub: Zola	

Subs not used: *Cudicini, Terry.*

SHEFF. WED.	
Srnicek ☆	8
Atherton	6
Hinchcliffe	7
Jonk	7
Walker	7
Sonner *Subbed: 62 mins (Haslam)*	6
Booth (booked) *Booked: 65 mins (foul); Subbed: 71 mins (Cresswell)*	5
Alexandersson (booked) *Booked: 73 mins (foul)*	5
Nolan	6
Briscoe *Subbed: 62 mins (Sibon)*	6
de Bilde	7
sub: Haslam	6
sub: Sibon	6
sub: Cresswell	

Subs not used: *Pressman, McKeever.*

MATCH FACTS

Shots On Target		
Chelsea	13-5	Sheff. Wed.
Shots Off Target		
Chelsea	8-6	Sheff. Wed.
Hit Woodwork		
Chelsea	0-0	Sheff. Wed.
Corners		
Chelsea	10-7	Sheff. Wed.

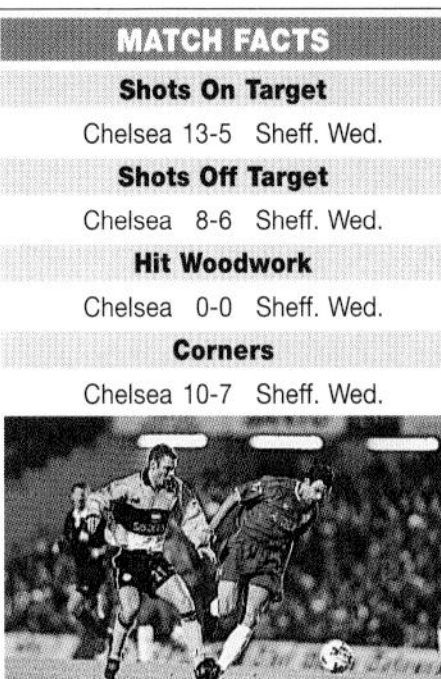

HOW THEY LINED UP

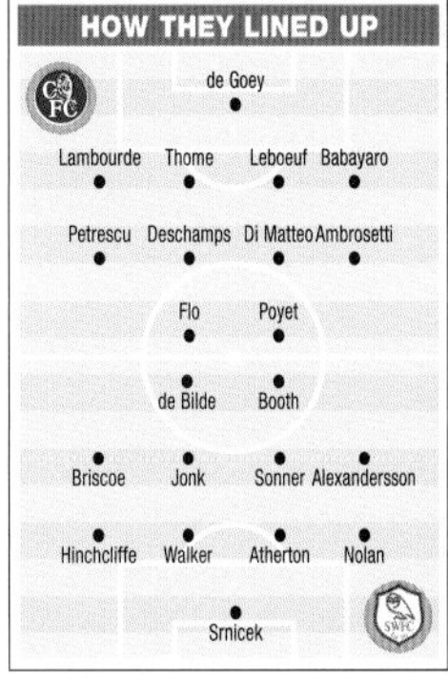

THIS WEEK...

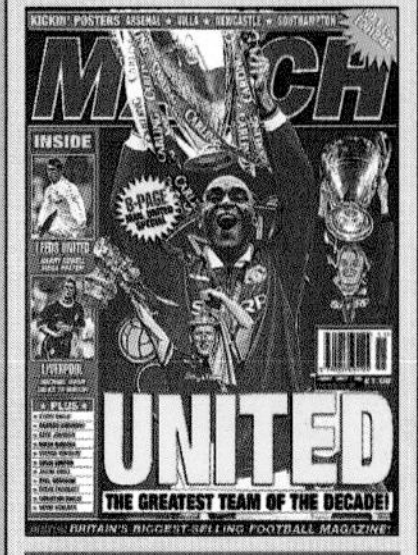

IN THE NEWS

CHELSEA: France centre-back **Frank Leboeuf**, who claimed the English game was unnecessarily violent earlier in the season, could face a five-match ban for allegedly stamping on Harry Kewell during The Blues' recent defeat at home to Leeds... The latest big name striker linked with Stamford Bridge is Roma ace **Marco Delvecchio**.

PREMIERSHIP: Everton supporters celebrate as Bill Kenwright buys The Toffees for £20 million... Liverpool's victory over Wimbledon is their seventh home win in a row. **Robbie Fowler** notches his 150th career goal for The Reds in the same game – some four months after claiming his 149th strike... Legendary singer Tom Jones turns down the opportunity to play the part of Manchester United legend Sir Matt Busby in a musical history of the Old Trafford club.

THE FINAL SCORE!

DECEMBER 26		
Coventry	3-2	Arsenal
Derby	0-2	**Aston Villa**
Everton	5-0	Sunderland
Leeds	2-1	Leicester
Man. United	4-0	Bradford
Newcastle	2-2	Liverpool
Sheff. Wed.	1-0	Middlesbrough
Southampton	1-2	**Chelsea**
Tottenham	4-0	Watford
Wimbledon	2-2	West Ham
DECEMBER 28		
Arsenal	2-0	Leeds
Bradford	0-0	Everton
Leicester	1-2	**Newcastle**
Liverpool	3-1	Wimbledon
Sunderland	2-2	Man. United
Watford	3-2	SoUthampton
West Ham	1-1	Derby
DECEMBER 29		
Aston Villa	1-1	Tottenham
Chelsea	3-0	Sheff. Wed.

TOP OF THE PREMIERSHIP

	P	W	D	L	Pts
1. Leeds	20	14	2	4	44
2. Man. United	19	13	4	2	43
3. Arsenal	20	12	3	5	39
7. Chelsea	**18**	**9**	**3**	**6**	**30**

JANUARY

 START OF MONTH **7th**  END OF MONTH **6th**

"I have few a medals already but the one I want most of all is the title. This season we're in the Champions League but it would be nice to be there as champions." Gustavo Poyet

A NEW YEAR AND A NEW CHALLENGE FOR CHELSEA – COULD THEY put their inconsistent Premiership form behind them and mount a serious challenge to the teams at the top of the league? There were certainly plenty of opportunities in January, with five league fixtures, a month's break from the Champions League and only the FA Cup to distract the side.

With this in mind, Coventry weren't exactly following the script by taking the lead twice at Highfield Road, but The Blues equalised on each occasion to earn a 2-2 draw. Their second away fixture in four days was at Bradford, who were desperately trying to prove their doubters wrong by maintaining their Premiership status. The Bantams took a step in the right direction by scoring after just two minutes of the kick-off and held Gianluca Vialli's side to a 1-1 draw after the visitors missed a number of chances.

Concerned by his team's lack of finishing power, the Chelsea boss drafted in former World Player Of The Year George Weah on loan from Italian giants AC Milan. The Liberian made an instant impact at Stamford Bridge, scoring a late headed winner on his debut after coming on as a substitute against Tottenham. But the renewed optimism was dampened in the next match, when Chelsea had to rely on another late strike, from captain Dennis Wise, to salvage a point at home after a disappointing display against Leicester.

The Blues continued their run in the FA Cup with a comfortable 2-0 victory against Nottingham Forest in the fourth round, then drew with a rejuvenated Aston Villa side in the Premiership. The month ended with a bad-tempered FA Cup fifth round tie with Leicester, but Chelsea ran out 2-1 winners with goals from Gustavo Poyet and George Weah. This left Vialli's team unbeaten in the new millennium, but their inability to kill teams off after dominating the games proved frustrating for the manager and supporters alike.

THE GAMES

Jan. 4 v **Coventry** (a)
Jan. 8 v **Bradford** (a)
Jan. 12 v **Tottenham** (h)
Jan. 15 v **Leicester** (h)
Jan. 19 v **Nott'm Forest** (h)
Jan. 22 v **Aston Villa** (a)
Jan. 30 v **Leicester** (h)

TRANSFERS IN

George Weah
Position: **Striker**
Fee: **Loan**
From: **AC Milan**

TRANSFERS OUT

Steve Hampshire
Position: **Striker**
Fee: **Free**
To: **Dunfermline**

MATCH facts

Matchman Of The Month

GEORGE WEAH
Average Rating: 8.00

Zola was the creative spark for Chelsea as they earned a point at Coventry.

Chelsea created a host of chances but couldn't kill the game off at Bradford.

Coventry City	(0)	2
 Chelsea	(0)	2

Competition: **FA Carling Premiership**
Date: **Tuesday January 4, 2000**
Attendance: **20,164**
Referee: **P Durkin** (Portland) 6

Game 31

THE GAME: Coventry had a frustrating evening at Highfield Road, with Chelsea twice coming from behind to deny them a fifth successive home win over The Blues. Chelsea seemed to be chasing the game from the start, though, and with this result it seems the club have lost their chance of finishing in the top three Champions League positions in the Premiership. Tore Andre Flo earned them the point – the Norwegian forward made it five goals in the last three games with two fine strikes, benefiting from superb approach play by Gianfranco Zola.

COVENTRY GOALS: Roussel *(54 mins):* The Belgian striker controlled the ball superbly then fired his shot past de Goey; **Keane** *(81 mins):* Powered home a close-range header after Roussel had again caused problems in the Chelsea defence.

CHELSEA GOALS: Flo *(55 mins):* Zola beat three Coventry challenges and pushed the ball across to Flo, who rifled home his 12th goal of the season; **Flo** *(82 mins):* Zola again created the opening for Flo, who showed sublime skill to chip the ball over the advancing Hedman from the right of the area.

MATCH RATING: ★★★ **LEAGUE POSITION: 7th**

"It's a strain on the team when they are involved in so many competitions, but on the other hand it's important that we are involved. We have to learn from Man. United and emulate the standards they've set." GRAEME LE SAUX

MATCH FACTS

Shots On Target		
Coventry	6-9	Chelsea
Shots Off Target		
Coventry	8-4	Chelsea
Hit Woodwork		
Coventry	0-0	Chelsea
Corners		
Coventry	4-3	Chelsea

HOW THEY LINED UP

Hedman
Telfer, Breen, Williams, Froggatt
Hadji, McAllister, Palmer, Chippo
Keane, Roussel
Flo, Zola
Poyet, Wise, Deschamps, Di Matteo
Babayaro, Desailly, Thome, Ferrer
de Goey

COVENTRY CITY

Player	Rating
Hedman	7
Williams	7
Telfer	6
Froggatt	6
Breen	6
McAllister	6
Hadji (booked) — *Booked: 57 mins (handball)*	7
Palmer ☆	8
Chippo	6
Keane (goal) — *Goal: 81 mins*	7
Roussel (goal) — *Goal: 54 mins; Subbed: 87 mins (Whelan)*	6
sub: *Whelan*	

Subs not used: *Norman, Eustace, Ogrizovic, Gustafsson.*

CHELSEA

Player	Rating
de Goey	6
Babayaro	7
Desailly	6
Ferrer	6
Thome	7
Deschamps — *Subbed: 78 mins (Morris)*	6
Poyet — *Subbed: 74 mins (Petrescu)*	6
Wise	7
Di Matteo (booked) — *Booked: 28 mins (foul); Subbed: 85 mins (Sutton)*	6
Flo (2 goals) ☆ — *Goals: 55, 82 mins*	8
Zola	7
sub: *Morris*	
sub: *Petrescu*	
sub: *Sutton*	

Subs not used: *Lambourde, Cudicini.*

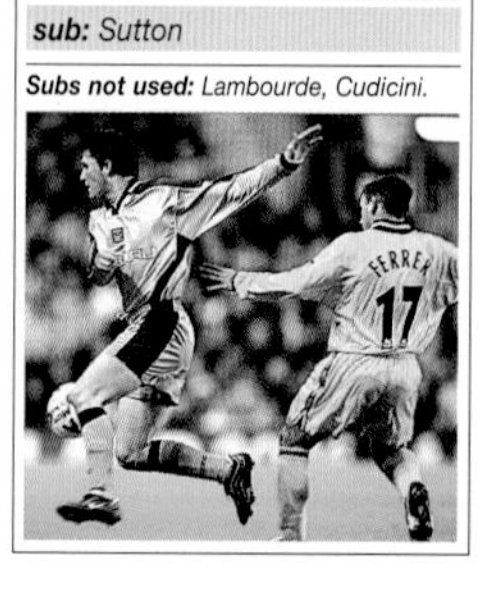

 **Bradford City** (1) 1

 **Chelsea** (0) 1

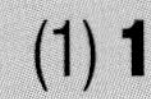

Competition: **FA Carling Premiership**
Date: **Saturday January 8, 2000**
Attendance: **18,276**
Referee: **A Wiley** (Burntwood) 7

THE GAME: The Premiership's relegation favourites, Bradford City, shocked Chelsea's international all-stars at Valley Parade by taking a surprise second-minute lead. Bantams striker Lee Mills got the early goal to give the home fans encouragement, but Chelsea dominated the play throughout and should have equalised long before they did. Dan Petrescu's second-half strike came after the visitors had squandered a host of good chances, with Gustavo Poyet cursing his bad luck on several occasions. It had been a disappointing start to the New Year for the travelling Blues supporters, and Gianluca Vialli would have been concerned by the return of only one goal from 34 shots, compared to Bradford's one goal from seven attempts.

BRADFORD GOAL: Mills *(2 mins):* Headed in from Dean Saunders' cross from the right for his fifth Premiership goal.
CHELSEA GOAL: Petrescu *(58 mins):* A throughball from Di Matteo sent Petrescu through to chip over the 'keeper.

MATCH RATING: ★★★★ **LEAGUE POSITION: 7th**

"To win the title in this country you need quality, strength and luck. People say that you make your own luck, but I don't know whether that is right or not." GUSTAVO POYET

BRADFORD CITY	
Clarke	☆9
Myers	6
McCall	7
Wetherall	7
Blake	7
Mills ⚽ *Goal: 2 mins*	8
O'Brien	7
Windass *Subbed: 62 mins (Beagrie)*	6
Halle	6
Redfearn	6
Saunders	7
sub: *Beagrie*	6

Subs not used: *Davison, Westwood, Lawrence, Rankin.*

CHELSEA	
de Goey	8
Petrescu ⚽ *Goal: 58 mins*	☆8
Babayaro	6
Deschamps	7
Poyet *Subbed: 84 mins (Morris)*	6
Sutton *Subbed: 68 mins (Zola)*	6
Wise *Subbed: 67 mins (Di Matteo)*	6
Ferrer	7
Flo	8
Terry	6
Thome	7
sub: *Di Matteo*	7
sub: *Zola*	7
sub: *Morris*	

Subs not used: *Cudicini, Lambourde.*

MATCH FACTS

Shots On Target		
Bradford	5-13	Chelsea
Shots Off Target		
Bradford	7-21	Chelsea
Hit Woodwork		
Bradford	0-0	Chelsea
Corners		
Bradford	6-4	Chelsea

HOW THEY LINED UP

Clarke
Halle, Wetherall, O'Brien, Myers
Windass, Redfearn, McCall, Blake
Mills, Saunders

Flo, Sutton
Poyet, Wise, Deschamps, Petrescu
Babayaro, Terry, Thome, Ferrer
de Goey

THIS WEEK...

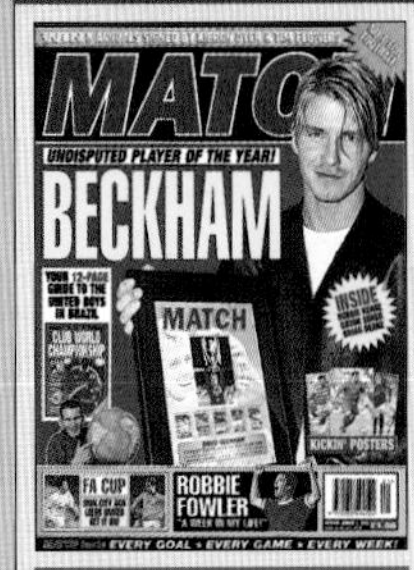

IN THE NEWS

CHELSEA: Nottingham Forest leave it late in a replay against lowly Oxford to clinch an FA Cup fourth round tie with The Blues... The 1-1 league draw with Bradford City is particularly disappointing to Chelsea fans. It was one of their two games in hand which they had hoped to win in order to get back in the title race... Lazio deny they are about to sign **Marcel Desailly**, who is out of action for a month with a shoulder injury... New £2.7 million signing from Sheffield Wednesday, **Emerson Thome**, will be eligible to play in Chelsea's Champions League campaign when it resumes in March... Former World Player Of The Year **George Weah** arrives at Stamford Bridge on loan from AC Milan.

PREMIERSHIP: Tottenham midfielder **Darren Anderton** turns down an increased pay offer of £24,000 a week... Aston Villa striker **Dion Dublin** breaks his neck against Sheffield Wednesday. Experts say the injury nearly put him in a wheelchair for life... Sunderland's **Thomas Sorensen** has agreed a new deal at the club despite interest from Lazio.

THE FINAL SCORE!

JANUARY 3		
Derby	2-0	Watford
Everton	2-2	Leicester
Leeds	1-2	**Aston Villa**
Newcastle	2-2	West Ham
Sheff. Wed.	1-1	Arsenal
Southampton	1-0	Bradford
Tottenham	1-0	Liverpool
Wimbledon	1-0	Sunderland
JANUARY 4		
Coventry	2-2	Chelsea
JANUARY 8		
Bradford	1-1	Chelsea

TOP OF THE PREMIERSHIP

	P	W	D	L	Pts
1. Leeds	21	14	2	5	44
2. Man. United	19	13	4	2	43
3. Arsenal	21	12	4	5	40
7. Chelsea	**20**	**9**	**5**	**6**	**32**

The attacking strength of Chelsea's full-backs was a big plus against Spurs.

Chelsea	(0) **1**
Tottenham	(0) **0**

Competition: **FA Carling Premiership**

Date: **Wednesday January 12, 2000**

Attendance: **34,969**

Referee: **N Barry** (Scunthorpe) 5

THE GAME: A stunning debut from substitute George Weah gave Chelsea a win they barely deserved at Stamford Bridge. With just three minutes left on the clock and a 0-0 stalemate looming in this London derby, the former World Player Of The Year scored with a precise header to secure three points for Vialli's Blues. Chelsea missed the influence of Marcel Desailly, Didier Deschamps and Gianfranco Zola and struggled to break down Tottenham's determined rearguard. The visitors, for their part, were denied by the expert reflexes of the reliable Ed de Goey, who pulled off a string of impressive saves. Tottenham manager George Graham summed up the match by saying, "Chelsea will be delighted. They won without playing well."

CHELSEA GOAL: Weah *(87 mins):* Lambourde found Wise in space on the edge of the Spurs area and the captain delivered a cross from the left for Weah to head the winner past Walker.

MATCH RATING: ★★★ **LEAGUE POSITION: 6th**

"I've signed on loan here at Chelsea for six months, but if I like it I won't be going back to Italy. I would have liked to have finished my career with AC Milan, but unfortunately it just wasn't possible." GEORGE WEAH

MATCH FACTS

Shots On Target		
Chelsea	9-8	Tottenham
Shots Off Target		
Chelsea	6-4	Tottenham
Hit Woodwork		
Chelsea	0-0	Tottenham
Corners		
Chelsea	5-5	Tottenham

HOW THEY LINED UP

CHELSEA	
de Goey	8
Petrescu	6
Leboeuf	5
Lambourde	7
Wise	6
Di Matteo	5
Flo *Subbed: 56 mins (Weah)*	6
Poyet *Subbed: 56 mins (Sutton)*	6
Terry	7
Thome	7
Harley	7
sub: *Sutton*	7
sub: *Weah* ⚽ *Goal: 87 mins*	☆ 9

Subs not used: *Cudicini, Ambrosetti, Morris.*

TOTTENHAM	
Walker	7
Carr	6
Campbell	☆ 8
Perry	7
Anderton	7
Sherwood	7
Iversen ▯ *Booked: 89 mins (unsporting behaviour)*	6
Edinburgh	7
Ginola	6
Armstrong ▯ *Booked: 48 mins (dissent)*	5
Clemence	6

Subs not used: *Baardsen, Fox, Dominguez, Young, Nielsen.*

Chelsea's two Wise men know the only Weah is up for The Blues.

Chelsea (0) 1
Leicester City (1) 1

Competition: **FA Carling Premiership**
Date: **Saturday January 15, 2000**
Attendance: **35,063**
Referee: **G Barber** (Tring) 6

THE GAME: Gianfranco Zola announced his return to the starting line-up in style by setting up a late equaliser for The Blues against Leicester at Stamford Bridge. The forward had been either dropped or rested for the last two games, but in his 150th appearance for the club he delivered a perfect cross for Dennis Wise to head home a late equaliser. Leicester, who played without many first-team regulars because of an injury crisis, may have been disappointed with a share of the points as they chased and harried the home side all afternoon. Their cause was helped by a surprisingly quiet George Weah, after an incredible debut in midweek, and his partnership with Zola often broke down without the necessary service from midfield.

CHELSEA GOAL: Wise *(86 mins):* Zola curled in a free-kick from just outside the area and Wise rose above the Leicester defence to head the ball into the back of the net.

LEICESTER GOAL: Taggart *(42 mins):* Oakes crossed for Taggart, who hit the woodwork with his first attempt, but the big defender scrambled home the rebound to make it 1-0.

MATCH RATING: ★★★★ **LEAGUE POSITION: 6th**

"That was the worst display I've seen from a Chelsea side for many a year." KEN BATES, CHELSEA CHAIRMAN

CHELSEA	
de Goey	7
Petrescu	7
Subbed: 46 mins (Poyet)	
Leboeuf	6
Deschamps	6
Subbed: 46 mins (Ambrosetti)	
Wise ⚽	6
Goal: 86 mins	
Di Matteo	6
Ferrer	6
Subbed: 65 mins (Flo)	
Zola	7
Thome	7
Weah	7
Harley	☆ 8
sub: Poyet	6
sub: Ambrosetti	5
sub: Flo	5

Subs not used: *Cudicini, Terry.*

LEICESTER CITY	
Arphexad	☆ 9
Sinclair	8
Taggart ⚽	7
Goal: 42 mins	
Heskey	7
Eadie	6
Gunnlaugsson	7
Subbed: 52 mins (Guppy)	
Gilchrist	6
Elliott	6
Marshall	6
Subbed: 38 mins (Fenton)	
Oakes	6
Zagorakis	6
sub: Fenton (booked)	6
Booked: 60 mins (foul)	
sub: Guppy	7

Subs not used: *Flowers, Thomas, Stewart.*

MATCH FACTS

Shots On Target		
Chelsea	7-8	Leicester
Shots Off Target		
Chelsea	7-1	Leicester
Hit Woodwork		
Chelsea	1-1	Leicester
Corners		
Chelsea	12-3	Leicester

HOW THEY LINED UP

THIS WEEK...

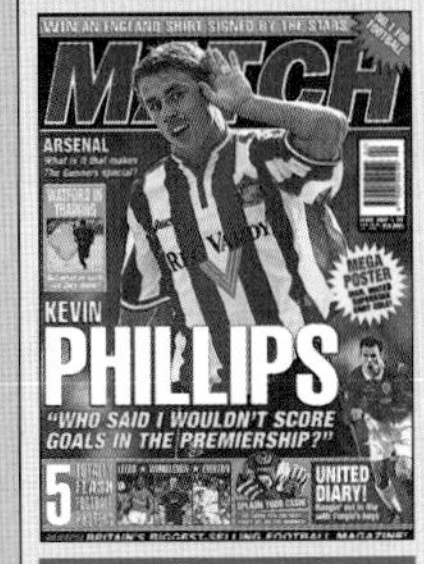

MATCH
ARSENAL
KEVIN
PHILLIPS
"WHO SAID I WOULDN'T SCORE GOALS IN THE PREMIERSHIP?"
UNITED DIARY!

IN THE NEWS

CHELSEA: Striker **George Weah** is instantly hailed as the answer to Chelsea's goalscoring problems as the big Liberian scores on his debut. Weah tells the media that Arsenal boss Arsene Wenger had a huge influence on him when he first left Africa to play for Monaco in France. The former AC Milan frontman says Wenger was like a father to him... The transfer of Dynamo Tblisi's **Rati Alexidze** to Stamford Bridge is now in doubt after the midfielder was refused a work permit... Leeds boss David O'Leary is rumoured to be lining up a £5 million offer for Blues striker **Chris Sutton**.

PREMIERSHIP: Manchester United midfielder **David Beckham** comes second in the World Player Of The Year awards. He is beaten into the runners-up spot by Barcelona and Brazil star **Rivaldo**... Persistent injury forces the former Sheffield Wednesday and England striker **David Hirst** to retire. Hirst had only managed a handful of appearances since joining Southampton... Sir Alex Ferguson has allowed 'keeper **Massimo Taibi** to join Serie A club Reggiana on loan until the end of the current season... Southampton defender **Claus Lundekvam** is the victim of a bizarre injury when he damages his back while cooking his morning bacon and eggs.

THE FINAL SCORE!

JANUARY 12		
Chelsea	1-0	Tottenham
JANUARY 15		
Arsenal	4-1	Sunderland
Chelsea	1-1	Leicester
Coventry	2-0	Wimbledon
Everton	2-2	Tottenham
Middlesbrough	1-4	**Derby**
Sheff. Wed.	2-0	Bradford
Watford	2-3	**Liverpool**
West Ham	1-1	Aston Villa

TOP OF THE PREMIERSHIP

	P	W	D	L	Pts
1. Leeds	21	14	2	5	44
2. Man. United	19	13	4	2	43
3. Arsenal	22	13	4	5	43
6. Chelsea	**22**	**10**	**6**	**6**	**36**

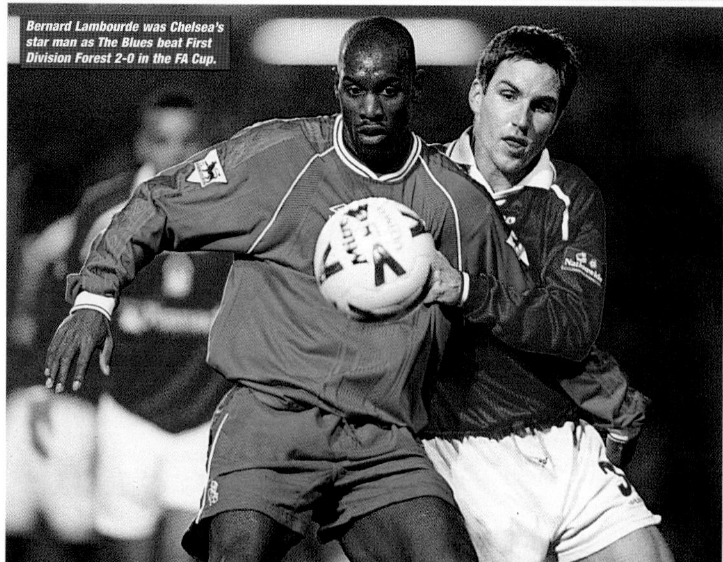

Bernard Lambourde was Chelsea's star man as The Blues beat First Division Forest 2-0 in the FA Cup.

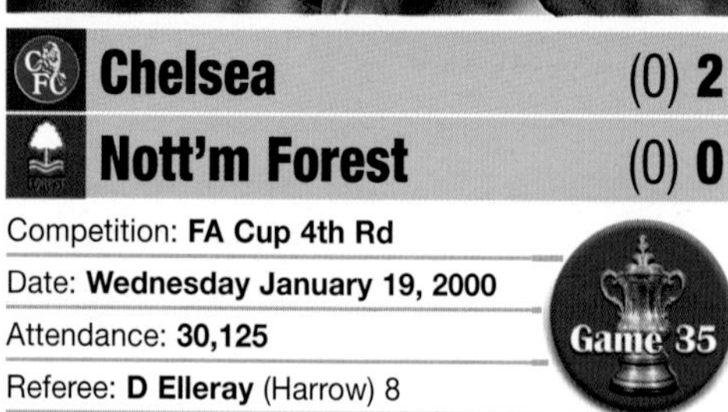

Chelsea (0) 2
Nott'm Forest (0) 0

Competition: **FA Cup 4th Rd**

Date: **Wednesday January 19, 2000**

Attendance: **30,125**

Referee: **D Elleray** (Harrow) 8

Game 35

THE GAME: Chelsea booked their place in the FA Cup fifth round but made hard work of it against struggling Nottingham Forest. The visitors, in 16th place in the First Division, should have been brushed aside comfortably at Stamford Bridge, but poor finishing let Gianluca Vialli's side down. The Blues made plenty of chances, but a combination of the woodwork and Forest's offside trap denied Gianluca Vialli's side from turning their superiority into goals. When Chelsea finally succeeded in finding the net, it was thanks to the sublime skill of Gianfranco Zola – providing his second crucial assist in two games – and substitute Jody Morris, who set up the second goal for Dennis Wise. This wasn't the most convincing display from The Blues, but they still progressed to the next round of the competition, with a home draw against Leicester awaiting them.

CHELSEA GOALS: Leboeuf *(57 mins):* Zola whipped in one of his trademark free-kicks from just outside the penalty area and Leboeuf rose unmarked to glance it in; **Wise** *(86 mins):* Morris danced his way into the penalty area and chipped the ball back from the touchline and into the six-yard box, where Wise was waiting to head the ball in, making it 2-0.

MATCH RATING: ★★★ **LEAGUE POSITION: 6th**

MATCH FACTS		
Shots On Target		
Chelsea	15-3	Nott'm Forest
Shots Off Target		
Chelsea	12-5	Nott'm Forest
Hit Woodwork		
Chelsea	1-0	Nott'm Forest
Corners		
Chelsea	10-1	Nott'm Forest

HOW THEY LINED UP

de Goey

Lambourde, Terry, Leboeuf, Harley

Petrescu, Deschamps, Wise, Poyet

Flo, Zola

Freedman, John

Brennan, Prutton, Bart-Williams, Gray

Rogers, Scimeca, Hjelde, Louis-Jean

Beasant

CHELSEA	
de Goey	8
Petrescu	7
Subbed: 90 mins (Percassi)	
Leboeuf ⚽	7
Goal: 57 mins	
Deschamps	6
Subbed: 69 mins (Morris)	
Poyet	6
Wise ⚽	7
Goal: 86 mins	
Flo	6
Lambourde	☆ 8
Zola	7
Terry	7
Harley	8
***sub:** Morris*	8
***sub:** Percassi*	

Subs not used: *Sutton, Ambrosetti, Cudicini.*

NOTTINGHAM FOREST	
Beasant	☆ 8
Louis-Jean	6
Booked: 17 mins (foul)	
Rogers	7
Hjelde	6
Scimeca	6
Bart-Williams	6
Freedman	6
John	7
Gray	6
Subbed: 63 mins (Harewood)	
Prutton	7
Brennan	7
***sub:** Harewood*	7

Subs not used: *Crossley, Bonalair, Dawson, Williams.*

Harley caught the eye for Chelsea, but Villa had more chances to win the game.

Aston Villa (0) 0
Chelsea (0) 0

Competition: **FA Carling Premiership**

Date: **Saturday January 22, 2000**

Attendance: **33,704**

Referee: **A Wilkie** (Chester-le-Street) 7

Game 36

THE GAME: Aston Villa increased their unbeaten run in the Premiership to six games, but after their recent improvement in form they were disappointed at failing to beat Chelsea at Villa Park. Chris Sutton and George Weah started the game up front together for the first time, with the Liberian showing flashes of brilliance early on, particularly when he flicked the ball over a confused Ugo Ehiogu and lashed the ball into the side-netting. Young full-back Jon Harley also impressed for Gianluca Vialli's charges, looking comfortable in defence – he cleared spectacularly off the line from Ehiogu – and effective going forward, with one 35-yard lob that bounced off Villa's crossbar. David James showed the form that has forced him back into contention for the England squad with several fine saves, while Ed de Goey had an even more eventful afternoon in the Chelsea goal. He allowed Emerson Thome's backpass to slip under his foot, then was lucky to collect the ball before it went over the line. Moments later he punched a clearance straight to Paul Merson, who laid the ball on a plate for Benito Carbone. Fortunately for The Blues, the Italian striker missed from close range and they came away satisfied with a point.

MATCH RATING: ★★★ **LEAGUE POSITION: 6th**

> **"We have to make sure we qualify for the Champions League by finishing in the top three of the Premiership. It'll be hard with so many other teams trying to qualify, but we have the ability to do it." DAN PETRESCU**

ASTON VILLA	
James	6
Watson	6
Subbed: 60 mins (Delaney)	
Southgate	7
Ehiogu	6
Barry	6
Wright	6
Taylor	7
Boateng	6
Merson	☆8
Joachim	5
Subbed: 46 mins (Vassell)	
Carbone	5
sub: *Delaney*	5
sub: *Vassell*	5
Subbed: 63 mins (Stone)	
sub: *Stone*	5

Subs not used: *Thompson, Cutler.*

CHELSEA	
de Goey	7
Lambourde	6
Leboeuf	7
Subbed: 53 mins (Hogh)	
Thome	7
Harley	6
Morris	6
Wise	5
Deschamps	5
Poyet	6
Subbed: 74 mins (Flo)	
Weah	☆8
Sutton	6
Subbed: 74 mins (Zola)	
sub: *Hogh*	6
sub: *Flo*	
sub: *Zola*	

Subs not used: *Cudicini, Ambrosetti.*

MATCH FACTS

Shots On Target		
Aston Villa	4-3	Chelsea
Shots Off Target		
Aston Villa	6-4	Chelsea
Hit Woodwork		
Aston Villa	0-1	Chelsea
Corners		
Aston Villa	10-1	Chelsea

HOW THEY LINED UP

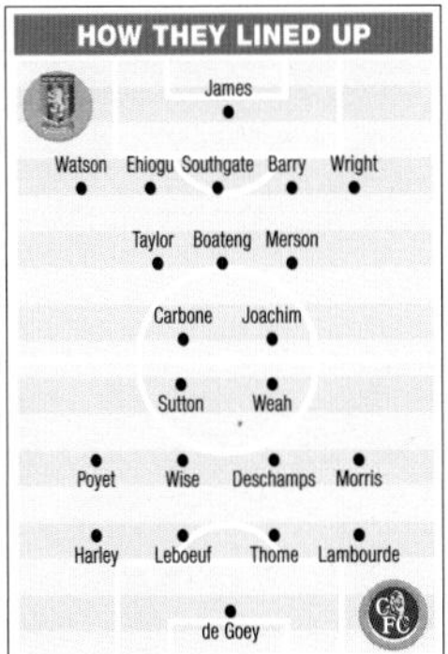

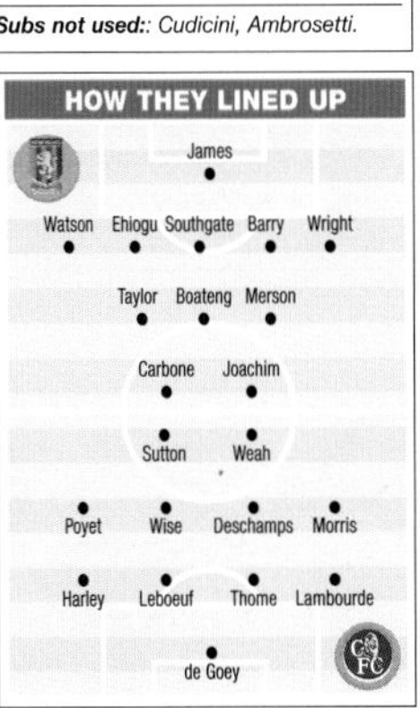

Chelsea (1) 2
Leicester City (0) 1

Competition: **FA Cup 5th Rd**

Date: **Sunday January 30, 2000**

Attendance: **30,141**

Referee: **G Poll** (Tring) 6

THE GAME: Breathtaking goals from Gus Poyet and George Weah secured victory for The Blues in this FA Cup fifth round clash, but the newspapers focused on other incidents in this bad-tempered clash. Referee Graham Poll handed out seven cautions and two red cards, including the dismissal of Dennis Wise in the last minute for a handball – the captain's second bookable offence. But in contrast to the Premiership meeting between the two sides earlier in January, Chelsea were always in command at Stamford Bridge. The victory took The Blues into the quarter-finals against Second Division side Gillingham, making them many people's favourites to win the competition.

CHELSEA GOALS: Poyet *(35 mins):* Wise delivered an awkward cross which Weah just managed to head back into Poyet's path for a spectacular flying volley; **Weah** *(50 mins):* Sutton delivered the perfect pass for Weah, who squeezed in front of his marker and rifled home a stunning strike.

LEICESTER GOAL: Elliott *(90 mins):* Wrong-footed the Chelsea defence before netting with a cool finish.

MATCH RATING: ★★★★★ **LEAGUE POSITION: 6th**

CHELSEA	
de Goey	7
Petrescu (booked)	7
Booked: 18 mins (foul)	
Hogh	6
Subbed: 46 mins (Terry)	
Desailly	7
Deschamps	7
Poyet (goal)	☆9
Goal: 35 mins	
Sutton (booked)	7
Booked: 25 mins (foul); Subbed: 70 mins (Flo)	
Wise (booked, sent off)	7
Booked: 24 mins (foul); Sent-off: 90 mins (second bookable offence: handball)	
Lambourde	7
Weah (goal)	8
Goal: 50 mins	
Harley	7
sub: *Terry*	7
sub: *Flo*	7

Subs not used: *Morris, Cudicini, Zola.*

LEICESTER	
Arphexad	7
Sinclair (booked)	7
Booked: 27 mins (foul)	
Taggart	☆8
Walsh (booked, sent off)	6
Booked: 50 mins (dissent); Sent-off: 61 mins (violent conduct)	
Heskey	7
Subbed: 78 mins (Gunnlaugsson)	
Eadie (booked)	7
Booked: 26 mins (unsporting behaviour)	
Savage	7
Gilchrist	6
Elliott (booked, goal)	7
Booked: 80 mins (dissent); Goal: 90 mins	
Impey	6
Subbed: 76 mins (Stewart)	
Zagorakis	6
Subbed: 76 mins (Fenton)	
sub: *Gunnlaugsson*	
sub: *Stewart*	
sub: *Fenton*	

Subs not used: *Flowers, Campbell.*

MATCH FACTS

Shots On Target		
Chelsea	5-3	Leicester
Shots Off Target		
Chelsea	5-4	Leicester
Hit Woodwork		
Chelsea	2-0	Leicester
Corners		
Chelsea	5-1	Leicester

HOW THEY LINED UP

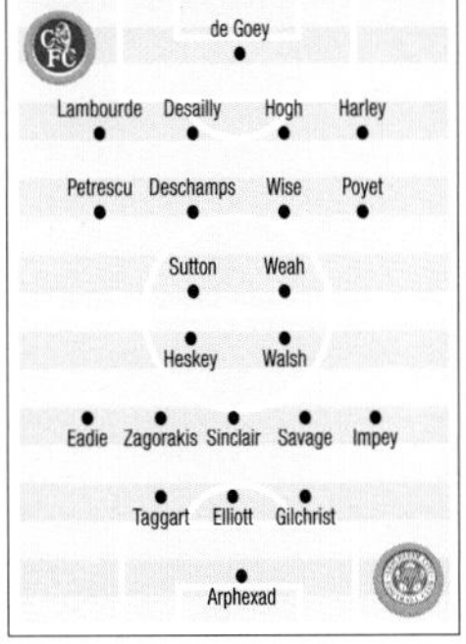

de Goey
Lambourde Desailly Hogh Harley
Petrescu Deschamps Wise Poyet
Sutton Weah
Heskey Walsh
Eadie Zagorakis Sinclair Savage Impey
Taggart Elliott Gilchrist
Arphexad

THIS WEEK...

IN THE NEWS

CHELSEA: Roberto Di Matteo will be out of action for around six weeks after discovering he broke his arm in the Premiership game with Leicester... Gianluca Vialli wants to bring in some younger players during the summer after admitting that the average age of his squad is too old... Vialli is said to be interested in Belgian striker **Luc Nilis**, who is out of contract in the summer and available on a free transfer. His PSV Eindhoven team-mate, **Ruud van Nistelrooy**, is also said to be a Chelsea target but there is stiff competition for the latter's signature... Left back **Jon Harley** caps his fine displays for The Blues by signing a new three-and-a-half year contract.

PREMIERSHIP: Fans of Sheffield Wednesday vent their anger at the four local MPs who called for the dismissal of Owls manager **Danny Wilson**... Liverpool chief Gerard Houllier, keen to strengthen his strikeforce following a number of injuries, has reportedly failed in a bid to sign Vitesse Arnhem's **Pierre van Hooijdonk** on loan... Man. United's **Denis Irwin** decides to retire from international football. The versatile 34-year-old defender won a total of 56 caps for the Republic Of Ireland.

THE FINAL SCORE!

JANUARY 22		
Aston Villa	0-0	Chelsea
Bradford	3-2	Watford
Derby	0-0	Coventry
Leicester	1-3	**West Ham**
Liverpool	0-0	Middlesbrough
Southampton	2-0	Everton
Tottenham	0-1	**Sheff. Wed.**
Wimbledon	2-0	Newcastle
JANUARY 23		
Sunderland	1-2	**Leeds**
JANUARY 24		
Man. United	1-1	Arsenal
JANUARY 29		
Man. United	1-0	Middlesbrough

TOP OF THE PREMIERSHIP

	P	W	D	L	Pts
1. Man. United	21	14	5	2	47
2. Leeds	22	15	2	5	47
3. Arsenal	23	13	5	5	44
6. Chelsea	**23**	**10**	**7**	**6**	**37**

FEBRUARY

START OF MONTH **6th** END OF MONTH **5th**

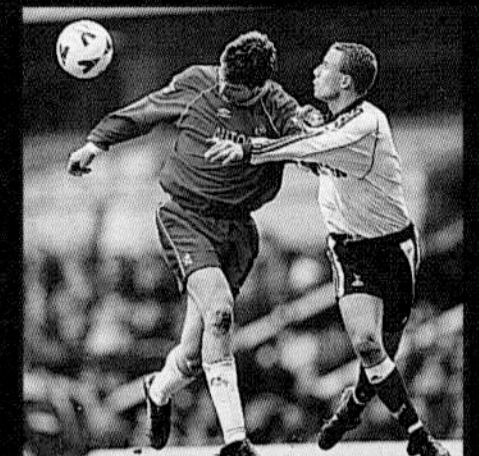

"I wanted to come and play in London. I like the football in England and that the fans always cheer for their team, whether they win the match or lose it." George Weah

WITH JUST OVER THREE MONTHS TO GO BEFORE THE END OF THE season, many critics had already written off Chelsea's championship hopes as they began the month in sixth place. But Blues manager Gianluca Vialli was desperate for his team to produce a late surge of winning form in order to secure a place in the 2000-2001 Champions League.

February was a successful period for Vialli's charges as they finally put together a string of victories, starting with a hard-fought 1-0 win over Spurs at White Hart Lane and completing the double over George Graham's side. Three late strikes at Stamford Bridge earned a further three points against Wimbledon, who made it very tough for The Blues in a physical encounter, but they showed character to overpower their London rivals 3-1.

Chelsea were drawn against Gillingham in the quarter-finals of the FA Cup and dispatched the Second Division side 5-0, despite being only 1-0 in front at half time. George Weah earned rave reviews even though he didn't get on the scoresheet, and it was no coincidence that the arrival of the talented Liberian had coincided with the team's upturn in form.

After earning a place in the FA Cup semi-finals, The Blues resumed their Premiership duties by gaining revenge on Watford after losing at Vicarage Road earlier in the campaign. Despite a gallant fight, Graham Taylor's side were beaten 2-1, with the winner coming from young defender Jon Harley, who was producing some excellent performances at left-back.

The only sour note in February was the disappointing 1-0 away defeat to Marseille in Group D of the Champions League, leaving Chelsea's hopes of making the quarter-finals hanging in the balance. But the Stamford Bridge faithful took heart from seeing their side's improved form in the Premiership and their continuing quest for silverware in the cup competitions.

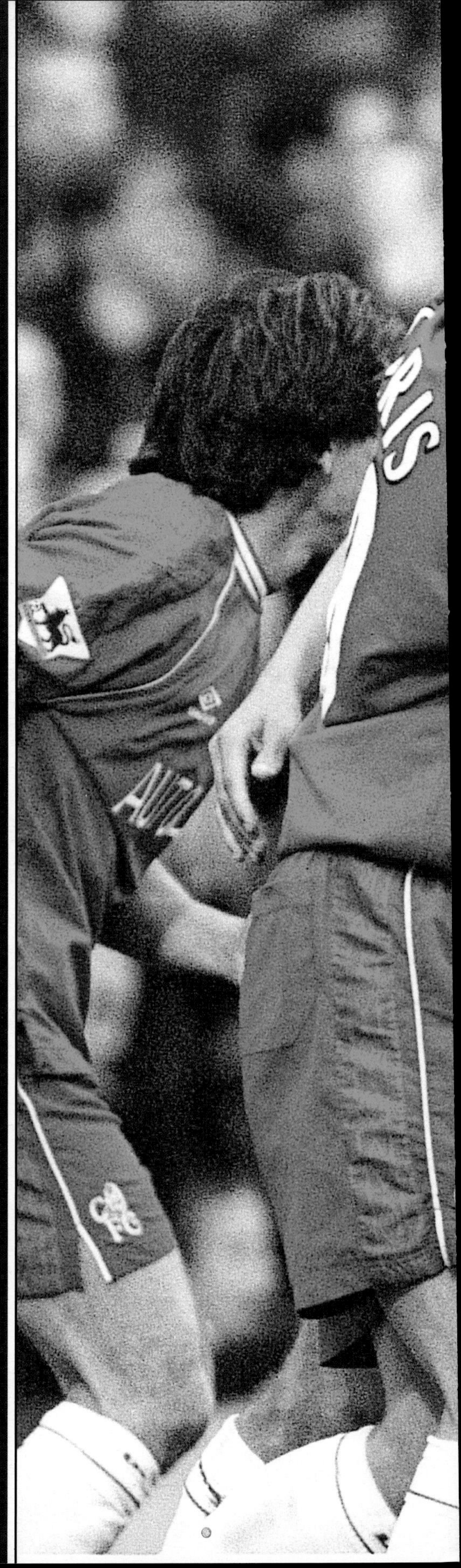

THE GAMES

Feb. 5 v **Tottenham** (a)

Feb. 12 v **Wimbledon** (h)

Feb. 20 v **Gillingham** (h)

Feb. 26 v **Watford** (h)

Feb. 29 v **Marseille** (a)

TRANSFERS IN

Rati Aleksidze
Position: **Midfield**
Fee: **£120,000**
From: **Dynamo Tblisi**

TRANSFERS OUT

Rhys Evans
Position: **Goalkeeper**
Fee: **Loan**
To: **Bristol Rovers**

Mikael Forssell
Position: **Striker**
Fee: **Loan**
To: **Crystal Palace**

MATCH facts
Matchman Of The Month

JON HARLEY
Average Rating: 7.66

George Weah enjoyed his second win against Spurs in the London derby.

Tottenham (0) 0
Chelsea (0) 1

Competition: **FA Carling Premiership**

Date: **Saturday February 5, 2000**

Attendance: **36,041**

Referee: **G Poll** (Tring) 7

Game 38

THE GAME: Bernard Lambourde was Chelsea's unlikely goal hero as The Blues maintained their record against Tottenham at White Hart Lane. The French defender's second-half strike meant Spurs were without a home victory over their London rivals in 22 meetings, dating back to 1987. But Chelsea didn't have everything their own way. Tottenham had the best of the first half and had 'keeper Ed de Goey to thank for keeping the scores level at the break. After Lambourde's goal early in the second half, the home side were unlucky not to restore parity after hitting the woodwork, but The Blues managed to protect their lead and extended their unbeaten run to ten games.

CHELSEA GOAL: Lambourde *(52 mins):* Wise took a quick free-kick around the wall to Lambourde, who lobbed it over stranded Tottenham 'keeper Walker from ten yards.

MATCH RATING: ★★★ **LEAGUE POSITION: 5th**

"The basis of any good team is to have a good defence. If you're not letting in any goals then you're in a better position to win games." GRAEME LE SAUX

MATCH FACTS		
Shots On Target		
Tottenham	3-4	Chelsea
Shots Off Target		
Tottenham	7-2	Chelsea
Hit Woodwork		
Tottenham	1-0	Chelsea
Corners		
Tottenham	7-4	Chelsea

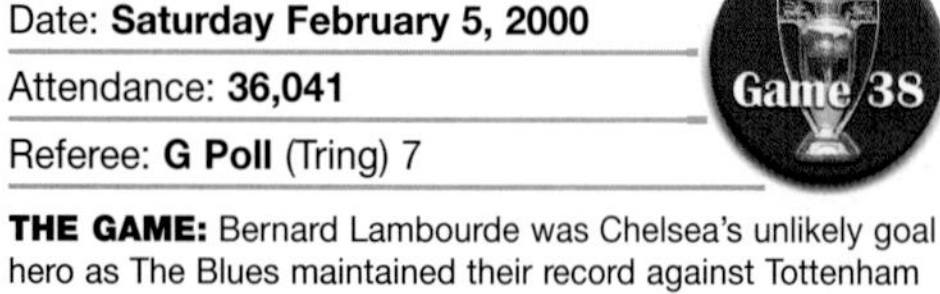

HOW THEY LINED UP

Walker
Carr, Perry, Campbell, Taricco
Anderton, Sherwood, Clemence, Ginola
Iversen, Armstrong
Sutton, Weah
Poyet, Wise, Deschamps, Petrescu
Harley, Desailly, Thome, Lambourde
de Goey

TOTTENHAM	
Walker	7
Carr	7
Taricco	6
Campbell	7
Perry	7
Anderton *Subbed: 85 mins (Nielsen)*	5
Sherwood	6
Iversen *Subbed: 79 mins (Korsten)*	6
Ginola	7
Armstrong	7
Clemence	☆8
sub: Nielsen	
sub: Korsten	

Subs not used: *Baardsen, Young, Scales.*

CHELSEA	
de Goey	7
Petrescu *Subbed: 84 mins (Morris)*	6
Desailly	6
Deschamps	6
Poyet *Booked: 74 mins (foul)*	6
Sutton *Subbed: 76 mins (Flo)*	6
Wise	☆8
Lambourde *Goal: 52 mins*	7
Thome	7
Weah	7
Harley	7
sub: Morris	
sub: Flo	

Subs not used: *Leboeuf, Cudicini, Zola.*

Sweet music for Chelsea as Jody Morris blows his own trumpet.

Chelsea (0) 3
Wimbledon (0) 1

Competition: **FA Carling Premiership**

Date: **Saturday, February 12, 2000**

Attendance: **34,826**

Referee: **P Jones** (Loughborough) 8

Game 39

THE GAME: A late fightback from The Blues extended their unbeaten run and demonstrated an encouraging consistency that was lacking in Chelsea's performances between August and December. Three goals in an impressive ten-minute spell wrapped up the points for the home side, but only after they had fallen behind to Wimbledon. Norwegian striker Andreas Lund found room in The Blues defence to volley in after 72 minutes and it looked like The Dons would leave Stamford Bridge with the three points. But with time running out Gus Poyet grabbed a late equaliser for Chelsea, who went on to destroy Wimbledon in the final ten minutes. Gianluca Vialli was pleased with the way his side eventually disposed of the opposition, but this was only after he brought on Gianfranco Zola and Tore Andre Flo to give Chelsea a three-man attack.

CHELSEA GOALS: Poyet *(78 mins)*: Weah knocked the ball down to Poyet, who scored with a right-foot volley from the edge of the area; **Weah** *(80 mins):* Morris crossed from the right for Weah to head home from eight yards; **Morris** *(88 mins):* Zola set up Morris, who unleashed a 25-yard piledriver.

WIMBLEDON GOAL: Lund *(72 mins):* Cort headed down Ardley's cross for Lund to volley home from five yards.

MATCH RATING: ★★★ **LEAGUE POSITION: 5th**

"Every player loves to score goals. Maybe I am just fortunate, but I have a real passion for scoring goals. There is nothing that gives a player greater pleasure than to score." GUSTAVO POYET

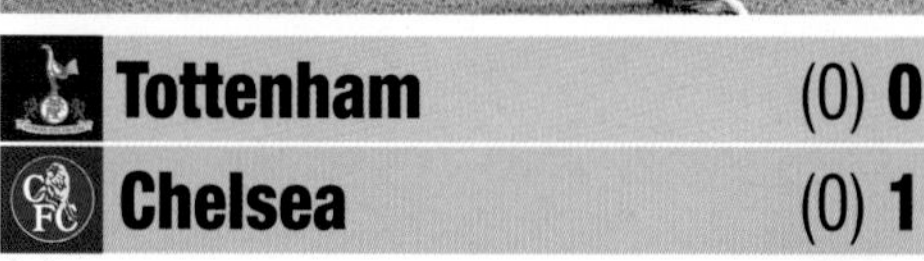

CHELSEA	
de Goey	7
Petrescu	7
Subbed: 62 mins (Zola)	
Leboeuf	6
Deschamps	5
Subbed: 70 mins (Flo)	
Poyet ⚽	8
Goal: 78 mins	
Sutton	6
Subbed: 70 mins (Morris)	
Wise	6
Lambourde	5
Thome	6
Weah ⚽	☆8
Goal: 80 mins	
Harley	8
sub: *Zola*	6
sub: *Flo*	7
sub: *Morris* ⚽	7
Goal: 88 mins	

Subs not used: *Cudicini, Clement.*

WIMBLEDON	
Sullivan	7
Cunningham	7
Kimble	7
Cort	7
Earle	7
Subbed: 83 mins (Francis)	
Euell	7
Andreson	6
Subbed: 68 mins (Ardley)	
Willmott	6
Andersen ▯	6
Booked: 82 mins (foul)	
Hreidarsson	☆8
Lund ▯ ⚽	7
Booked: 44 mins (foul); Goal: 72 mins	
sub: *Ardley*	6
sub: *Francis*	

Subs not used: *Leaburn, Heald, Badir.*

MATCH FACTS

Shots On Target	
Chelsea 5-3 Wimbledon	
Shots Off Target	
Chelsea 9-5 Wimbledon	
Hit Woodwork	
Chelsea 0-0 Wimbledon	
Corners	
Chelsea 5-2 Wimbledon	

HOW THEY LINED UP

Chelsea (1) 5
Gillingham (0) 0

Competition: **FA Cup Quarter-Final**

Date: **Sunday February 20, 2000**

Attendance: **34,205**

Referee: **P Durkin** (Portland) 8

THE GAME: Chelsea took a step closer to their first piece of silverware of the campaign by beating giantkillers Gillingham. Five goals showed the gap between Premiership and Second Division football, even though The Gills had already disposed of Bradford and Sheffield Wednesday. The first half was a tight affair, even after The Blues took an early lead, but they failed to capitalise on it in the opening period. After the break it was a different story, and after John Terry scored the second goal it was a question of how many Chelsea would score before the end. The win took The Blues into the FA Cup semi-final to face Newcastle – the losing finalists in the previous two years.

CHELSEA GOALS: Flo *(17 mins):* Poyet found Flo unmarked at the far post to head home; **Terry** *(49 mins):* A corner from Zola was met by the head of Terry for his first Chelsea goal; **Weah** *(50 mins):* Weah rose above Saunders to plant the ball into the back of the net; **Zola** *(penalty 85 mins):* Browning pulled down Morris in the area and Zola drilled the penalty into the left-hand corner; **Morris** *(87 mins):* Sutton headed the ball back into the path of Morris and though the midfielder's first shot hit the bar, he drove his second chance home.

MATCH RATING: ★★★★ **LEAGUE POSITION: 5th**

CHELSEA	
de Goey	7
Desailly	6
Deschamps	6
Poyet	6
Flo ⚽	7
Goal: 17 mins; Subbed: 74 mins (Ambrosetti)	
Morris ⚽	7
Goal: 87 mins	
Lambourde	6
Zola ⚽	7
Goal: 85 mins (pen)	
Terry ⚽	7
Goal: 49 mins; Subbed: 74 mins (Clement)	
Weah ⚽	☆8
Goal: 50 mins; Subbed: 77 mins (Sutton)	
Harley ▯	7
Booked: 39 mins (foul)	
sub: *Ambrosetti*	
sub: *Clement*	
sub: *Sutton*	

Subs not used: *Petrescu, Cudicini.*

GILLINGHAM	
Bartram	☆8
Edge	5
Smith	7
Ashby	7
Butters	7
Southall	5
Subbed: 78 mins (Browning)	
Hessenthaler	7
Saunders	5
Pennock	5
Subbed: 46 mins (Asaba)	
Lewis ▯	6
Booked: 27 mins (foul)	
Thomson	6
Subbed: 54 mins (Nosworthy)	
sub: *Asaba*	7
sub: *Nosworthy*	6
sub: *Browning*	

Subs not used: *Hodge, Mitten.*

MATCH FACTS

Shots On Target	
Chelsea 13-3 Gillingham	
Shots Off Target	
Chelsea 7-7 Gillingham	
Hit Woodwork	
Chelsea 2-0 Gillingham	
Corners	
Chelsea 9-2 Gillingham	

HOW THEY LINED UP

de Goey
Lambourde Desailly Terry Harley
Morris Deschamps Poyet
Weah Flo Zola
Lewis Thomson
Smith Hessenthaler Saunders
Edge Ashby Butters Pennock Southall
Bartram

THIS WEEK...

IN THE NEWS

CHELSEA: Paolo Maldini says he wants to move to Chelsea after the Euro 2000 Championships... Boss Gianluca Vialli has re-registered as a player... France defender **Frank Leboeuf** is handed a four-match ban for getting sent-off against Leeds and being involved in an incident with Harry Kewell.

PREMIERSHIP: Former England manager Glenn Hoddle takes over at Southampton... Man. United finalise a four-year sponsorship deal with Vodafone worth around £30 million... Sir Alex Ferguson publicly criticises his players for their rash protests after conceding a penalty against Middlesbrough.

THE FINAL SCORE!

FEBRUARY 2		
Sheff. Wed.	0-1	**Man. United**
FEBRUARY 5		
Aston Villa	4-0	Watford
Bradford	2-1	Arsenal
Derby	3-3	Sheff. Wed.
Leicester	2-1	Middlesbrough
Liverpool	3-1	Leeds
Man. United	3-2	Coventry
Southampton	2-1	West Ham
Sunderland	2-2	Newcastle
Tottenham	0-1	**Chelsea**
FEBRUARY 6		
Wimbledon	0-3	**Everton**
FEBRUARY 12		
Chelsea	3-1	Wimbledon
Coventry	3-2	Sunderland
Everton	2-1	Derby
Leeds	1-0	Tottenham
Newcastle	3-0	Man. United
Sheff. Wed.	0-1	**Southampton**
Watford	1-1	Leicester
West Ham	5-4	Bradford
FEBRUARY 13		
Arsenal	0-1	**Liverpool**
FEBRUARY 14		
Middlesbrough	0-4	**Aston Villa**
FEBRUARY 19		
Middlesbrough	2-0	Coventry
FEBRUARY 20		
Leeds	0-1	**Man. United**

TOP OF THE PREMIERSHIP

	P	W	D	L	Pts
1. Man. United	24	16	5	3	53
2. Leeds	24	16	2	6	50
3. Liverpool	25	14	5	6	47
5. Chelsea	**25**	**12**	**7**	**6**	**43**

Harley celebrates his first goal in a Chelsea shirt in the 2-1 win over Watford.

Marseille's three-pronged attack caused plenty of problems for The Blues.

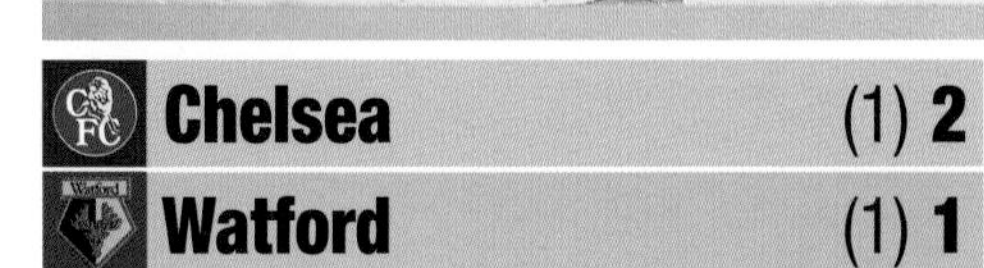

Chelsea	(1)	2
Watford	(1)	1

Competition: **FA Carling Premiership**

Date: **Saturday February 26, 2000**

Attendance: **34,920**

Referee: **S Dunn** (Bristol) 7

THE GAME: Fifteen places separated Chelsea and Watford in the league table at the start of this game but there was little to choose between the sides in this game at Stamford Bridge. The Blues gained revenge for their 1-0 defeat by The Hornets earlier in the season, but it wasn't the most convincing display from Gianluca Vialli's charges. Without George Weah or Chris Sutton to lead the attack, it was left to defenders Jon Harley and Marcel Desailly to score their first goals of the campaign against the Premiership's bottom club. Desailly's strike in the first minute should have been the catalyst for a simple Blues win but Watford's equaliser caused some anxious moments. The decisive goal was scored by Harley, in fine form after his midweek England Under-21 debut, who popped up midway through the second half to secure three points for Vialli's men.

CHELSEA GOALS: Desailly *(1 min):* Zola's curled free-kick found Desailly in the area and the defender flicked his header in from six yards; **Harley** *(65 mins):* Petrescu's cross from the right found Harley on the edge of the six-yard box and the defender headed past Chamberlain for his first Blues goal.

WATFORD GOAL: Smart *(38 mins):* A long-range shot by Helguson could only be parried by de Goey, allowing Smart to race into the box and rifle the ball home from close range.

MATCH RATING: ★★★ **LEAGUE POSITION: 5th**

MATCH FACTS

Shots On Target	
Chelsea 8-10 Watford	

Statistic	Chelsea	Watford
Shots On Target	8	10
Shots Off Target	7	9
Hit Woodwork	0	3
Corners	6	3

HOW THEY LINED UP

Chelsea: de Goey; Lambourde, Desailly, Thome, Harley; Petrescu, Deschamps, Morris, Poyet; Zola, Flo

Watford: Smart, Helguson; Kennedy, Hyde, Palmer, Wooter; Gibbs, Williams, Page, Bonnot; Chamberlain

CHELSEA	
de Goey	7
Petrescu	7
Desailly ⚽ *Goal: 1 min*	7
Deschamps	5
Poyet	5
Flo	6
Morris ▯ *Booked: 90 mins (foul)*	7
Lambourde *Subbed: 57 mins (Ferrer)*	5
Zola	6
Thome	6
Harley ⚽ *Goal: 65 mins*	☆ 8
sub: Ferrer	6

Subs not used: *Ambrosetti, Cudicini, Dalla Bona, Wolleaston.*

WATFORD	
Chamberlain	5
Kennedy	6
Page	7
Palmer	7
Hyde ▯ *Booked: 52 mins (foul)*	6
Smart ⚽ *Goal: 38 mins*	☆ 8
Wooter *Subbed: 80 mins (Ngonge)*	7
Gibbs	5
Bonnot *Subbed: 87 mins (Miller)*	5
Williams	5
Helguson ▯ *Booked: 85 mins (ungentlemanly conduct)*	7
sub: Ngonge	
sub: Miller	

Subs not used: *Robinson, Day, Smith.*

Marseille (1) 1
Chelsea (0) 0

Competition: **Champs League Group D**

Date: **Tuesday February 29, 2000**

Attendance: **30,000**

Referee: **R Pedersen** (Norway) 7

Game 42

THE GAME: Chelsea were beaten for only the second time in this season's Champions League by a Marseille side which seemed to raise their game against The Blues. The troubled club were placed precariously above the relegation zone in the French First Division but still looked dangerous going forward on home soil and caused plenty of problems to Chelsea by playing three men up front. The early part of the match was played at a ferocious pace, with both sides looking dangerous on the counter-attack and missing some golden chances to take the lead in the first ten minutes. Cyrille Pouget failed to capitalise on some great work by his Marseille team-mates, while Blues striker Gianfranco Zola missed a golden chance from six yards just moments later. The visitors paid the price for their wayward finishing when Robert Pires surprised Ed de Goey with a powerful strike that rebounded off both posts and into the Chelsea net. In the second half, the French side again looked dangerous on the counter-attack, but it was The Blues who came closer to scoring, with Chris Sutton and Gustavo Poyet denied by fine saves from Stephane Trevisan.

MARSEILLE GOAL: Pires *(16 mins):* Running down the right wing, Pires spotted 'keeper de Goey wandering from his near post and hit a shot which flew off both posts before going in.

MATCH RATING: ★★ **LEAGUE POSITION: 5th**

MARSEILLE	
Trevisan	7
Blondeau	7
Pires ⚽ *Goal: 16 mins*	7
Brando	6
Pouget *Subbed: 72 mins (De La Pena)*	6
Dalmat	☆8
Leroy	7
Cyprien	7
Bakayoko *Subbed: 90 mins (Moses)*	6
Luccin	6
Abardonado	7
sub: De La Pena	
sub: Moses	

Subs not used: *Carrasso, Issa, Martin, Martini, Keita.*

CHELSEA	
de Goey	6
Petrescu	6
Leboeuf	5
Desailly	6
Deschamps *Subbed: 62 mins (Di Matteo)*	5
Poyet	5
Wise	6
Ferrer *Subbed: 81 mins (Morris)*	☆7
Flo *Subbed: 81 mins (Sutton)*	5
Zola	5
Harley	6
sub: Di Matteo	6
sub: Morris	
sub: Sutton	

Subs not used: *Cudicini, Lambourde, Thome, Ambrosetti.*

MATCH FACTS

Shots On Target		
Marseille	2-4	Chelsea
Shots Off Target		
Marseille	5-4	Chelsea
Hit Woodwork		
Marseille	0-0	Chelsea
Corners		
Marseille	6-6	Chelsea

HOW THEY LINED UP

Trevisan

Cyprien Luccin Abardonado

Blondeau Brando Leroy Dalmat

Pires Bakayoko Pouget

Zola Flo

Poyet Wise Deschamps Petrescu

Harley Leboeuf Desailly Ferrer

de Goey

THIS WEEK...

IN THE NEWS

CHELSEA: Georgia international **Rati Alexidze** is hoping to make a good impression at Stamford Bridge – three years after his first spell at the club. The 21-year-old striker spent six months at the club under former boss Ruud Gullit but is now ready to make an impact after receiving a work permit... The Blues say that any punishment they hand out to Nigeria defender **Celestine Babayaro** for his late return from the African Nations Cup will be kept 'in-house'... Press reports suggest The Blues may have to offload striker **Tore Andre Flo** to land in-demand Dutchman **Ruud van Nistelrooy**... Romania defender **Dan Petrescu** has agreed a new two-year deal to stay at Stamford Bridge.

PREMIERSHIP: Newcastle United captain **Alan Shearer** announces his intention to quit international football after Euro 2000 because he wants to concentrate on his club career and spend more time with his family... Newspapers are rife with transfer speculation about **David Beckham** after his bust-up with Sir Alex Ferguson... Leicester City beat Tranmere Rovers 2-1 in the 2000 Worthington Cup Final at Wembley, becoming the first club in England to qualify for Europe next season.

THE FINAL SCORE!

FEBRUARY 26		
Arsenal	3-1	Southampton
Bradford	1-1	Aston Villa
Chelsea	2-1	Watford
Coventry	0-1	**Tottenham**
Middlesbrough	0-0	Leeds
Sheff. Wed.	0-2	**Newcastle**
Sunderland	1-1	Derby
West Ham	0-4	**Everton**
Wimbledon	2-2	Man. United

TOP OF THE PREMIERSHIP

	P	W	D	L	Pts
1. Man. United	26	17	6	3	57
2. Leeds	26	16	3	7	51
3. Arsenal	26	14	5	7	47
5. Chelsea	**26**	**13**	**7**	**6**	**46**

MARCH

 START OF MONTH **5th**  END OF MONTH **4th**

"We would like to think we're going to win something this season – for the fans, for ourselves and for the club. You never know, I wouldn't put it past us." Jody Morris

AS THE SEASON APPROACHED A CRUCIAL PERIOD THE BLUES HAD no room for error. They needed to continue their fine form in the Premiership to keep up with the leading pack and battle for vital points in Group D of the Champions League to progress into the quarter-finals. Despite criticism from the press concerning the side's inconsistent displays, Chelsea were still in contention for three trophies, which was more than most teams could boast.

In a dress rehearsal for the forthcoming FA Cup semi-final, The Blues beat Newcastle by a single goal to give Gianluca Vialli's charges a psychological edge, but the Chelsea manager was keen to play down the significance of Gustavo Poyet's winner. Four days later, Vialli's side recorded a vital win over Marseille at Stamford Bridge to put them in a strong position in the second Champions League phase, with Ed de Goey performing heroics to keep out the French side. However, a slip up in the Premiership followed as Chelsea could only draw at home to an Everton side severely depleted by injuries.

The Champions League campaign continued positively though, as Dutch side Feyenoord were beaten 3-1 – despite an Ed de Goey error that allowed the Dutch to equalise and threaten an undeserved victory on their home turf. Chelsea's win, which guaranteed Viall's team a place in the knockout phase of the tournament, meant the home tie with Lazio became academic – which was fortunate as the Italians turned on the style to win a thrilling game 2-1. In the draw for the quarter-finals, The Blues were pitted against tournament favourites Barcelona, an awesome prospect which provided the Londoners with their sternest test of the season to date.

Clearly distracted by the glamour of Europe, Chelsea drew their remaining league fixtures – away to West Ham and at home to Southampton – meaning they had only won six out of a possible 12 Premiership points in March.

THE GAMES

Mar. 4 v **Newcastle** (a)

Mar. 8 v **Marseille** (h)

Mar. 11 v **Everton** (h)

Mar. 14 v **Feyenoord** (a)

Mar. 18 v **West Ham** (a)

Mar. 22 v **Lazio** (h)

Mar. 25 v **Southampton** (h)

TRANSFERS IN

None

TRANSFERS OUT

John Terry
Position: **Defender**
Fee: **Loan**
To: **Nottingham Forest**

MATCH facts

Matchman Of The Month

FRANK LEBOEUF
Average Rating: 7.33

Newcastle United	(0) **0**
Chelsea	(1) **1**

Competition: **FA Carling Premiership**

Date: **Saturday March 4, 2000**

Attendance: **36,448**

Referee: **M Riley** (Leeds) 7

THE GAME: In a dress-rehearsal for the FA Cup semi-final, Chelsea gained the psychological advantage over Newcastle by winning 1-0 at St James' Park. Continuing their impressive run of form since Christmas, The Blues lifted themselves from a below-par Champions League performance in midweek to end Bobby Robson's unbeaten home run since taking over as manager in September. Man Of The Match Gus Poyet scored the only goal of the game to lift his side into third place in the Premiership and in contention for a Champions League place. Newcastle's best chance fell to Kieron Dyer, and the England midfielder thought he had equalised midway through the first half, but his shot was brilliantly deflected over the crossbar by Blues 'keeper Ed de Goey to hand Chelsea victory.

CHELSEA GOAL: Poyet *(21 mins):* A wayward pass by Lee was intercepted by Di Matteo, who fed Morris on the left. His cross found Poyet, who got in front of Howey to head home.

MATCH RATING: ★★ **LEAGUE POSITION: 3rd**

"It's important for us to qualify for Europe via the league. We can't rely on winning the FA Cup or the Champions league, so it's important for us to win as many games as we can in the Premiership." JON HARLEY

NEWCASTLE UNITED	
Given	6
Barton	7
Domi *Subbed: 46 mins (Solano)*	5
Howey	6
Dyer	5
Shearer	6
Speed	6
Hughes	6
Ferguson	5
Dabizas	☆8
Lee *Subbed: 75 mins (Ketsbaia)*	5
sub: *Solano*	6
sub: *Ketsbaia*	

Subs not used: *Harper, Gavilan, Fumaca.*

CHELSEA	
de Goey	7
Babayaro	6
Leboeuf	9
Poyet ⚽ *Goal: 21 mins*	☆9
Sutton *Subbed: 72 mins (Flo)*	6
Wise	6
Di Matteo *Subbed: 48 mins (Petrescu)*	7
Ferrer	6
Morris	7
Zola	7
Thome	7
sub: *Petrescu*	7
sub: *Flo*	

Subs not used: *Ambrosetti, Cudicini, Terry.*

MATCH FACTS

Shots On Target		
Newcastle	5-5	Chelsea
Shots Off Target		
Newcastle	8-3	Chelsea
Hit Woodwork		
Newcastle	0-0	Chelsea
Corners		
Newcastle	4-3	Chelsea

HOW THEY LINED UP

Given

Barton Dabizas Howey Hughes Domi

Dyer Speed Lee

Ferguson Shearer

Sutton Zola

Poyet Wise Morris Di Matteo

Babayaro Leboeuf Thome Ferrer

de Goey

Poyet celebrates scoring his seventh league goal of the season at St James' Park.

Dennis Wise's winning strike took Vialli's side a step nearer to the Champions League quarter-finals.

Chelsea (1) 1
Marseille (0) 0

Competition: **Champs League Group D**
Date: **Wednesday March 8, 2000**
Attendance: **33,206**
Referee: **J Fernandez Marin** (Spain) 5

Game 44

THE GAME: Blues 'keeper Ed de Goey erased the memories of his nightmare in Marseille with a string of spectacular saves to play an important role in Chelsea's elevation to the top of Group D. The big Dutchman pulled off a series of point-blank saves to earn his 23rd clean sheet of the season and preserve Chelsea's interest in the Champions League. The match was a close affair, with both sides looking capable of sneaking the three points. But it was Blues skipper Dennis Wise who gave his side a slender advantage with a close-range finish midway through the first half. Former Everton striker Ibrahim Bakayoko looked most likely to bring Marseille level, but he was unable to break down Chelsea's defence, leaving The Blues on the verge of the quarter-finals with two games to play in Group D.

CHELSEA GOAL: Wise *(26 mins):* Flo delivered an inviting cross from the left and Zola headed into Wise's path for the captain to slide the ball in from close range.

MATCH RATING: ★★★ **LEAGUE POSITION:** 3rd

"I'm enjoying my football and I'm playing well. I'm just doing what I've always done, but people have noticed me more in the games where I've done well and scored goals. Everyone's said how well I've done." DENNIS WISE

MATCH FACTS

Shots On Target
Chelsea 10-7 Marseille

Shots Off Target
Chelsea 6-7 Marseille

Hit Woodwork
Chelsea 0-1 Marseille

Corners
Chelsea 6-8 Marseille

HOW THEY LINED UP

de Goey
Ferrer, Desailly, Leboeuf, Babayaro
Morris, Deschamps, Wise, Poyet
Flo, Zola

Pouget, Bakayoko, Pires
Dalmat, Leroy, Brando
Perez, Abardonado, Luccin, Cyprien
Trevisan

CHELSEA

Player	Rating
de Goey ☆	9
Babayaro	5
Leboeuf (booked)	5
Booked: 39 mins (foul)	
Desailly	6
Deschamps (booked)	5
Booked: 8 mins (foul); Subbed: 79 mins (Di Matteo)	
Poyet	6
Wise (goal)	8
Goal: 26 mins	
Ferrer	7
Flo	5
Morris	7
Zola	6
Subbed: 79 mins (Harley)	
sub: *Harley*	
sub: *Di Matteo*	

Subs not used: *Cudicini, Sutton, Thome, Ambrosetti, Lambourde.*

MARSEILLE

Player	Rating
Trevisan	7
Perez	6
Subbed: 38 mins (Fischer)	
Pires	6
Brando	6
Pouget (booked)	6
Booked: 51 mins (foul)	
Dalmat	6
Leroy	7
Cyprien	6
Subbed: 66 mins (De La Pena)	
Bakayoko ☆	8
Luccin	6
Abardonado	6
sub: *Fischer* (booked)	7
Booked: 88 mins (foul)	
sub: *De La Pena*	7

Subs not used: *Carrasso, Martin, Moses, Keita, Martini.*

THIS WEEK...

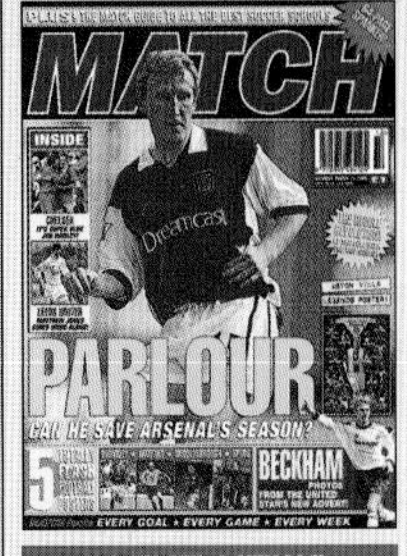

IN THE NEWS

CHELSEA: Frank Leboeuf has decided to retire from international football in 2002 and end his career at Stamford Bridge. The French defender has also revealed that Chelsea's Champions League opponents Marseille tried to sign him earlier in the season... BSkyB add Chelsea to their portfolio of clubs, buying 9.9 per cent of the Stamford Bridge club for a fee of £40 million. Sky also has a stake in Manchester United, Leeds, Sunderland and Manchester City.

PREMIERSHIP: Newcastle place a £10 million price tag on winger and Peru captain **Nolberto Solano** after rumours surface of a pending approach from Manchester United. The 26-year-old is thought to have recently rejected a new contract at St James' Park... Manchester United boss Sir Alex Ferguson says that teams play over-defensively against them in Europe, making it difficult for The Red Devils to play their usual attacking game... **Stan Collymore** scores a superb hat-trick on his home debut for Leicester City to crush opponents Sunderland 5-2 at Filbert Street. Liverpool agree to pay £11 million for Foxes striker **Emile Heskey**, ending months of speculation about the England striker's future.

THE FINAL SCORE!

MARCH 4		
Derby	4-0	Wimbledon
Everton	1-1	Sheff. Wed.
Man. United	1-1	Liverpool
Newcastle	0-1	**Chelsea**
Southampton	1-1	Middlesbrough
Tottenham	1-1	Bradford
Watford	1-2	**West Ham**
MARCH 5		
Aston Villa	1-1	Arsenal
Leeds	3-0	Coventry
Leicester	5-2	Sunderland
MARCH 8		
West Ham	2-0	Southampton

TOP OF THE PREMIERSHIP

	P	W	D	L	Pts
1. Man. United	27	17	7	3	58
2. Leeds	27	17	3	7	54
3. Chelsea	**27**	**14**	**7**	**6**	**49**
4. Liverpool	26	14	6	6	48

Roberto Di Matteo couldn't inspire a win against an injury-hit Everton side.

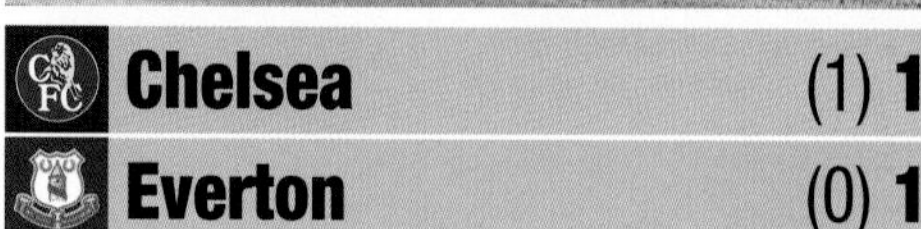

Chelsea (1) 1
Everton (0) 1

Competition: **FA Carling Premiership**

Date: **Saturday March 11, 2000**

Attendance: **35,113**

Referee: **D Elleray** (Harrow) 6

THE GAME: Chelsea failed to take advantage of a weakened Everton side and had to settle for a point in this encounter at Stamford Bridge. Everton had a number of players out through injury and were without leading striker Kevin Campbell, so it seemed like the three points were a formality, but The Blues underestimated their determined visitors. Neither side created many opportunities early on in the game, but it was Chelsea who took the lead with one of their first real attacks. Captain Dennis Wise benefitted from good work by Roberto Di Matteo and Chris Sutton to place a firm shot past Paul Gerrard for his ninth goal of the season. But The Blues let Everton back into the game in the second half and allowed Danny Cadamarteri to equalise. Both sides had opportunities to win the game in the closing stages, with Ed de Goey making an outstanding save from American striker Joe-Max Moore, and Jody Morris aiming his header straight at 'keeper Paul Gerrard.

CHELSEA GOAL: Wise *(30 mins):* Di Matteo and Sutton combined to set up Wise and the England midfielder made no mistake with a 20-yard shot past Everton 'keeper Gerrard.

EVERTON GOAL: Cadamarteri *(69 mins):* Gough headed the ball down into Cadamarteri's path and the Everton striker was able to stab the ball home from close range.

MATCH RATING: ★★ **LEAGUE POSITION: 3rd**

MATCH FACTS		
Shots On Target		
Chelsea	5-4	Everton
Shots Off Target		
Chelsea	9-5	Everton
Hit Woodwork		
Chelsea	0-0	Everton
Corners		
Chelsea	2-0	Everton

HOW THEY LINED UP

Chelsea: de Goey; Ferrer, Thome, Leboeuf, Harley; Di Matteo, Morris, Wise, Babayaro; Sutton, Zola

Everton: Moore, Hughes, M; Barmby, Pembridge, Collins, Cadamarteri; Dunne, Gough, Weir, Xavier; Gerrard

CHELSEA	
de Goey	7
Babayaro	6
Leboeuf	6
Sutton	4
Wise ⚽ *Goal: 30 mins*	☆8
Di Matteo	7
Ferrer	6
Morris	5
Zola *Subbed: 46 mins (Flo)*	5
Thome	7
Harley *Subbed: 72 mins (Poyet)*	6
sub: Flo	6
sub: Poyet	

Subs not used: *Ambrosetti, Cudicini, Terry.*

EVERTON	
Gerrard	7
Gough *Booked: 77 mins (foul)*	6
Collins	7
Barmby *Booked: 77 mins (dissent)*	7
Pembridge	4
Weir	7
Dunne	5
Cadamarteri ⚽ *Goal: 69 mins*	☆8
Hughes, M	5
Xavier	5
Moore	5

Subs not used: *Myhre, Watson, Gemmill, Jevons, Ward.*

Get in! Tore Andre Flo secures a place in the quarter-finals of the Champions League.

Feyenoord (0) 1
Chelsea (1) 3

Competition: **Champs League Group D**

Date: **Tuesday March 14, 2000**

Attendance: **45,000**

Referee: **E Fisker** (Denmark) 6

THE GAME: Chelsea became the first English team to qualify for the quarter-finals of the European Champions League with a masterful display in Holland. The Blues had dominated the last encounter between the two teams at Stamford Bridge in November and did exactly the same in this return match. But the visitors had an early setback when Frank Leboeuf missed a penalty following a clumsy challenge on Tore Andre Flo in the area. Gianfranco Zola scored a sublime goal towards the end of the first half to delight the travelling fans and give The Blues a deserved lead. Feyenoord managed to equalise after the break through a mistake by 'keeper Ed de Goey, but it did nothing to stop Chelsea's attacking instincts. They responded immediately with a Dennis Wise header before Tore Andre Flo sealed the victory with a fine individual strike. The result left Chelsea two points clear at the top of Group D with only Lazio left to play. The Blues were almost certain of a place in the quarter-finals and only defeat in the final game, combined with a big Feyenoord win against Marseille, could end their hopes.

FEYENOORD GOAL: Kalou *(57 mins):* De Goey palmed out Rzasa's cross and Kalou was on hand to score the equaliser.

CHELSEA GOALS: Zola *(39 mins):* Received a header from Flo, then turned and struck a superb shot past Dudek which went in off the left-hand post; **Wise** *(64 mins):* A cross from the left by Babayaro was placed perfectly for Wise to head past Dudek; **Flo** *(69 mins):* Poyet's throughball found Flo in space on the right and the big Norwegian beat Konterman before coolly placing a right-foot drive past Dudek.

MATCH RATING: ★★★ **LEAGUE POSITION: 3rd**

FEYENOORD	
Dudek	7
Rzasa	7
van Gastel	6
Bosvelt (yellow card)	7
Booked: 67 mins (foul)	
van Wonderen	7
Cruz	☆8
Tomasson	7
Konterman	7
Paauwe	5
Subbed: 46 mins (Kalou)	
de Visser	6
Subbed: 69 mins (Samardzic)	
van Gobbel	6
sub: Kalou (goal)	6
Goal: 57 mins	
sub: Samardzic	6

Subs not used: *Graafland, Gyan, de Haan, Korneev, van Vossen.*

CHELSEA	
de Goey	8
Petrescu	7
Babayaro	7
Leboeuf	7
Desailly	8
Deschamps	7
Poyet	8
Subbed: 77 mins (Morris)	
Wise (goal)	☆9
Goal: 64 mins	
Di Matteo	7
Flo (goal)	8
Goal: 69 mins	
Zola (goal)	8
Goal: 39 mins; Subbed: 90 mins (Ambrosetti)	
sub: Morris	
sub: Ambrosetti	

Subs not used: *Cudicini, Hogh, Sutton, Harley, Thome.*

MATCH FACTS

Shots On Target		
Feyenoord	2-12	Chelsea
Shots Off Target		
Feyenoord	4-3	Chelsea
Hit Woodwork		
Feyenoord	0-0	Chelsea
Corners		
Feyenoord	0-8	Chelsea

HOW THEY LINED UP

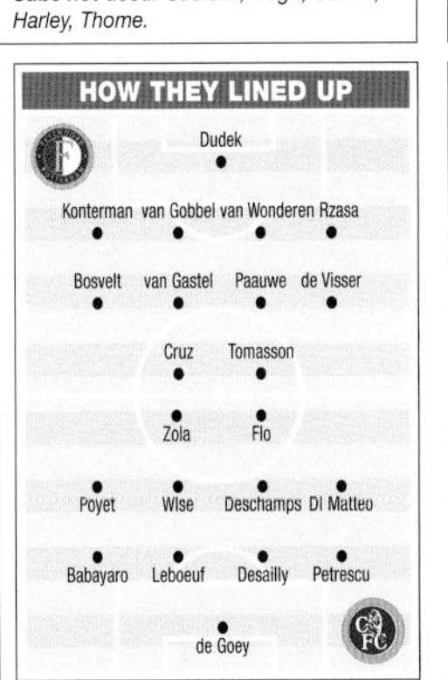

West Ham United (0) 0
Chelsea (0) 0

Competition: **FA Carling Premiership**
Date: **Saturday March 18, 2000**
Attendance: **26,041**
Referee: **S Dunn** (Bristol) 6

THE GAME: Chelsea's impressive form in Europe again failed to translate into success at home as they were held to a 0-0 stalemate by West Ham. It extended the team's unbeaten run in the Premiership to 12 games, but their hopes of claiming a top-three place received another body blow at Upton Park. Both teams had chances in the first half, with Craig Forrest denying Dan Petrescu after 26 minutes and Paolo Di Canio threatening to break the deadlock. The game changed after the interval when Igor Stimac was red-carded for his second bookable foul of the game, which encouraged the home side to tighten their defence and prevent the visitors from stealing the points. Tore Andre Flo almost succeeded towards the end of the game but his header was saved and it ended goalless.

MATCH RATING: ★★★ **LEAGUE POSITION: 4th**

> **"The Premiership is a totally different style of football and needs a different approach. We suffered at the start of the season because we didn't cope with the change from Champions League to Premiership."** JODY MORRIS

WEST HAM UNITED	
Forrest	7
Stimac (yellow card) (red card)	6
Booked: 45 mins (unsporting behaviour); Sent-off: 70 mins (second bookable offence: foul)	
Ferdinand	8
Lomas	7
Lampard	7
Foe (yellow card)	7
Booked: 88 mins (foul)	
Moncur (yellow card)	☆9
Booked: 18 mins (foul); Subbed: 86 mins (Cole)	
Minto	8
di Canio	8
Sinclair	7
Wanchope	6
Subbed: 59 mins (Kitson)	
sub: Kitson	
Subbed: 77 mins (Ruddock)	
sub: Ruddock	
sub: Cole	

Subs not used: *Feuer, Keller.*

CHELSEA	
de Goey	7
Petrescu	6
Subbed: 65 mins (Poyet)	
Babayaro	7
Leboeuf	7
Desailly	7
Deschamps	7
Wise	☆9
Ferrer	7
Flo (yellow card)	7
Booked: 45 mins (unsporting behaviour); Subbed: 82 mins (Sutton)	
Morris (yellow card)	7
Booked: 52 mins (foul); Subbed: 82 mins (Di Matteo)	
Zola	8
sub: Poyet	6
sub: Sutton	
sub: Di Matteo	

Subs not used: *Cudicini, Thome.*

MATCH FACTS

Shots On Target		
West Ham	3-5	Chelsea
Shots Off Target		
West Ham	9-2	Chelsea
Hit Woodwork		
West Ham	1-0	Chelsea
Corners		
West Ham	3-4	Chelsea

HOW THEY LINED UP

THIS WEEK...

IN THE NEWS

CHELSEA: Coach Gianluca Vialli has revealed his wish to stay in English football for at least two more years, saying: "I want to stay here at Chelsea and help them to become the best club in Europe". The Stamford Bridge supremo has ruled out an £18 million move for highly-rated Dutch striker **Ruud van Nistelrooy**.

PREMIERSHIP: Man. United crush Fiorentina 3-1 in the Champions League. Sir Alex Ferguson says it's one of the best displays during his time at the club...Graeme Souness returns to English football as the new coach of Blackburn Rovers... **Georgi Kinkladze** says he wants a permanent move to Derby after showing impressive form while on loan from Dutch giants Ajax.

THE FINAL SCORE!

MARCH 11		
Aston Villa	1-0	Coventry
Chelsea	1-1	Everton
Liverpool	1-1	Sunderland
Man. United	3-1	Derby
Newcastle	1-0	Watford
Sheff. Wed.	3-1	West Ham
Tottenham	7-2	Southampton
Wimbledon	2-1	Leicester
MARCH 12		
Bradford	1-2	**Leeds**
Middlesbrough	2-1	Arsenal
MARCH 15		
Coventry	1-0	Everton
Liverpool	0-0	Aston Villa
MARCH 18		
Coventry	4-0	Bradford
Derby	0-2	**Liverpool**
Leicester	0-2	**Man. United**
Southampton	2-0	Aston Villa
Sunderland	1-1	Middlesbrough
Watford	1-0	Sheff. Wed.
West Ham	0-0	Chelsea
MARCH 19		
Arsenal	2-1	Tottenham
Leeds	4-1	Wimbledon

TOP OF THE PREMIERSHIP

	P	W	D	L	Pts
1. Man. United	29	19	7	3	64
2. Leeds	28	18	3	7	57
3. Liverpool	29	15	8	6	53
4. Chelsea	**29**	**14**	**9**	**6**	**51**

Chelsea	(1)	**1**
Lazio	(0)	**2**

Competition: **Champs League Group D**

Date: **Wednesday March 22, 2000**

Attendance: **34,260**

Referee: **M Melo Pereira** (Portugal) 6

THE GAME: Chelsea saw their one-goal lead demolished by Lazio at Stamford Bridge but they still finished as runners-up in Group D to secure a place in the quarter-finals. Gus Poyet's fantastic strike put The Blues in front on the stroke of half time but this brought out the best in Lazio. The Italian giants were awesome to watch in the second half and quality goals from Filippo Inzaghi and Sinisa Mihajlovic were enough to send the Italians through as group winners. Chelsea, having finished in second place, went into the draw knowing they had a one in three chance of meeting the winners of Group B and current European Cup holders Manchester United.

CHELSEA GOAL: Poyet *(45 mins):* A mistake in the Lazio defence allowed Deschamps to intercept the ball and supply Poyet, who hit a left-foot shot into the top right-hand corner.

LAZIO GOALS: Inzaghi *(55 mins):* Nedved broke through on the left-wing after good work in midfield and set up Inzaghi, who fired home a low shot for the equaliser; **Mihajlovic** *(66 mins):* Curled a brilliant free-kick over the wall which dipped viciously into the top left-hand corner of de Goey's goal.

MATCH RATING: ★★★★ **LEAGUE POSITION: 4th**

CHELSEA	
de Goey	6
Petrescu	7
Babayaro *Subbed: 73 mins (Morris)*	6
Leboeuf *Booked: 34 mins (foul); Subbed: 61 mins (Hogh)*	7
Desailly	6
Deschamps	6
Poyet *Goal: 45 mins*	☆7
Di Matteo *Booked: 4 mins (foul); Subbed: 73 mins (Harley)*	6
Ferrer	7
Flo	6
Zola	7
sub: Hogh	
sub: Harley *Booked: 88 mins (foul)*	
sub: Morris	

Subs not used: *Cudicini, Thome, Sutton, Ambrosetti.*

LAZIO	
Marchegiani	7
Negro	7
Mihajlovic *Goal: 66 mins*	☆8
Simeone	7
Pancaro	6
Nedved	8
Stankovic *Booked: 46 mins (Boksic)*	6
Inzaghi *Goal: 55 mins; Subbed: 68 mins (Salas)*	7
Veron	7
Couto *Booked: 34 mins (unsporting behaviour); Sent-off 83 mins (second bookable offence: foul)*	6
Almeyda	7
sub: Boksic	7
sub: Salas *Subbed: 88 mins (Gottardi)*	6
sub: Gottardi	

Subs not used: *Ballotta, Sensini, Conceicao, Mancini.*

CHAMPIONS LEAGUE

FINAL STANDINGS GROUP D

	P	W	D	L	Pts
1. Lazio	6	3	2	1	11
2. Chelsea	**6**	**3**	**1**	**2**	**10**
3. Feyenoord	6	2	2	2	8
4. Marseille	6	1	1	4	4

MATCH FACTS

Shots On Target		
Chelsea	7-5	Lazio
Shots Off Target		
Chelsea	3-10	Lazio
Hit Woodwork		
Chelsea	1-0	Lazio
Corners		
Chelsea	2-4	Lazio

HOW THEY LINED UP

de Goey

Ferrer Desailly Leboeuf Babayaro

Petrescu Deschamps Di Matteo Poyet

Flo Zola

Inzaghi

Nedved Stankovic Veron Simeone Almeyda

Pancaro Mihajlovic Couto Negro

Marchegiani

Defeat at home to Lazio meant Chelsea finished second in the Champions League Group D.

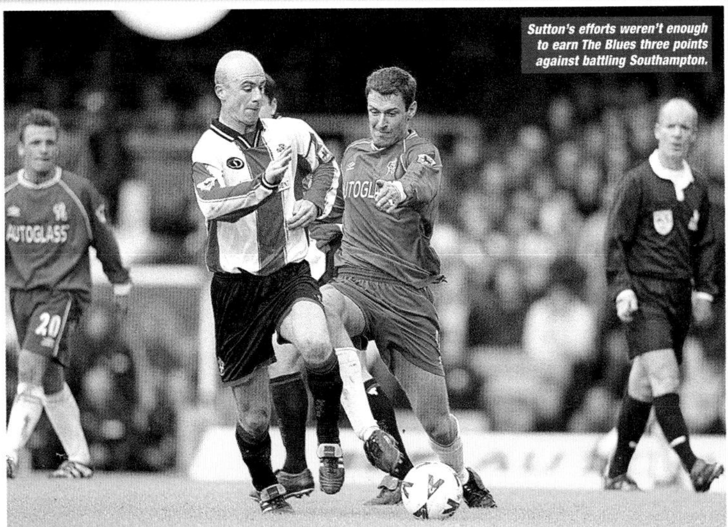
Sutton's efforts weren't enough to earn The Blues three points against battling Southampton.

Chelsea (0) 1
Southampton (0) 1

Competition: **FA Carling Premiership**

Date: **Saturday March 25, 2000**

Attendance: **34,956**

Referee: **D Gallagher** (Banbury) 8

Game 49

THE GAME: The Blues were spared an embarrassing home defeat in this match thanks to an own goal from Southampton centre-back Dean Richards. The former Wolves defender had been outstanding in soaking up Chelsea's pressure, but it was a header past his own 'keeper that gave The Blues a share of the points. Wanting to avoid a tired display after being beaten by Lazio in midweek, Gianluca Vialli made six changes for his side's 49th game of the season. But while The Blues had three strikers on show and 19 shots at goal, their poor finishing let the team down. Chelsea fans were frustrated that their heroes couldn't reproduce their European form in the Premiership, but Vialli's team had other prizes to chase as the campaign moved into April. Being drawn against Barcelona in the quarter-finals of the Champions League and Newcastle in the semi-finals of the FA Cup at Wembley was obvious consolation for the side's inconsistent form in the Premiership.

CHELSEA GOAL: Richards *(own goal 74 mins):* Harley's fine cross into the Southampton penalty area was headed past his own 'keeper by defender Richards.

SOUTHAMPTON GOAL: Tessem *(67 mins):* Controlled the ball brilliantly then drove a fine shot into the left-hand corner.

MATCH RATING: ★★★ **LEAGUE POSITION: 4th**

MATCH FACTS

Shots On Target		
Chelsea	8-5	Southampton
Shots Off Target		
Chelsea	11-2	Southampton
Hit Woodwork		
Chelsea	2-0	Southampton
Corners		
Chelsea	10-3	Southampton

HOW THEY LINED UP

de Goey

Ferrer, Thome, Desailly, Harley

Petrescu, Wise, Morris

Weah, Sutton, Zola

Pahars, Davies

Oakley, Marsden, Kachloul, Tessem

Bridge, El Khalej, Richards, Dodd

Jones

CHELSEA

Player	Rating
de Goey	6
Petrescu	7
Desailly	6
Sutton *Subbed: 73 mins (Poyet)*	4
Wise	5
Ferrer	5
Morris	5
Zola *Subbed: 86 mins (Ambrosetti)*	6
Thome	5
Weah	☆7
Harley	7
sub: *Poyet*	
sub: *Ambrosetti*	

Subs not used: *Hogh, Di Matteo, Cudicini.*

SOUTHAMPTON

Player	Rating
Jones	7
Dodd	7
Marsden	7
Richards ⚽ *Own Goal: 74 mins*	☆8
Oakley	7
Davies	6
Pahars	7
Bridge	6
Tessem ⚽ *Goal: 67 mins*	7
El Khalej	6
Kachloul	7

Subs not used: *Lundekvam, Le Tissier, Moss, Benali, Soltvedt.*

THIS WEEK...

IN THE NEWS

CHELSEA: Defender **Graeme Le Saux** has returned to training after five months on the sidelines with an ankle injury... The club is set to face a disciplinary hearing to discuss an incident that occurred in the players' tunnel last month against Wimbledon... **Gus Poyet** could miss up to 18 matches over the next 18 months if Uruguay require his services for World Cup 2002 qualifying games. **Celestine Babayaro** could also be missing for a month at the beginning of next season after Nigeria succeed in qualifying for the 2000 Olympic Games, which start in September.

PREMIERSHIP: Sunderland end a disastrous run of 12 games without a win as **Kevin Phillips** grabs a winner against Everton... **Jamie Redknapp** marks his first game back for over four months with a headed winner against Newcastle as The Reds hit a rich vein of form at exactly the right time... Former Middlesbrough star **Fabrizio Ravanelli** says he'd love to come back to Boro one day as a manager... Man. United, Chelsea and Arsenal have all been linked with an audacious £18 million move for PSV Eindhoven striker **Ruud van Nistelrooy.**

THE FINAL SCORE!

MARCH 25		
Aston Villa	2-0	Derby
Bradford	0-4	**Man. United**
Chelsea	1-1	Southampton
Liverpool	2-1	Newcastle
Middlesbrough	1-0	Sheff. Wed.
Sunderland	2-1	Everton
Watford	1-1	Tottenham
MARCH 26		
Arsenal	3-0	Coventry
Leicester	2-1	Leeds
West Ham	2-1	Wimbledon

TOP OF THE PREMIERSHIP

	P	W	D	L	Pts
1. Man. United	30	20	7	3	67
2. Leeds	30	19	3	8	60
3. Liverpool	30	16	8	6	56
5. Chelsea	**30**	**14**	**10**	**6**	**52**

APRIL

 START OF MONTH **5th**  END OF MONTH **5th**

"The Champions League is something all players want to be part of. I've enjoyed playing against all the good teams, but the Barcelona game is massive." Dennis Wise

CHELSEA FACED AN INCREDIBLE FIXTURE LIST IN APRIL, WITH NINE crucial games in just 29 days. Gianluca Vialli's side was chasing three major targets this month – the FA Cup Final, the Champions League semi-final and a top-three position in the league. To fulfil their ambitions The Blues needed to triumph over a resurgent Newcastle side, Spanish giants Barcelona and Premiership heavyweights Manchester United, Leeds and Liverpool.

A 1-0 win against Leeds at the start of the month improved Chelsea's league standing and pushed the title towards Old Trafford, but The Blues had other concerns. Few people gave them a chance against the Spaniards but Chelsea turned in a superb display to take a 3-1 lead to the Nou Camp.

Before the second leg in Spain, The Blues had a massive game against Newcastle in the FA Cup semi-final. In a thrilling encounter at Wembley, excellent goalkeeping from Ed de Goey and two goals from Gustavo Poyet saw Chelsea through to the final to face Aston Villa. Gianluca Vialli's side continued their 16-game unbeaten run by beating Coventry at Stamford Bridge, but a defeat by Premiership strugglers Sheffield Wednesday was a major blow ahead of their return leg against Barcelona in the Champions League. The Catalan side fielded an awesome display of attacking talent, clearly stating their intention to claw back the 3-1 deficit from the first leg. Inspired by Luis Figo they reversed the scoreline from Stamford Bridge and showed their true class in extra-time to win the tie 6-4 on aggregate.

Deflated, The Blues returned to the Premiership and dropped two points at home to Middlesbrough, leaving them fifth in the table. The next game saw them travel to newly-crowned champions Manchester United, losing 3-2 after being in a winning position. At least a month of mixed emotions ended on a high when The Blues beat Liverpool 2-0 at Stamford Bridge.

THE GAMES

Apr. 1 v **Leeds** (a)

Apr. 5 v **Barcelona** (h)

Apr. 9 v **Newcastle** (n)

Apr. 12 v **Coventry** (h)

Apr. 15 v **Sheff. Wed.** (a)

Apr. 18 v **Barcelona** (a)

Apr. 22 v **Middlesbrough** (h)

Apr. 24 v **Man. United** (a)

Apr. 29 v **Liverpool** (h)

TRANSFERS IN

None

TRANSFERS OUT

None

MATCH facts

Matchman Of The Month

GEORGE WEAH
Average Rating: 7.00

Jon Harley lets fly to grab the only goal of the game in the win at Elland Road.

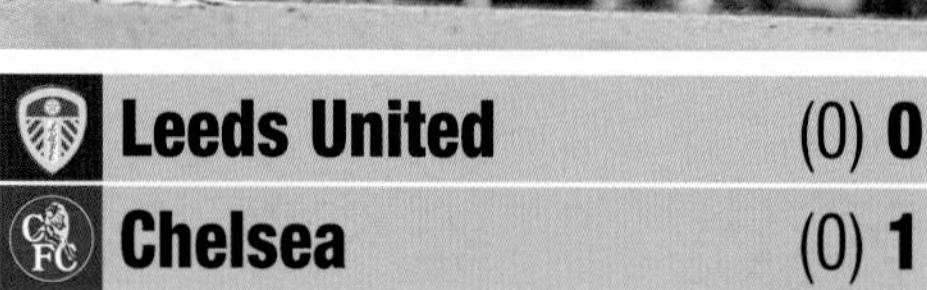

Leeds United	(0) **0**
Chelsea	(0) **1**

Competition: **FA Carling Premiership**

Date: **Saturday April 1, 2000**

Attendance: **40,162**

Referee: **J Winter** (Stockton) 7

Game 50

THE GAME: The Blues maintained their unbeaten run in the Premiership as Jon Harley's second-half goal gave Chelsea all three points at Elland Road. In doing so, Gianluca Vialli's men dealt a mortal blow to Leeds' championship aspirations and virtually handed the Premiership crown to Manchester United. It also strengthened Chelsea's hopes of securing a Champions League place with seven games remaining in the league. After a tentative first half, The Blues started to look dangerous and Man Of The Match Harley nearly scored with a curling effort after 54 minutes, only for Nigel Martyn to pull off an excellent save. But the England Under-21 star wasn't to be denied for long and showed great confidence to score the only goal of the game eight minutes later. Tempers threatened to boil over soon after, but Chelsea kept their cool to record a vital win.

CHELSEA GOAL: Harley *(62 mins):* A pass from Sutton into the box found Harley on the left and the defender slotted the ball under Martyn's body at the near post.

MATCH RATING: ★★★ LEAGUE POSITION: 5th

"Young players like myself learn a lot from the foreign players here. It makes you a better player so when you do get your chance, you're as ready as you'll ever be to play in the first team." JON HARLEY

MATCH FACTS

Shots On Target
Leeds 5-4 Chelsea
Shots Off Target
Leeds 12-5 Chelsea
Hit Woodwork
Leeds 0-0 Chelsea
Corners
Leeds 12-4 Chelsea

HOW THEY LINED UP

Martyn

Kelly Woodgate Radebe Harte

Bowyer Bakke McPhail Wilcox

Smith Kewell

Sutton Weah

Babayaro Wise Morris Di Matteo

Harley Thome Leboeuf Ferrer

de Goey

LEEDS UNITED

Player	Rating
Martyn	6
Kelly	6
Woodgate	7
Radebe	5
Harte	6
Bowyer *Booked: 85 mins (dissent)*	5
Bakke	☆8
McPhail	7
Wilcox *Subbed: 74 mins (Huckerby)*	7
Smith *Booked: 85 mins (foul)*	5
Kewell	5
sub: *Huckerby*	

Subs not used: *Haaland, Robinson, Mills, Jones.*

CHELSEA

Player	Rating
de Goey	7
Ferrer	7
Leboeuf	8
Thome	7
Wise	7
Morris *Booked: 37 mins (foul)*	7
Di Matteo	7
Harley *Goal: 62 mins; Subbed: 88 mins (Lambourde)*	☆9
Babayaro	7
Weah	5
Sutton *Booked: 90 mins (foul)*	6
sub: *Lambourde*	

Subs not used: *Hogh, Cudicini, Dalla Bona, Zola.*

THIS WEEK...

IN THE NEWS

CHELSEA: Defender **Graeme Le Saux** has suffered complications in his recovery from a long-term ankle injury. Hopes were raised that the left-back may return to action this month, but Gianluca Vialli has conceded that Le Saux may not return until next season... In-demand **Ruud van Nistelrooy** says he'd prefer a move to Chelsea than Manchester United or Arsenal. The striker's club, PSV Eindhoven, have extended his transfer deadline while he makes a decision about his future... The Blues have been linked with talented Inter Milan trio **Nicola Ventola**, **Javier Zanetti** and **Sebastien Frey**.

PREMIERSHIP: The Premiership launches new plans to fine players up to four weeks' wages if they step out of line... Leicester new boy **Stan Collymore** breaks his leg when his studs catch in the turf as he plays a pass in the game away to Derby, but the striker insists that he'll be back for the start of next season... Aston Villa forward **Benito Carbone** dismisses claims he is demanding £40,000 a week to stay at Villa Park... Arsenal veteran **Nigel Winterburn** seems likely to leave The Gunners in the summer after losing his place to Brazilian **Silvinho**... West Ham's teenage star **Joe Cole** has signed a new contract which could earn him £3 million in four seasons.

THE FINAL SCORE!

APRIL 1		
Coventry	0-3	**Liverpool**
Everton	4-2	Watford
Leeds	0-1	**Chelsea**
Man. United	7-1	West Ham
Newcastle	2-0	Bradford
Southampton	1-2	**Sunderland**
Wimbledon	1-3	**Arsenal**
APRIL 2		
Derby	3-0	Leicester
APRIL 3		
Tottenham	2-3	**Middlesbrough**

TOP OF THE PREMIERSHIP

	P	W	D	L	Pts
1. Man. United	31	21	7	3	70
2. Leeds	31	19	3	9	60
3. Liverpool	31	17	8	6	59
4. Chelsea	**31**	**15**	**10**	**6**	**55**

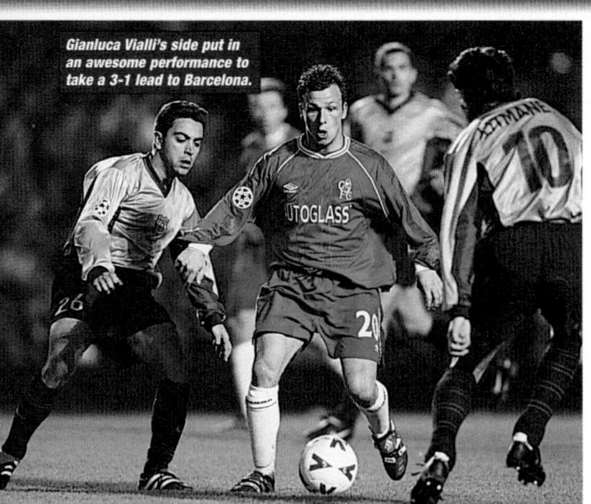

Gianluca Vialli's side put in an awesome performance to take a 3-1 lead to Barcelona.

FROM THE PAGES OF MATCH

On the eve of **CHELSEA**'s Champions League quarter-final with Barcelona, **GRAEME LE SAUX** and **DAN PETRESCU** told **MATCH** about the club's experiences in Europe this season.

Have you been surprised by your success in Europe?
Dan says: *"Not really, and I'm sure over the next year we'll be even more successful in Europe. The success was one of the main reasons I signed a new contract with Chelsea."*
Graeme says: *"The team have done very well in Europe and we've started to pick up our Premiership form now as well. We wanted to take our form from the European games into the domestic competitions and we've done that."*

Has Vialli's knowledge of European football helped?
Dan says: *"Yes, when we play against a team in Europe we know a lot about them. We watch videos of how they play and Luca talks about how they work as a team. We know what they can do and that's why we do well against them."*

Can you go on to win the Champions League from here?
Graeme says: *"It's difficult to say because every team is capable of beating everyone else. It's down to who's the best team on the night, but as long as we prepare well and apply ourselves, our big-name players should make a difference."*

Which teams do you think are your biggest threats?
Dan says: *"Barcelona and Lazio are probably the strongest teams still in the competition. But now that we've qualified for the quarter-finals, I think we can go all the way."*

Chelsea	(3)	3
 Barcelona	(0)	1

Competition: **Champs Lge QF 1st leg**

Date: **Wednesday April 5, 2000**

Attendance: **33,662**

Referee: **M Merk** (Germany) 5

THE GAME: Three goals in the space of just eight incredible minutes put Chelsea on course to record a memorable win at Stamford Bridge. Barcelona were unbeaten in the Champions League until this game but were torn apart by Gianluca Vialli's side. It was the Spanish champions who exerted most of the early pressure but The Blues came back well, with Gianfranco Zola causing all sorts of problems in the visitors' defence. He gave Chelsea the lead after 29 minutes, curling an absolutely magical free-kick over the wall and into the corner of the net. A shell-shocked Barcelona then conceded two goals in quick succession from Tore Andre Flo to put Gianluca Vialli's side in the driving seat, but Luis Figo made it 3-1 early in the second half to set up a mouthwatering return leg in the Nou Camp.

CHELSEA GOALS: Zola *(29 mins):* Curled a quite magical free-kick over the wall and into the net; **Flo** *(33 mins):* Zola struck a precision cross from the right-wing for Flo to tap in from close range; **Flo** *(37 mins):* Spotted Hesp off his line and chipped the 'keeper from the edge of the box.

BARCELONA GOAL: Figo *(54 mins)*: Rivaldo, out wide on the left, delivered a precision pass from the left for Portuguese international Figo to score from the edge of the six-yard box.

MATCH RATING: ★★★★★ **LEAGUE POSITION: 4th**

CHELSEA	
de Goey	8
Petrescu	7
Booked: 16 mins (foul); Subbed: 71 mins (Di Matteo)	
Babayaro	6
Desailly	8
Deschamps	8
Wise	8
Ferrer	8
Flo	9
Goals: 33, 37 mins; Subbed: 90 mins (Sutton)	
Morris	7
Zola	☆ 9
Goal: 29 mins; Booked: 48 mins (foul)	
Thome	8
sub: Di Matteo	
sub: Sutton	

Subs not used: *Cudicini, Hogh, Poyet, Lambourde, Harley.*

BARCELONA	
Hesp	6
Abelardo	6
Figo	☆ 8
Booked: 29 mins (foul); Goal: 54 mins	
Cocu	6
Booked: 51 mins (foul)	
Kluivert	6
Subbed: 71 mins (Dani)	
Rivaldo	7
Bogarde	6
de Boer, F	6
Xavi	7
Gabri	7
Booked: 31 mins (foul)	
Puyol	7
Subbed: 46 mins (Litmanen)	
sub: Litmanen	6
sub: Dani	

Subs not used: *Arnau, Reiziger, Dehu, Guardiola, Simao Sabrosa.*

MATCH FACTS

	Shots On Target	
Chelsea	6-7	Barcelona
	Shots Off Target	
Chelsea	4-5	Barcelona
	Hit Woodwork	
Chelsea	0-0	Barcelona
	Corners	
Chelsea	4-5	Barcelona

HOW THEY LINED UP

de Goey

Ferrer, Thome, Desailly, Babayaro

Petrescu, Deschamps, Wise, Morris

Zola, Flo

Rivaldo, Kluivert

Figo, Cocu, Xavi, Gabri

Bogarde, de Boer, F, Abelardo, Puyol

Hesp

THIS WEEK...

IN THE NEWS

CHELSEA: Former Barcelona boss Bobby Robson tips the Spanish giants to be far too powerful for Chelsea at Stamford Bridge and warns Vialli that to try and contain them would be suicidal. After the game Robson describes Chelsea's 3-1 win as 'awesome' but warns The Blues that they may need to score at least one goal in the Nou Camp to ensure progress to the semi-finals, such is the potency of Barcelona's attacking threat.

PREMIERSHIP: John Hartson's big-money transfer to Tottenham from Wimbledon breaks down after the Welshman fails a medical... Liverpool striker **Emile Heskey** is subjected to lengthy verbal racist abuse from opposition fans in an England Under-21s play-off game against Yugoslavia in Barcelona... Tottenham captain **Sol Campbell** reveals Manchester United made a £17 million bid for him earlier in the season... Brazilian defender **Roberto Carlos** says that **David Beckham** is 'slow' and 'lacking in ability' after Manchester United's 0-0 Champions League draw with Real Madrid in the Bernabeu... Leicester striker **Stan Collymore** says he could now be fit for the end of the season after dislocating his ankle and fracturing his leg in the recent game against Derby... French Footballer Of The Year **Sylvain Wiltord** has expressed an interest in joining Arsenal.

THE FINAL SCORE!

	APRIL 5	
Sheff. Wed	0-1	**Aston Villa**
	APRIL 8	
Bradford	1-2	**Southampton**
Leicester	1-1	Everton
Sunderland	2-1	Wimbledon
Watford	0-0	Derby

TOP OF THE PREMIERSHIP

	P	W	D	L	Pts
1. Man. United	31	21	7	3	70
2. Leeds	31	19	3	9	60
3. Liverpool	31	17	8	6	59
5. Chelsea	**31**	**15**	**10**	**6**	**55**

"Everybody – we're going to win the cup..." Gustavo Poyet gets into the party spirit at Wembley.

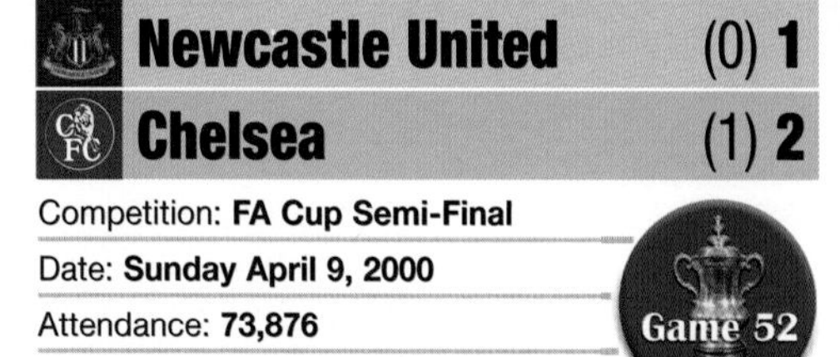

Competition: **FA Cup Semi-Final**

Date: **Sunday April 9, 2000**

Attendance: **73,876**

Referee: **D Gallagher** (Banbury) 6

Game 52

THE GAME: Gustavo Poyet was Chelsea's hero as he scored two goals against Newcastle to book their place in the FA Cup Final to face Aston Villa. The Blues made six changes from the side that beat Barcelona and lacked the fluency they showed in midweek. Newcastle looked the better side at Wembley but George Weah and Chris Sutton combined for Poyet to score the opening goal. The Magpies got a deserved equaliser in the second half, but Poyet's clinical finishing just six minutes later sent The Blues into the final as hot favourites to lift the cup.

NEWCASTLE GOAL: Lee *(65 mins):* Shearer crossed from the right to Lee, who scored with a header from close range.

CHELSEA GOALS: Poyet *(16 mins):* A superb Chelsea move ended with a brilliant finish from the Uruguayan into the top right-hand corner; **Poyet** *(71 mins):* Harley crossed to Poyet, who scored with a strong header past Given from eight yards.

MATCH RATING: ★★★★ **LEAGUE POSITION: 5th**

MATCH FACTS

Shots On Target		
Newcastle	8-4	Chelsea
Shots Off Target		
Newcastle	6-5	Chelsea
Hit Woodwork		
Newcastle	0-0	Chelsea
Corners		
Newcastle	11-2	Chelsea

HOW THEY LINED UP

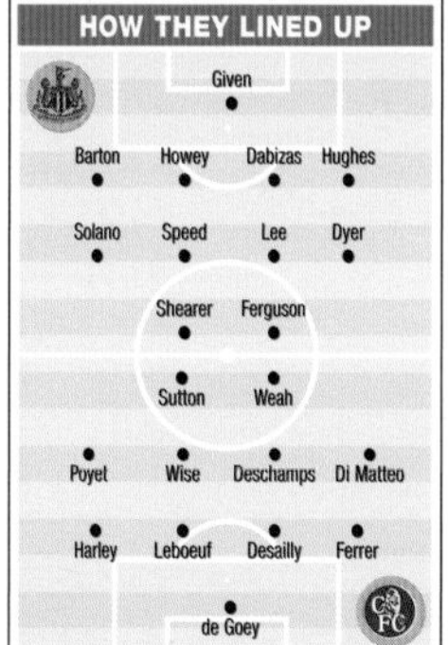

NEWCASTLE UNITED	
Given	7
Barton	7
Hughes	6
Subbed: 79 mins (Ketsbaia)	
Howey	7
Dabizas	7
Solano	8
Speed	7
Lee ⚽	7
Goal: 65 mins	
Dyer	8
Shearer	☆8
Ferguson	6
Subbed: 38 mins (Domi)	
sub: Domi	7
sub: Ketsbaia	

Subs not used: *Harper, Goma, Gavilan.*

CHELSEA	
de Goey	8
Ferrer	7
Subbed: 74 mins (Petrescu)	
Harley	7
Leboeuf	7
Desailly	7
Di Matteo	6
Deschamps ▯	7
Booked: 75 mins (foul)	
Wise	8
Poyet ⚽⚽	☆9
Goals: 16, 71 mins	
Sutton	5
Subbed: 46 mins (Flo)	
Weah	7
Subbed: 79 mins (Zola)	
sub: Flo	6
sub: Petrescu	
sub: Zola	

Subs not used: *Cudicini, Hogh.*

Gianfranco Zola's strike sealed a valuable three points against Coventry.

Chelsea (0) 2
Coventry City (1) 1

Competition: **FA Carling Premiership**

Date: **Wednesday April 12, 2000**

Attendance: **33,316**

Referee: **G Poll** (Tring) 8

Game 53

THE GAME: Liberian striker George Weah provided a ray of sunshine to prevent this rain-drenched midweek fixture from being a washout. A heavy pitch at Stamford Bridge prevented Chelsea from playing their natural passing game and this was particularly evident in the first half as they went behind after Gary McAllister's long-range strike. The inspired second-half introduction of George Weah changed the game. Weah was unstoppable in Chelsea's attack and set up both of the home team's goals, including a superb move to present Gianfranco Zola with his first Premiership goal in 26 games. The win sent The Blues into fourth place in the league and a step closer to qualifying for the 2000-2001 Champions League campaign.

CHELSEA GOALS: Hendry *(own goal 52 mins):* Ambrosetti crossed to Weah, who headed goalwards with Hendry getting the final touch; **Zola** *(57 mins):* Weah darted into the Coventry area and knocked the ball back for Zola, on the edge of the box, who unleashed an unstoppable right-foot strike.

COVENTRY GOAL: McAllister *(17 mins):* Hendry laid the ball back for McAllister, who scored past de Goey from 25 yards.

MATCH RATING: ★★ **LEAGUE POSITION: 4th**

> **"There are a few players who still don't understand the significance of sport. They just play for the money. Most of them do not understand that sport can bring peace, unification and reconciliation." GEORGE WEAH**

Sheffield Wednesday	(0)	**1**
Chelsea	(0)	**0**

Competition: **FA Carling Premiership**

Date: **Saturday April 15, 2000**

Attendance: **21,743**

Referee: **P Durkin** (Portland) 7

THE GAME: Chelsea's hectic fixture schedule caught up with them at Hillsborough, with Sheffield Wednesday ending their unbeaten record since the beginning of the year. Relegation favourites Wednesday overran a lethargic Chelsea side in the first half, with The Blues distracted by the forthcoming clash with Barcelona in the Nou Camp. The decisive moment of the game came early in the second half when Gilles de Bilde was felled by Ed de Goey and Wim Jonk scored from the penalty spot. This sparked Chelsea into life, with George Weah hitting the post twice in as many minutes, but the visitors couldn't claw back a goal to escape their seventh league defeat.

SHEFFIELD WEDNESDAY GOAL: Jonk *(penalty 51 mins)*: de Bilde was upended by de Goey, who was lucky to escape with a booking, and Jonk confidently converted the spot-kick.

MATCH RATING: ★★★ **LEAGUE POSITION: 4th**

"We're not putting the strikers through on goal as much as we did last year and I think it's because defences are dropping so deep. That's the main reason the clear-cut chances haven't come." JODY MORRIS

CHELSEA	
de Goey	7
Petrescu	6
Leboeuf	7
Poyet	6
Subbed: 50 mins (Ambrosetti)	
Wise	6
Di Matteo	6
Subbed: 54 mins (Dalla Bona)	
Flo	4
Subbed: 50 mins (Weah)	
Morris	5
Zola ⚽	7
Goal: 57 mins	
Thome	7
Harley	6
sub: *Weah*	☆8
sub: *Dalla Bona*	6
sub: *Ambrosetti*	6

Subs not used: *Hogh, Hitchcock.*

COVENTRY CITY	
Hedman	7
Shaw	7
Keane	5
Whelan	6
Subbed: 77 mins (Zuniga)	
McAllister ⚽	☆8
Goal: 17 mins	
Hadji	6
Subbed: 78 mins (Burrows)	
Telfer	6
Froggatt	6
Chippo	6
Quinn	6
Hendry ⚽	6
Own Goal: 52 mins	
sub: *Zuniga*	
sub: *Burrows*	

Subs not used: *Ogrizovic, Breen, Eustace.*

SHEFFIELD WEDNESDAY	
Pressman	7
Haslam	7
Atherton	7
Walker	7
Hinchcliffe	7
Alexandersson	6
Jonk ⚽	☆8
Goal: 51 mins	
Horne	6
Subbed: 65 mins (Briscoe)	
Quinn	7
Booth	7
de Bilde	6
Subbed: 73 mins (Sibon)	
sub: *Briscoe*	6
sub: *Sibon*	

Subs not used: *Srnicek, Sonner, Cresswell.*

CHELSEA	
de Goey ▯	7
Booked: 51 mins (foul)	
Petrescu	6
Subbed: 46 mins (Dalla Bona)	
Desailly ▯	7
Booked: 81 mins (foul)	
Thome	6
Babayaro	6
Ambrosetti	6
Subbed: 71 mins (Flo)	
Morris	6
Subbed: 46 mins (Deschamps)	
Poyet	☆8
Lambourde	6
Sutton	6
Weah	7
sub: *Dalla Bona*	6
sub: *Deschamps*	6
sub: *Flo*	

Subs not used: *Hogh, Hitchcock.*

MATCH FACTS

Shots On Target		
Chelsea	3-2	Coventry
Shots Off Target		
Chelsea	11-3	Coventry
Hit Woodwork		
Chelsea	0-0	Coventry
Corners		
Chelsea	8-3	Coventry

HOW THEY LINED UP

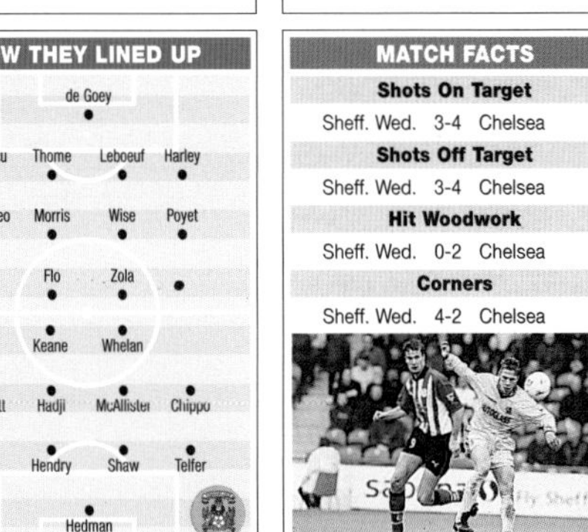

MATCH FACTS

Shots On Target		
Sheff. Wed.	3-4	Chelsea
Shots Off Target		
Sheff. Wed.	3-4	Chelsea
Hit Woodwork		
Sheff. Wed.	0-2	Chelsea
Corners		
Sheff. Wed.	4-2	Chelsea

HOW THEY LINED UP

Pressman

Haslam, Atherton, Walker, Hinchcliffe

Alexandersson, Jonk, Horne, Quinn

Booth, de Bilde

Sutton, Weah

Ambrosetti, Poyet, Morris, Petrescu

Babayaro, Desailly, Thome, Lambourde

de Goey

THIS WEEK...

IN THE NEWS

CHELSEA: Celestine Babayaro may be unavailable for The Blues' Champions League second leg clash with Barcelona after being caught up in another club versus country row... England defender **Graeme Le Saux** hopes to resume full training in three weeks' time after a frustrating spell out on the sidelines... Coach Gianluca Vialli is keeping a close eye on Argentina international **Javier Zanetti** and **Stephane Dalmat** of Marseille.

PREMIERSHIP: Man. United's attempt to defend their Champions League crown ends in a 3-2 defeat at Old Trafford against Spanish side Real Madrid. Red Devils boss Sir Alex Ferguson responds quickly to the quarter-final defeat, moving to strengthen his squad by making a phenomenal £19 million bid for sought-after PSV Eindhoven striker **Ruud van Nistelrooy**.

THE FINAL SCORE!

APRIL 9		
Aston Villa	1-0	Leeds
Liverpool	2-0	Tottenham
APRIL 10		
Middlesbrough	3-4	**Man. United**
APRIL 12		
Chelsea	2-1	Coventry
West Ham	2-1	Newcastle
Wimbledon	0-2	**Sheff. Wed.**
APRIL 15		
Coventry	2-1	Middlesbrough
Derby	1-2	**West Ham**
Everton	4-0	Bradford
Man. United	4-0	Sunderland
Newcastle	0-2	**Leicester**
Sheff. Wed.	1-0	Chelsea
Southampton	2-0	Watford
Tottenham	2-4	**Aston Villa**

TOP OF THE PREMIERSHIP

	P	W	D	L	Pts
1. Man. United	33	23	7	3	76
2. Liverpool	32	18	8	6	62
3. Leeds	32	19	3	10	60
4. Chelsea	**33**	**16**	**10**	**7**	**58**

	Barcelona	(2) 5
	Chelsea	(0) 1

Barcelona win 6-4 on aggregate AET.

Competition: **Champs Lge QF 2nd leg**

Date: **Tuesday April 18, 2000**

Attendance: **98,000**

Referee: **A Frisk** (Sweden) 7

THE GAME: Barcelona swept Chelsea aside in an awesome performance at the Nou Camp to knock The Blues out of the Champions League. The Catalan side's away goal in the first leg proved crucial and they fielded an extraordinary array of attacking talent with the express aim of scoring goals. Barca pulled the tie back to 3-3 before Tore Andre Flo restored his side's slim lead. It didn't stop the home side – Dani equalised with seven minutes left, and Rivaldo and Patrick Kluivert broke the hearts of the Blues fans by making it 6-4 after extra-time.

BARCELONA GOALS: Rivaldo *(24 mins):* Deflected free-kick from 25 yards; **Figo** *(45 mins):* Slotted the ball past de Goey after a rebound from Kluivert's shot; **Dani** *(83 mins):* Sent the game into extra-time with a header from a free-kick; **Rivaldo** *(penalty 99 mins):* Slotted into the bottom left-hand corner; **Kluivert** *(104 mins):* Headed home a cross from the right.

CHELSEA GOAL: Flo *(60 mins)*: Hesp's clearance fell to Flo, on the edge of the box, who sent a low shot into the net.

MATCH RATING: ★★★★★ **LEAGUE POSITION: 4th**

BARCELONA	
Hesp	6
Zenden *Subbed: 72 mins (Dani)*	7
de Boer, F	7
Reiziger *Subbed: 106 mins (Sergi)*	8
Puyol *Subbed: 86 mins (Abelardo)*	7
Cocu	7
Guardiola	7
Gabri	8
Rivaldo ⚽⚽ *Goals: 24 mins, 99 mins (pen)*	8
Kluivert ⚽ *Goal: 104 mins*	8
Figo ⚽ ▯ *Goal: 45 mins; Booked: 53 mins (foul)*	☆ 10
sub: *Dani* ⚽ *Goal: 83 mins*	6
sub: *Sergi*	6
sub: *Abelardo*	6

***Subs not used:** Arnau, Xavi, Litmanen, Simao Sabrosa.*

CHELSEA	
de Goey	7
Babayaro ▮ *Sent-off: 98 mins (professional foul)*	7
Desailly	6
Leboeuf	6
Ferrer ▯ *Booked: 1 min (foul); Subbed: 46 mins (Lambourde)*	6
Morris	7
Wise ▯ *Booked: 48 mins (foul)*	7
Deschamps *Subbed: 102 mins (Petrescu)*	7
Di Matteo	6
Zola *Subbed: 120 mins (Poyet)*	7
Flo ⚽ *Goal: 60 mins*	7
sub: *Lambourde*	6
sub: *Petrescu*	6
sub: *Poyet*	

***Subs not used:** Cudicini, Thome, Ambrosetti, Sutton.*

MATCH FACTS

Shots On Target		
Barcelona	12-6	Chelsea
Shots Off Target		
Barcelona	9-2	Chelsea
Hit Woodwork		
Barcelona	2-0	Chelsea
Corners		
Barcelona	8-3	Chelsea

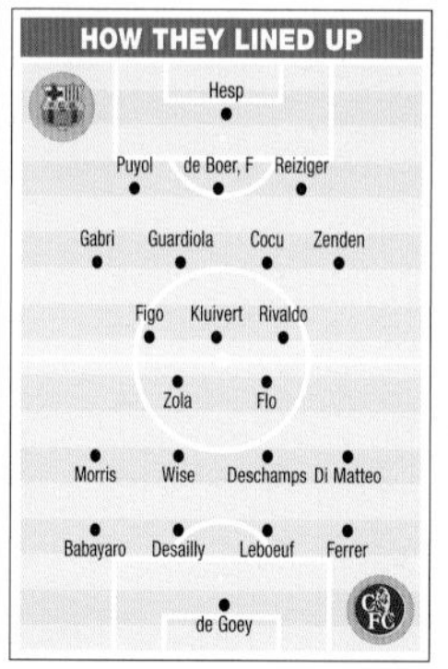

HOW THEY LINED UP

Hesp
Puyol, de Boer, F, Reiziger
Gabri, Guardiola, Cocu, Zenden
Figo, Kluivert, Rivaldo
Zola, Flo
Morris, Wise, Deschamps, Di Matteo
Babayaro, Desailly, Leboeuf, Ferrer
de Goey

The despair is all too clear on Dennis Wise's face after Champions League elimination at the hands of Barcelona.

TWO POINTS DROPPED AT HOME TO BATTLING BORO

Ambrosetti was the only shining light in the draw with Middlesbrough.

Chelsea	(1)	**1**
Middlesbrough	(1)	**1**

Competition: **FA Carling Premiership**

Date: **Saturday April 22, 2000**

Attendance: **34,467**

Referee: **U Rennie** (Sheffield) 6

Game 56

THE GAME: The prospect of another season of Champions League football slipped further from Chelsea's grasp as their European hangover continued at Stamford Bridge. The home team looked tired after their midweek disappointment and by failing to carve out a win they missed the chance to go third in the Premiership. Chelsea started off brightly, with Gustavo Poyet having a goal disallowed for offside before grabbing a 10th minute lead. The Blues were dominant in the first half and should have extended their lead, so it was a real surprise when Hamilton Ricard scored an equaliser shortly before half time. The second period began in the same vein, with Chris Sutton and Gabriele Ambrosetti both going close for Chelsea. But Middlesbrough fought their way back into the match with Ricard and Paul Ince going close to scoring a winner. Neither side could impose themselves on the game, but while a draw was a fair result, Chelsea considered this as two points lost.

CHELSEA GOAL: Poyet *(10 mins):* Wise swung in a corner and Poyet rose above the Boro defence to head home.

MIDDLESBROUGH GOAL: Ricard *(37 mins):* Ziege's corner was met by Festa but the ball fell to Ricard, who volleyed it into the back of the net from close range.

MATCH RATING: ★★ **LEAGUE POSITION: 5th**

MATCH FACTS

	Shots On Target	
Chelsea	6-4	Middlesbrough
	Shots Off Target	
Chelsea	5-6	Middlesbrough
	Hit Woodwork	
Chelsea	1-0	Middlesbrough
	Corners	
Chelsea	6-8	Middlesbrough

HOW THEY LINED UP

de Goey

Lambourde, Desailly, Thome, Melchiot

Wise, Deschamps, Poyet, Ambrosetti

Sutton, Zola

Deane, Ricard

Ziege, Mustoe, Ince, Summerbell

Festa, Vickers, Cooper, Fleming

Schwarzer

CHELSEA

Player	Rating
de Goey	5
Melchiot	5
Subbed: 72 mins (Harley)	
Thome	6
Desailly	5
Lambourde	4
Poyet ⚽	5
Goal: 10 mins	
Deschamps	5
Subbed: 62 mins (Morris)	
Wise	6
Ambrosetti	☆7
Sutton	5
Zola	6
Subbed: 62 mins (Flo)	
sub: *Morris*	5
sub: *Flo*	4
sub: *Harley*	

Subs not used: *Cudicini, Leboeuf.*

MIDDLESBROUGH

Player	Rating
Schwarzer	5
Fleming 🟨	6
Booked: 58 mins (foul)	
Vickers	5
Festa	5
Mustoe	4
Ince	☆7
Deane	5
Ziege	6
Ricard ⚽	6
Goal: 37 mins; Subbed: 79 mins (Campbell)	
Summerbell	4
Cooper	4
sub: *Campbell*	

Subs not used: *Beresford, Stamp, Maddison, Juninho.*

THIS WEEK...

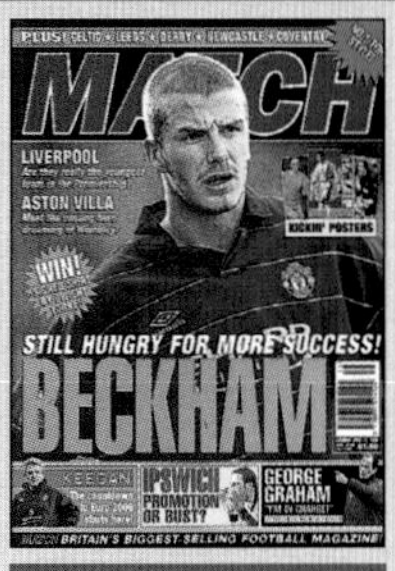

IN THE NEWS

CHELSEA: The Blues could face a possible points deduction if the FA act upon Paul Durkin's match report after the recent encounter with Sheffield Wednesday. **Marcel Desailly, Didier Deschamps** and **Emerson Thome** were among a number of Chelsea players who vented their anger at the referee after the final whistle.

PREMIERSHIP: Manchester United regain their Premiership title after convincingly beating Southampton 3-1 at The Dell... Arsenal succeed in making it through to the UEFA Cup Final to face Galatasaray, who conquered Leeds United in the semi-final... West Ham rubbish reports linking **Rio Ferdinand**, their £15 million-rated England defender, with a move to Leeds in the close season... Manchester United's veteran full-back **Denis Irwin** has signed a new one-year contract at the club which will keep him at Old Trafford until the end of the 2000-2001 season.

THE FINAL SCORE!

	APRIL 16	
Leeds	0-4	**Arsenal**
Wimbledon	1-2	**Liverpool**
	APRIL 19	
Leicester	0-1	**Tottenham**
	APRIL 21	
Bradford	4-4	Derby
Everton	0-0	Liverpool
	APRIL 22	
Aston Villa	2-2	Leicester
Chelsea	1-1	Middlesbrough
Sheff. Wed.	0-2	**Sunderland**
Southampton	1-3	**Man. United**
Tottenham	2-0	Wimbledon
West Ham	5-0	Coventry
	APRIL 23	
Aston Villa	2-2	Leicester
Watford	2-3	**Arsenal**

TOP OF THE PREMIERSHIP

	P	W	D	L	Pts
1. Man. United	34	24	7	3	79
2. Liverpool	34	19	9	6	66
3. Arsenal	32	18	6	8	60
5. Chelsea	**34**	**16**	**11**	**7**	**59**

Nicky Butt and Dennis Wise battle for possession in Chelsea's 3-2 defeat at Old Trafford.

Manchester United (2) 3
Chelsea (2) 2

Competition: **FA Carling Premiership**

Date: **Monday April 24, 2000**

Attendance: **61,593**

Referee: **S Dunn** (Bristol) 6

THE GAME: Newly-crowned champions Manchester United avenged their embarrassing 5-0 defeat at Stamford Bridge in October by beating Chelsea at Old Trafford. The Red Devils went ahead through Dwight Yorke after charging down Ed de Goey's clearance. The Blues fought back, though, equalising through Dan Petrescu before Gianfranco Zola gave Chelsea a half-time lead. But United refused to lie down on home soil and further goals from Dwight Yorke and Ole Gunnar Solskjaer meant The Blues left Old Trafford empty-handed once again.

MANCHESTER UNITED GOALS: Yorke *(10 mins):* Charged down a de Goey clearance from eight yards and saw the ball rebound into the net; **Solskjaer** *(39 mins):* Finished from the edge of the penalty area, hitting a low shot to the 'keeper's right; **Yorke** *(69 mins):* Scored with a right-foot tap-in from four yards after Beckham's drive was parried by de Goey.

CHELSEA GOALS: Petrescu *(22 mins):* Rifled home an angled right-foot shot from six yards to the right of van der Gouw; **Zola** *(36 mins):* The striker's right-foot shot from eight yards looped over van der Gouw's head and into the net.

MATCH RATING: ★★★ **LEAGUE POSITION: 5th**

MATCH FACTS

	Shots On Target	
Man. United	6-7	Chelsea
	Shots Off Target	
Man. United	8-7	Chelsea
	Hit Woodwork	
Man. United	0-1	Chelsea
	Corners	
Man. United	6-3	Chelsea

HOW THEY LINED UP

van der Gouw

Neville, G · Johnsen · Silvestre · Neville, P

Beckham · Butt · Keane · Giggs

Yorke · Solskjaer

Zola · Flo

Ambrosetti · Wise · Deschamps · Petrescu

Melchiot · Leboeuf · Thome · Lambourde

de Goey

MANCHESTER UNITED

Player	Rating
van der Gouw	7
Neville, G *Subbed: 32 mins (Berg)*	6
Neville, P	5
Johnsen	6
Silvestre	6
Keane *Subbed: 50 mins (Scholes)*	7
Beckham *Booked: 61 mins (foul)*	7
Butt	6
Yorke *Goals: 10, 69 mins*	☆8
Solskjaer *Booked: 37 mins (foul); Goal: 39 mins; Subbed: 63 mins (Cruyff)*	7
Giggs	7
sub: *Berg*	6
sub: *Scholes*	6
sub: *Cruyff*	6

Subs not used: *Fortune, Sheringham.*

CHELSEA

Player	Rating
de Goey	5
Petrescu *Goal: 22 mins; Subbed: 74 mins (Sutton)*	7
Leboeuf	6
Deschamps *Subbed: 46 mins (Morris)*	5
Wise	7
Melchiot	6
Ambrosetti *Subbed: 46 mins (Harley)*	5
Flo	7
Lambourde *Booked: 47 mins (foul)*	7
Zola *Goal: 36 mins*	7
Thome	☆8
sub: *Morris*	6
sub: *Harley*	5
sub: *Sutton*	

Subs not used: *Hogh, Cudicini.*

BLUES RISE TO THE OCCASION TO BEAT LIVERPOOL

Thome came off the bench to protect Chelsea's 2-0 lead at Stamford Bridge.

 **Chelsea** (2) **2**

 **Liverpool** (0) **0**

Competition: **FA Carling Premiership**

Date: **Saturday April 29, 2000**

Attendance: **34,957**

Referee: **G Barber** (Tring) 6

THE GAME: Chelsea's players picked up the gauntlet thrown down by coach Gianluca Vialli after the disappointment of the previous game to humble a buoyant Liverpool side which was unbeaten in 13 outings. The pace and passion that had been lacking in recent games suddenly came to the fore with two brilliantly-taken goals early in the first half from Roberto Di Matteo and George Weah. The visitors, who had not won at Stamford Bridge since 1989, had no answer to this powerful and purposeful display in front of a delighted home crowd.

CHELSEA GOALS: Weah *(2 mins):* Almost straight from the kick-off, Di Matteo picked out Weah who unleashed a superb right-foot drive past Westerveld; **Di Matteo** *(14 mins):* Weah neatly touched the ball on to Di Matteo, who was waiting by the penalty spot to score with his left foot.

MATCH RATING: ★★★★ **LEAGUE POSITION: 5th**

"I'm training with some of the best players in the world every day and I don't feel nervous training with them, so why should I be worried about playing in the kind of big games they've succeeded in?" JODY MORRIS

CHELSEA	
de Goey	6
Babayaro	5
Subbed: 46 mins (Poyet)	
Leboeuf	6
Desailly	☆ 9
Wise	7
Melchiot	7
Di Matteo ⚽	8
Goal: 14 mins	
Morris ▯	6
Booked: 18 mins (foul); Subbed: 70 mins (Thome)	
Zola	7
Weah ⚽	8
Goal: 2 mins; Subbed: 81 mins (Sutton)	
Harley	7
sub: *Poyet*	7
sub: *Thome*	7
sub: *Sutton*	

Subs not used: *Cudicini, Ambrosetti.*

LIVERPOOL	
Westerveld	7
Henchoz	7
Heskey	6
Owen	6
Hyypia	7
Berger	6
Hamann	☆ 8
Subbed: 65 mins (Camara)	
Matteo	6
Carragher	5
Murphy	6
Subbed: 75 mins (Fowler)	
Gerrard	6
Subbed: 51 mins (Redknapp)	
sub: *Redknapp*	5
sub: *Camara*	6
sub: *Fowler*	

Subs not used: *Song, Nielsen.*

MATCH FACTS

Shots On Target	
Chelsea 3-2 Liverpool	
Shots Off Target	
Chelsea 3-8 Liverpool	
Hit Woodwork	
Chelsea 0-0 Liverpool	
Corners	
Chelsea 5-7 Liverpool	

HOW THEY LINED UP

de Goey

Melchiot, Desailly, Leboeuf, Harley

Di Matteo, Morris, Wise, Babayaro

Zola, Weah

Heskey, Owen

Berger, Hamann, Gerrard, Murphy

Matteo, Hyypia, Henchoz, Carragher

Westerveld

THIS WEEK...

IN THE NEWS

CHELSEA: French side Lyon are rumoured to be set for a move for **Frank Leboeuf**... Promising young Inter Milan striker **Adrian Mitu** is a summer target for The Blues... Gianluca Vialli has hit out at his expensively assembled side after defeat to Man. United seriously hit their Champions League hopes for next season. "We were too casual and sloppy," Vialli said. "If you ask me if we have any realistic chance of reaching the Champions League next season, I'd say no."

PREMIERSHIP: Manchester United chairman Martin Edwards says the club may have to sell one of their star strikers to recoup some of **Ruud van Nistelrooy**'s £19 million transfer fee. Days later, the move collapses when the Dutchman fails a medical... Charlton clinch the First Division championship with a 1-1 draw at Blackburn... Arsenal winger **Marc Overmars** has been linked with a big-money move to Spanish giants Barcelona, with Ronald and Frank de Boer said to be going in the other direction.

THE FINAL SCORE!

APRIL 24		
Derby	2-0	Southampton
Man. United	3-2	Chelsea
Sunderland	0-1	**Bradford**
APRIL 29		
Aston Villa	1-1	Sunderland
Chelsea	2-0	Liverpool
Everton	0-1	**Arsenal**
Newcastle	2-0	Coventry
Southampton	1-2	**Leicester**
Tottenham	1-1	Derby
Watford	2-3	**Man. United**
West Ham	0-1	**Middlesbrough**
APRIL 30		
Bradford	3-0	Wimbledon
Sheff. Wed.	0-3	**Leeds**

TOP OF THE PREMIERSHIP

	P	W	D	L	Pts
1. Man. United	36	26	7	3	85
2. Arsenal	34	20	6	8	66
3. Liverpool	35	19	9	7	66
5. Chelsea	**36**	**17**	**11**	**8**	**62**

MAY

START OF MONTH **5th** END OF MONTH **5th**

"Aston Villa are a very good side. We know we'll have to play better than we did in the semi-final against Newcastle last month if we're going to win the Cup." Tore Andre Flo

WITH THE FA CUP FINAL AN OBVIOUS DISTRACTION, CHELSEA HAD to play out their final league games with one eye on Wembley. A 2-1 reverse at Arsenal ended their hopes of clinching a European spot in the league, but The Blues finished their Premiership season on a high by thrashing Derby 4-0 to finish fifth. This meant Gianluca Vialli's team had to beat Aston Villa in the final to qualify for European football in the following campaign.

With the 1999-2000 Premiership season over, Blues supporters turned their attentions to the biggest cup game in the world. The last ever FA Cup Final to be played beneath the Twin Towers pitted Chelsea, who had won the cup in 1997, against seven-times winners Aston Villa. It was a clash between two talented sides that were both capable of thrilling neutrals with their attacking flair. Villa had finished the season well, while some observers suggested Chelsea's European adventure had left them deflated.

Both teams played out a cautious first half but Gianluca Vialli's charges stepped up a gear after the break and had a Dennis Wise goal disallowed within ten minutes of the restart. Then, with just 17 minutes remaining at Wembley, Roberto Di Matteo – who had spent much of the first half of the season on the sidelines – lashed home the winner after Villa goalkeeper David James had fumbled Gianfranco Zola's free-kick.

It was Di Matteo's second strike in successive FA Cup-winning Chelsea teams, having grabbed the quickest goal in FA Cup Final history against Middlesbrough in 1997. Both sides went close to scoring before the end – George Weah for Chelsea and Benito Carbone for Villa – but it was the blue half of Wembley which was jubilant at the final whistle. Inspirational captain Dennis Wise collected the famous trophy, accompanied by his baby son, to sign off the 1999-2000 season in the best way possible.

THE GAMES

May. 6 v **Arsenal** (a)

May. 14 v **Derby** (h)

May. 20 v **Aston Villa** (n)

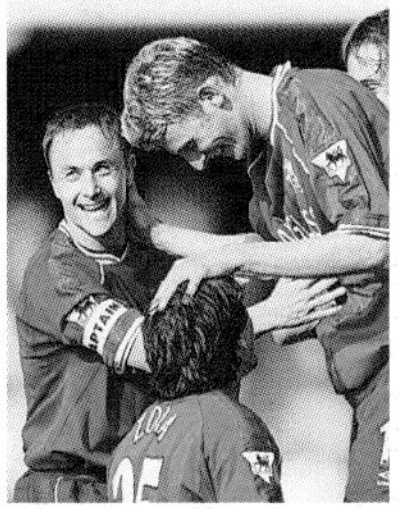

TRANSFERS IN

None

TRANSFERS OUT

None

MATCH facts

Matchman Of The Month

GIANFRANCO ZOLA
Average Rating: 7.00

Arsenal	(1) **2**
Chelsea	(0) **1**

Competition: **FA Carling Premiership**

Date: **Saturday May 6, 2000**

Attendance: **38,119**

Referee: **M Reed** (Birmingham) 8

THE GAME: Gianluca Vialli's men went to Highbury knowing that defeat would put them out of contention for a European place in the Premiership, but The Blues couldn't prevent their second defeat of the season against The Gunners. This was Arsenal's eighth consecutive win in the league and Chelsea found them in uncompromising mood. Thierry Henry won the battle of the Frenchmen by beating both Frank Leboeuf and Marcel Desailly to score a goal either side of half time. The visitors had de Goey to thank for keeping them in the match in the second half, with Henry looking dangerous every time he picked up the ball and ran at The Blues defence. Chelsea were always chasing the game, but they pulled a goal back after 79 minutes through Gustavo Poyet's 17th of the season. Unfortunately it was too little too late and Chelsea continued their record of never winning at Highbury in the Premiership.

ARSENAL GOALS: Henry *(22 mins):* Raced to collect a fine throughball, rounded de Goey and made no mistake with his cool finish; **Henry** *(48 mins):* Dispossessed fellow countryman Desailly before slotting the ball past de Goey from ten yards.

CHELSEA GOAL: Poyet *(79 mins):* Controlled the ball with his chest and shot low into the bottom left-hand corner.

MATCH RATING: ★★★★ **LEAGUE POSITION: 5th**

ARSENAL	
Seaman	7
Dixon	7
Vieira	8
Adams	7
Bergkamp *Subbed: 68 mins (Kanu)*	6
Overmars *Subbed: 46 mins (Winterburn)*	6
Henry (goal) (booked) (goal) *Goals: 22, 48 mins; Booked: 32 mins (dissent)*	☆ 9
Parlour	7
Silvinho	7
Petit *Subbed: 76 mins (Luzhny)*	7
Grimandi	8
sub: *Kanu*	6
sub: *Winterburn*	7
sub: *Luzhny*	

Subs not used: *Manninger, Malz.*

CHELSEA	
de Goey	7
Leboeuf *Subbed: 39 mins (Thome)*	7
Desailly	7
Wise	6
Melchiot	7
Di Matteo	7
Flo	6
Morris *Subbed: 60 mins (Deschamps)*	5
Lambourde	7
Zola *Subbed: 60 mins (Poyet)*	6
Weah	☆ 7
sub: *Thome* (booked) *Booked: 53 mins (foul)*	6
sub: *Deschamps*	6
sub: *Poyet* (goal) (booked) *Goal: 79 mins; Booked 79 mins (dissent)*	7

Subs not used: *Sutton, Cudicini.*

MATCH FACTS
Shots On Target
Arsenal 11-5 Chelsea
Shots Off Target
Arsenal 4-6 Chelsea
Hit Woodwork
Arsenal 0-1 Chelsea
Corners
Arsenal 7-4 Chelsea

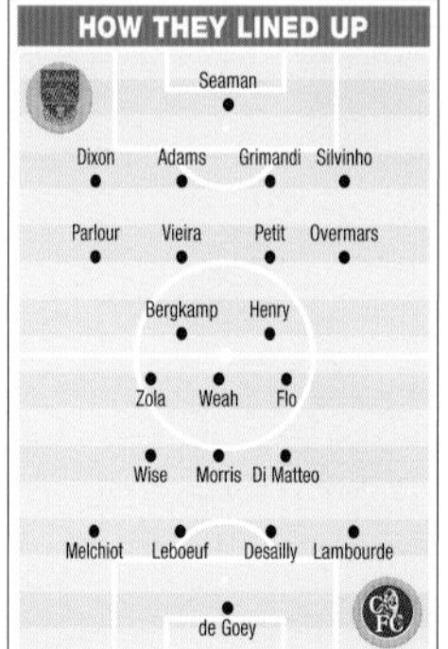

HOW THEY LINED UP

Seaman

Dixon Adams Grimandi Silvinho

Parlour Vieira Petit Overmars

Bergkamp Henry

Zola Weah Flo

Wise Morris Di Matteo

Melchiot Leboeuf Desailly Lambourde

de Goey

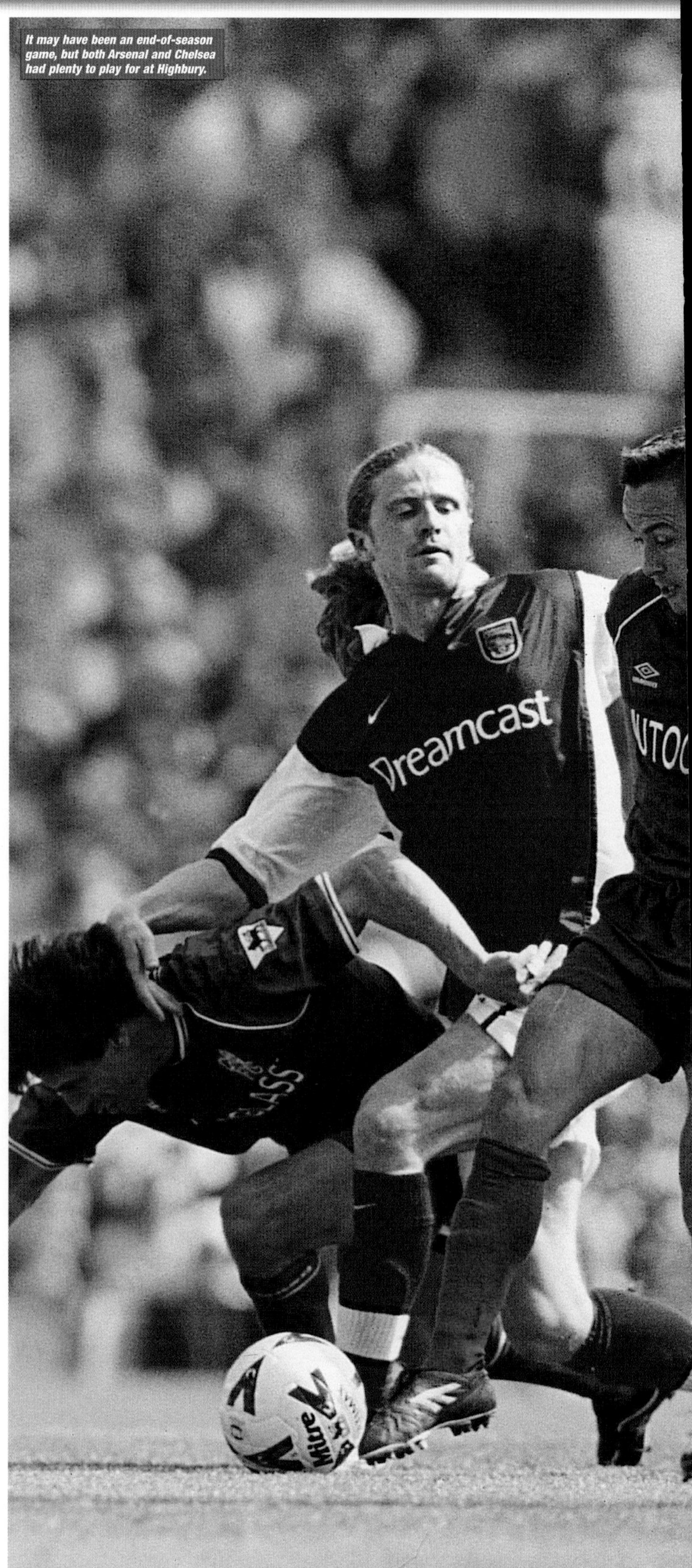

It may have been an end-of-season game, but both Arsenal and Chelsea had plenty to play for at Highbury.

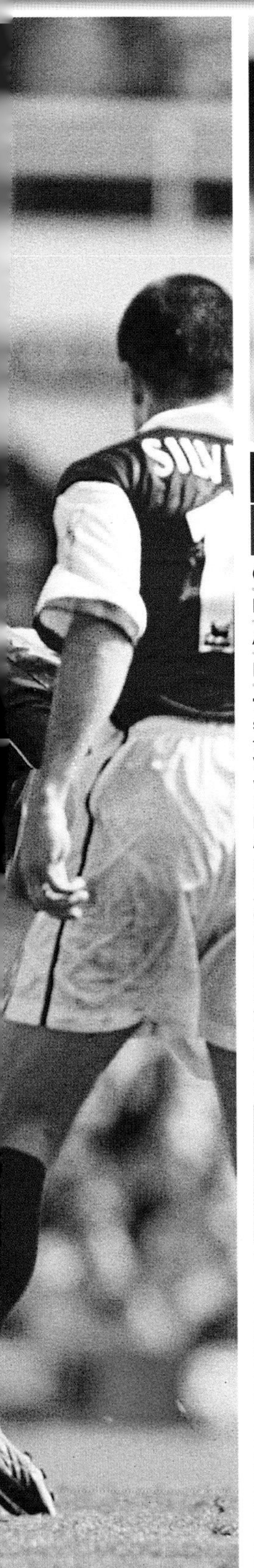

The classic big man-small man partnership pays dividends in the 4-0 win over Derby.

Chelsea	(0)	4
Derby County	(0)	0

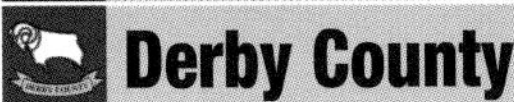

Competition: **FA Carling Premiership**

Date: **Sunday May 14, 2000**

Attendance: **35,084**

Referee: **J Winter** (Stockton) 7

Game 60

THE GAME: The Blues ended their Premiership campaign in style as they brushed aside Derby at Stamford Bridge. Despite their forthcoming FA Cup Final against Aston Villa, Gianluca Vialli chose a near full-strength side, resting only Ed de Goey, who had been an ever-present in the league until this match. In the end, four goals didn't reflect the dominance that the home team enjoyed, with the sides going in level at half time. After scoring four second-half goals, Chelsea finished in fifth place, below the four European placings, and would have to rely on winning the FA Cup for their passport into Europe.

CHELSEA GOALS: Zola *(47 mins):* Shrugged off the Derby defence to lift the ball over Poom and into the left-hand corner of the net; **Poyet** *(55 mins):* Zola delivered a perfect corner for Poyet to rise and head into Derby's goal from close range; **Di Matteo** *(69 mins):* Collected Wise's looping throughball on the edge of the box and unleashed a 20-yard, right-foot volley beyond Poom; **Flo** *(90 mins):* Melchiot crossed from the right of the Derby area for Flo to cheekily backheel into the net.

MATCH RATING: ★★★★ **LEAGUE POSITION: 5th**

"I think the players enjoyed themselves. I saw a lot of happiness out there on the pitch, but Derby seemed to give up after they'd conceded the first goal, so it was quite easy to create opportunities." GIANLUCA VIALLI

MATCH FACTS

Shots On Target		
Chelsea	10-3	Derby
Shots Off Target		
Chelsea	5-4	Derby
Hit Woodwork		
Chelsea	2-0	Derby
Corners		
Chelsea	11-5	Derby

HOW THEY LINED UP

Cudicini

Ferrer, Desailly, Leboeuf, Babayaro

Di Matteo, Deschamps, Wise, Poyet

Flo, Zola

Burton, Christie, Sturridge

Johnson, Bohinen, Burley

Dorigo, Elliott, Laursen, Delap

Poom

CHELSEA

Player	Rating
Cudicini	7
Babayaro	6
Leboeuf	5
Desailly *Subbed: 56 mins (Terry)*	6
Deschamps	5
Poyet ⚽ *Goal: 55 mins; Subbed: 64 mins (Ambrosetti)*	7
Wise	7
Di Matteo ▯ ⚽ *Booked: 40 mins (foul); Goal: 69 mins*	7
Ferrer *Subbed: 32 mins (Melchiot)*	6
Flo ⚽ *Goal: 90 mins*	7
Zola ⚽ *Goal: 47 mins*	☆8
sub: Terry	6
sub: Ambrosetti	6
sub: Melchiot	7

Subs not used: *de Goey, Morris.*

DERBY COUNTY

Player	Rating
Poom	☆9
Dorigo	5
Johnson	5
Sturridge	5
Burton	5
Delap *Subbed: 64 mins (Jackson)*	5
Christie	6
Bohinen *Subbed: 64 mins (Murray)*	6
Laursen	5
Elliott *Subbed: 56 mins (Riggott)*	5
Burley	7
sub: Jackson	5
sub: Murray	5
sub: Riggott	5

Subs not used: *Boertien, Oakes.*

THIS WEEK...

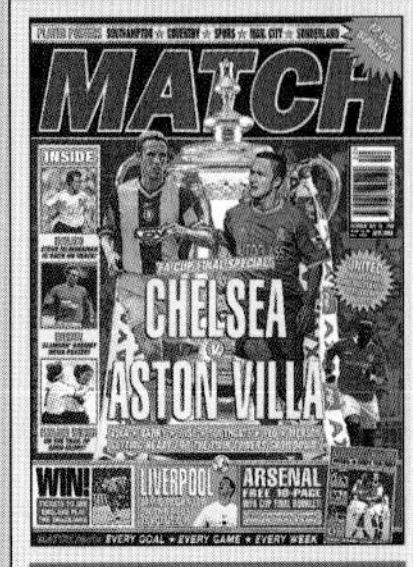

IN THE NEWS

CHELSEA: Lyon have dismissed reports that France centre-back **Frank Leboeuf** is to join them in the summer. Club president Jean Michel Aulas says: "Discussions have not even begun with Frank Leboeuf. We need to buy a great defender but it will not be him".

PREMIERSHIP: The relegation struggle proves to be even more exciting than the title race in the end, with Sheffield Wednesday, Watford and Wimbledon saying goodbye to the top-flight.

THE FINAL SCORE!

MAY 2		
Arsenal	2-1	West Ham
Middlesbrough	2-2	Newcastle
MAY 3		
Leeds	3-1	Watford
Liverpool	0-2	**Leicester**
MAY 6		
Arsenal	2-1	Chelsea
Coventry	4-1	Sheff. Wed.
Derby	0-0	Newcastle
Leicester	3-0	Bradford
Man. United	3-1	Tottenham
Middlesbrough	1-1	Watford
Sunderland	1-0	West Ham
Wimbledon	2-2	Aston Villa
MAY 7		
Liverpool	0-0	Southampton
MAY 8		
Leeds	1-1	Everton
MAY 9		
Arsenal	3-3	Sheff. Wed.
MAY 14		
Aston Villa	0-1	**Man. United**
Bradford	1-0	Liverpool
Chelsea	4-0	Derby
Everton	0-2	**Middlesbrough**
Newcastle	4-2	Arsenal
Sheff. Wed.	4-0	Leicester
Southampton	2-0	Wimbledon
Tottenham	3-1	Sunderland
Watford	1-0	Coventry
West Ham	0-0	Leeds

TOP OF THE PREMIERSHIP

	P	W	D	L	Pts
1. Man. United	38	28	7	3	91
2. Arsenal	38	22	7	9	73
3. Leeds	38	21	6	11	69
5. Chelsea	**38**	**18**	**11**	**9**	**65**

Chelsea win the last ever FA Cup Final at Wembley before it is redeveloped.

FROM THE PAGES OF MATCH

Some people think the FA Cup Final isn't the same as it once was. But **CHELSEA**'s all-star players were more than happy to tell **MATCH** how much it meant to them to lift the famous trophy.

Gianfranco Zola says: *"I think the team wanted to end the season properly. We did not do well in the league, but we'd done well in the FA Cup until the final. We were going to try our very best to win the cup and put everything right this season for ourselves and the fans as well."*

Mario Melchiot says: *"It was a great day. I've played in the cup final in Holland but the FA Cup is totally different. There is so much history in the competition and to be a part of it all is a dream for any player."*

Roberto Di Matteo says: *"I love Wembley, it's a great place for me and a great place for Chelsea. It's been a frustrating season for me personally so I didn't think I'd end up scoring the winner in the final. It's a great honour to have scored goals in two different FA Cup Finals."*

Tore Andre Flo says: *"The FA Cup is something you dream of as a young boy in Norway. It's not just a dream for kids in England to play in the cup final at Wembley. I know the rest of the foreign players at Chelsea feel the same as I do. It's the FA Cup – what more can you say?"*

Dennis Wise says: *"I'm sure this team will stay together next season and hopefully we can build on this win. I think next season we'll be looking for the Premiership title."*

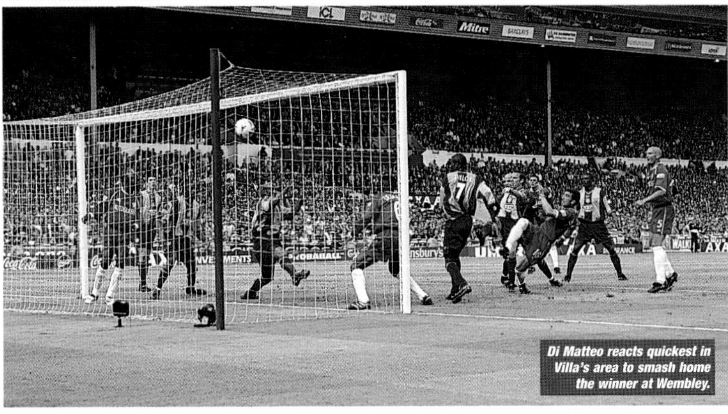

Di Matteo reacts quickest in Villa's area to smash home the winner at Wembley.

Aston Villa	(0)	**0**
Chelsea	(0)	**1**

Competition: **FA Cup Final**

Date: **Saturday May 20, 2000**

Attendance: **78,217**

Referee: **G Poll** (Tring) 7

Game 61

THE GAME: The 119th FA Cup Final wasn't a classic match, but a second-half goal from Roberto Di Matteo was enough to give Chelsea their third FA Cup trophy in the last ever final to be held under Wembley's Twin Towers. Di Matteo, who holds the record for scoring the fastest goal in the final, cemented his position as a Chelsea legend with the second-half winner after a fumble by Aston Villa 'keeper David James. It was no more than Chelsea's greater skill and invention deserved, but they were often frustrated by an organised and adventurous Villa side. The first half of the final was a dour affair, with both defences coping well and Frank Leboeuf in outstanding form for Chelsea. Both sides stepped up a gear after the break, but it was The Blues who exerted more pressure and it eventually paid off with Di Matteo's decisive goal. Dennis Wise collected the trophy in front of the jubilant Chelsea fans to end another eventful season at Stamford Bridge, with victory in the FA Cup finally securing the club's place in Europe.

CHELSEA GOAL: Di Matteo *(73 mins):* Zola's free-kick from the left was fumbled by James and the ball fell at the feet of Di Matteo, who gleefully smashed home the winning goal.

MATCH RATING: ★★★ **LEAGUE POSITION: 5th**

"I don't think we had a good first half. We defended well but we didn't attack well. We didn't move properly and we just couldn't find each other on the pitch. But the good thing was that we were patient." FRANK LEBOEUF

MATCH FACTS

Shots On Target		
Aston Villa	1-2	Chelsea
Shots Off Target		
Aston Villa	5-3	Chelsea
Hit Woodwork		
Aston Villa	0-0	Chelsea
Corners		
Aston Villa	6-1	Chelsea

HOW THEY LINED UP

James

Delaney, Ehiogu, Southgate, Barry, Wright

Taylor, Boateng, Merson

Dublin, Carbone

Zola, Weah

Poyet, Wise, Deschamps, Di Matteo

Babayaro, Leboeuf, Desailly, Melchiot

de Goey

ASTON VILLA	
James	6
Ehiogu	6
Southgate	7
Barry	6
Booked: 16 mins (foul)	
Delaney	6
Taylor	6
Subbed: 77 mins (Stone)	
Boateng	☆8
Booked: 89 mins (foul)	
Merson	5
Wright	6
Subbed: 87 mins (Hendrie)	
Dublin	5
Carbone	5
Subbed: 77 mins (Joachim)	
sub: *Stone*	
sub: *Hendrie*	
sub: *Joachim*	

Subs not used: *Samuel, Enckelman.*

CHELSEA	
de Goey	6
Melchiot	7
Booked: 18 mins (foul)	
Desailly	6
Leboeuf	☆8
Babayaro	7
Di Matteo	7
Goal: 73 mins	
Wise	6
Booked: 25 mins (foul)	
Deschamps	7
Poyet	6
Booked: 50 mins (foul)	
Zola	7
Subbed: 89 mins (Morris)	
Weah	5
Subbed: 87 mins (Flo)	
sub: *Flo*	
sub: *Morris*	

Subs not used: *Harley, Terry, Cudicini.*

THIS WEEK...

IN THE NEWS

CHELSEA: Gianfranco Zola has pledged his future to The Blues following talk of a move back to Italy... On loan **George Weah** could leave Stamford Bridge in the close-season because of his wage demands... **Dan Petrescu** says he wants to see out the rest of his career with Chelsea. The Romanian utility player, who has been at the club since 1995, says he has never wanted a move and is prepared to stay and fight for his place in the first-team... By winning the FA Cup Chelsea reward their fans for their superb support and guarantee European football in the UEFA Cup next season... After missing out on the Champions League, reports say **Didier Deschamps** wants a move away from Stamford Bridge in the summer. "I want to play in the Champions League next season," says the veteran France midfielder. "I've heard a rumour about me going to Lyon as player-manager, but that just made me laugh."

PREMIERSHIP: Roy Keane is named as the PFA and Football Writers' Footballer Of The Year for his outstanding performances in Manchester United's midfield this season... West Ham's star striker **Paolo di Canio** says he doesn't know what more he can do to get in the Italy squad for Euro 2000 after his fantastic season for The Hammers... Leeds United's draw on the final day against West Ham is enough to earn them Champions League football in 2000-2001... Liverpool finish fourth after losing to Bradford at Valley Parade and take their place in the draw for the UEFA Cup. Former Liverpool star **Steve McManaman** scores a goal and plays a starring role in Real Madrid's 3-1 European Cup Final win over Valencia. It also looks like McManaman has played his way back into the reckoning for a place in England's Euro 2000 squad... Despite his poor performance in the FA Cup Final against Chelsea, **David James** receives a call-up to Kevin Keegan's 28-man squad for the friendly matches against Brazil and Ukraine.

1999-2000 SQUAD Games/Goals

NAME	LGE	CL	FA	WC	TOTAL
1. Ed **de Goey**	37/0	16/0	6/0	0/0	**59/0**
2. Dan **Petrescu**	29/4	15/1	3/0	0/0	**47/5**
3. Celestine **Babayaro**	25/0	15/2	1/0	0/0	**41/2**
4. Jes **Hogh**	9/0	5/0	2/0	1/0	**17/0**
5. Frank **Leboeuf**	28/2	14/1	4/1	0/0	**46/4**
6. Marcel **Desailly**	23/1	16/0	4/0	0/0	**43/1**
7. Didier **Deschamps**	27/0	14/1	6/0	0/0	**47/1**
8. Gustavo **Poyet**	33/10	14/2	6/6	0/0	**53/18**
9. Chris **Sutton**	28/1	7/1	4/1	0/0	**39/3**
10. Pierluigi **Casiraghi**	0/0	0/0	0/0	0/0	**0/0**
11. Dennis **Wise**	30/4	15/4	5/2	0/0	**50/10**
12. Bjarne **Goldbaek**	6/0	2/0	0/0	1/0	**9/0**
13. Kevin **Hitchcock**	0/0	0/0	0/0	0/0	**0/0**
14. Graeme **Le Saux**	8/0	4/0	0/0	1/0	**13/0**
15. Mario **Melchiot**	5/0	0/0	1/0	0/0	**6/0**
16. Roberto **Di Matteo**	18/2	9/0	3/2	1/0	**31/4**
17. Albert **Ferrer**	25/0	14/1	2/0	0/0	**41/1**
18. Gabriele **Ambrosetti**	16/0	5/1	1/0	1/0	**22/1**
19. Tore Andre **Flo**	34/10	16/8	6/1	1/0	**57/19**
20. Jody **Morris**	30/3	11/0	4/1	1/0	**46/4**
21. Bernard **Lambourde**	15/2	2/0	3/0	1/0	**21/2**
22. Mark **Nicholls**	0/0	1/0	0/0	1/0	**2/0**
23. Carlo **Cudicini**	1/0	1/0	0/0	1/0	**3/0**
24. Samuele **Dalla Bona**	2/0	1/0	0/0	0/0	**3/0**
25. Gianfranco **Zola**	33/4	15/3	5/1	0/0	**53/8**
26. John **Terry**	4/0	0/0	4/1	1/0	**9/1**
27. Nick **Crittenden**	0/0	0/0	0/0	0/0	**0/0**
28. Robert **Wolleaston**	1/0	0/0	0/0	1/0	**2/0**
29. Neil **Clement**	0/0	0/0	1/0	0/0	**1/0**
30. Emerson **Thome**	20/0	1/0	0/0	0/0	**21/0**
31. George **Weah**	11/3	0/0	4/2	0/0	**15/5**
32. Mikael **Forssell**	0/0	1/0	0/0	1/0	**2/0**
33. Luca **Percassi**	0/0	0/0	1/0	0/0	**1/0**
34. Jon **Harley**	17/2	4/0	5/0	0/0	**26/2**

PREMIERSHIP MATCHMAN OF THE SEASON

PAOLO DI CANIO WAS NAMED THE PREMIERSHIP MATCHMAN OF the season after a sensational 1999-2000 with West Ham, but a host of Blues stars made it into the top 150 players of 1999-2000. Surprisingly, for a side that finished fifth, Chelsea's Matchman Of The Season Gustavo Poyet could only finish in 56th place despite an average rating of 6.77 out of ten. A consistent performer in the Blues midfield, Poyet's impressive return of 18 goals, including some memorable strikes, deservedly made him Chelsea's top player – he was also given six Star Ratings, more than anyone else at the club. Close behind Poyet was Dan Petrescu in 63rd place with an average of 6.75 out of ten. His consistency and versatility were vital to Gianluca Vialli's side in their quest for glory last season. Chelsea skipper Dennis Wise finished in 75th position. A natural leader, Wise put in some superb performances at the heart of the Blues midfield and scored some vital goals, especially in Europe, on his way to earning an average rating of 6.70. Also inside the top 100 players were Gianfranco Zola – with an average of 6.61 in joint 96th position – and Marcel Desailly, whose average of 6.60 saw him finish in 100th place. Ed de Goey, in joint 132nd position with an average of 6.51, and Emerson Thome, in 146th place with a rating of 6.47, completed an impressive Chelsea contingent in last season's top 150 Premiership players.

Pos.	Player	GP	SR	AVE
1.	**PAOLO DI CANIO** *West Ham United*	**29**	**13**	**7.48**
2.	**Roy Keane** *Manchester United*	29	6	7.24
3.	**Paul Merson** *Aston Villa*	29	10	7.17
4.	**Harry Kewell** *Leeds United*	36	13	7.16
5.	**Thierry Henry** *Arsenal*	30	8	7.16
6.	**Neil Sullivan** *Wimbledon*	37	9	7.13
7.	**Dean Richards** *Southampton*	35	11	7.05
8.	**Tim Sherwood** *Tottenham Hotspur*	25	4	7.04
9.	**Don Hutchison** *Everton*	29	6	7.03
10.	**Ryan Giggs** *Manchester United*	30	5	7.03
11.	**Paul Ince** *Middlesbrough*	32	10	7.00
12.	**John Collins** *Everton*	34	8	7.00
13.	**Chris Makin** *Sunderland*	34	5	7.00
14.	**David Beckham** *Manchester United*	31	5	7.00
15.	**Jaap Stam** *Manchester United*	33	2	7.00
16.	**Richard Gough** *Everton*	29	2	7.00
17.	**David Ginola** *Tottenham Hotspur*	36	7	6.97
18.	**Carl Cort** *Wimbledon*	34	4	6.97
19.	**Nikos Dabizas** *Newcastle United*	29	4	6.96
=	**Sol Campbell** *Tottenham Hotspur*	29	4	6.96
21.	**Patrick Vieira** *Arsenal*	30	3	6.96
22.	**Darren Anderton** *Tottenham Hotspur*	22	6	6.95
23.	**Jamie Redknapp** *Liverpool*	19	4	6.94
24.	**Sami Hyypia** *Liverpool*	38	5	6.92
25.	**Matt Elliott** *Leicester City*	37	7	6.91
26.	**Muzzy Izzet** *Leicester City*	32	4	6.90
27.	**Rob Lee** *Newcastle United*	30	4	6.90
28.	**Ben Thatcher** *Wimbledon*	20	3	6.90
29.	**Gary McAllister** *Coventry City*	38	8	6.89
30.	**Niall Quinn** *Sunderland*	35	7	6.88
31.	**Stefan Schwarz** *Sunderland*	27	3	6.88
32.	**Martin Keown** *Arsenal*	27	0	6.88
33.	**Rio Ferdinand** *West Ham United*	33	3	6.87
34.	**Lucas Radebe** *Leeds United*	31	3	6.87
35.	**Thomas Sorensen** *Sunderland*	37	4	6.86
36.	**Kenny Cunningham** *Wimbledon*	37	2	6.86
37.	**Kevin Phillips** *Sunderland*	36	7	6.83

38.	**Neil Lennon** *Leicester City*	31	5	6.83
39.	**Trevor Sinclair** *West Ham United*	36	3	6.83
40.	**Fredrik Ljungberg** *Arsenal*	24	3	6.83
41.	**Hermann Hreidarsson** *Wimbledon*	24	2	6.83
42.	**Christian Ziege** *Middlesbrough*	29	5	6.82
43.	**Mart Poom** *Derby County*	28	4	6.82
44.	**Lee Dixon** *Arsenal*	28	1	6.82
45.	**Magnus Hedman** *Coventry City*	35	6	6.80
46.	**Juninho** *Middlesbrough*	25	6	6.80
47.	**Emmanuel Petit** *Arsenal*	26	3	6.80
48.	**Paul Butler** *Sunderland*	31	3	6.80
49.	**Tony Adams** *Arsenal*	21	0	6.80
50.	**Robbie Earle** *Wimbledon*	24	3	6.79
51.	**Mark Schwarzer** *Middlesbrough*	37	7	6.78
52.	**David Wetherall** *Bradford City*	38	4	6.78
53.	**Chris Perry** *Tottenham Hotspur*	37	2	6.78
54.	**Warren Barton** *Newcastle United*	33	2	6.78
55.	**Gareth Southgate** *Aston Villa*	31	8	6.77
56.	**GUSTAVO POYET** *Chelsea*	**31**	**6**	**6.77**
57.	**Marcus Gayle** *Wimbledon*	36	5	6.77
58.	**Paul Scholes** *Manchester United*	31	4	6.77
59.	**Gilles Grimandi** *Arsenal*	27	0	6.77
60.	**Stephen Carr** *Tottenham Hotspur*	34	5	6.76
61.	**Kevin Campbell** *Everton*	26	1	6.76
62.	**Frank Lampard** *West Ham United*	34	0	6.76
63.	**DAN PETRESCU** *Chelsea*	**28**	**4**	**6.75**
64.	**Chris Armstrong** *Tottenham Hotspur*	29	2	6.75
65.	**David Seaman** *Arsenal*	24	1	6.75
66.	**Eirik Bakke** *Leeds United*	27	4	6.74
=	**Titi Camara** *Liverpool*	27	4	6.74
68.	**Jonathan Woodgate** *Leeds United*	34	1	6.73
69.	**Steve Bould** *Sunderland*	19	1	6.73
70.	**Gary Speed** *Newcastle United*	36	2	6.72
71.	**Oyvind Leonhardsen** *Tottenham Hotspur*	22	0	6.72
72.	**Emile Heskey** *Liverpool*	35	6	6.71
73.	**Matt Clarke** *Bradford City*	21	3	6.71
74.	**Marc Overmars** *Arsenal*	30	7	6.70
75.	**DENNIS WISE** *Chelsea*	**30**	**4**	**6.70**
76.	**Nordin Wooter** *Watford*	20	3	6.70
77.	**Mustapha Hadji** *Coventry City*	33	7	6.69
78.	**Alan Shearer** *Newcastle United*	36	4	6.69
79.	**Andy Cole** *Manchester United*	26	4	6.69
80.	**Denis Irwin** *Manchester United*	25	1	6.68
81.	**Paulo Wanchope** *West Ham United*	34	6	6.67
82.	**Nolberto Solano** *Newcastle United*	30	5	6.66
83.	**John Moncur** *West Ham United*	21	1	6.66
84.	**Brian Deane** *Middlesbrough*	29	3	6.65
=	**Kieron Dyer** *Newcastle United*	29	3	6.65
86.	**Pavel Srnicek** *Sheffield Wednesday*	20	3	6.65
87.	**Silvinho** *Arsenal*	29	0	6.65
88.	**Steven Gerrard** *Liverpool*	28	4	6.64
89.	**Paul Jones** *Southampton*	31	3	6.64
90.	**Ian Walker** *Tottenham Hotspur*	38	2	6.63
91.	**Nigel Winterburn** *Arsenal*	22	0	6.63
92.	**Nick Barmby** *Everton*	37	7	6.62
93.	**Igor Stimac** *West Ham United*	24	1	6.62
94.	**Seth Johnson** *Derby County*	36	5	6.61
95.	**Dean Saunders** *Bradford City*	31	5	6.61

96.	**Ugo Ehiogu** *Aston Villa*	31	2	6.61
=	**GIANFRANCO ZOLA** *Chelsea*	**31**	**2**	**6.61**
98.	**Nigel Martyn** *Leeds United*	38	2	6.60
99.	**David Unsworth** *Everton*	33	2	6.60
100.	**MARCEL DESAILLY** *Chelsea*	**23**	**2**	**6.60**
101.	**Teddy Sheringham** *Manchester United*	20	2	6.60
102.	**Henning Berg** *Manchester United*	20	1	6.60
103.	**Dwight Yorke** *Manchester United*	31	4	6.58
104.	**Steffen Iversen** *Tottenham Hotspur*	36	3	6.58
105.	**Stephen McPhail** *Leeds United*	24	3	6.58
106.	**Gerry Taggart** *Leicester City*	31	2	6.58
107.	**Richard Shaw** *Coventry City*	29	2	6.58
108.	**Andrew Impey** *Leicester City*	28	2	6.57
109.	**Kevin Pressman** *Sheffield Wednesday*	19	2	6.57
110.	**Ian Harte** *Leeds United*	33	0	6.57
111.	**Steve Guppy** *Leicester City*	30	2	6.56
112.	**Didier Domi** *Newcastle United*	23	2	6.56
113.	**Marc-Vivien Foe** *West Ham United*	25	1	6.56
114.	**Robert Page** *Watford*	36	6	6.55
115.	**Patrik Berger** *Liverpool*	34	6	6.55
116.	**Mark Hughes** *Everton*	29	3	6.55
117.	**Ole Gunnar Solskjaer** *Manchester United*	20	2	6.55
118.	**Steve Palmer** *Watford*	38	1	6.55
119.	**Lee Bowyer** *Leeds United*	31	4	6.54
120.	**Michael Owen** *Liverpool*	24	3	6.54
121.	**Eric Roy** *Sunderland*	22	2	6.54
=	**Shaka Hislop** *West Ham United*	22	2	6.54
123.	**Michael Gray** *Sunderland*	33	0	6.54
124.	**Ray Parlour** *Arsenal*	30	2	6.53
125.	**Paul Williams** *Coventry City*	28	2	6.53
126.	**Stuart McCall** *Bradford City*	34	2	6.52
127.	**Stephen Clemence** *Tottenham Hotspur*	19	1	6.52
128.	**David Weir** *Everton*	34	0	6.52
129.	**Jo Tessem** *Southampton*	23	0	6.52
130.	**Robbie Keane** *Coventry City*	31	4	6.51
131.	**Robbie Savage** *Leicester City*	35	3	6.51
132.	**Jason Euell** *Wimbledon*	37	0	6.51
=	**ED DE GOEY** *Chelsea*	**37**	**0**	**6.51**
134.	**Darryl Powell** *Derby County*	31	0	6.51
135.	**Jacob Laursen** *Derby County*	36	2	6.50
136.	**Matthew Oakley** *Southampton*	28	1	6.50
137.	**Dominic Matteo** *Liverpool*	32	0	6.50
138.	**Aaron Hughes** *Newcastle United*	24	0	6.50
139.	**Gary Neville** *Manchester United*	22	0	6.50
140.	**Robbie Blake** *Bradford City*	25	4	6.48
141.	**Dietmar Hamann** *Liverpool*	27	1	6.48
=	**Nicky Butt** *Manchester United*	27	1	6.48
143.	**Steve Lomas** *West Ham United*	25	1	6.48
144.	**Horacio Carbonari** *Derby County*	29	0	6.48
=	**Mauricio Taricco** *Tottenham Hotspur*	29	0	6.48
146.	**EMERSON THOME** *Chelsea/Sheff. Wed.*	**36**	**5**	**6.47**
147.	**Sander Westerveld** *Liverpool*	36	3	6.47
148.	**Alan Thompson** *Aston Villa*	19	2	6.47
149.	**Richard Johnson** *Watford*	21	1	6.47
150.	**Peter Beagrie** *Bradford City*	34	0	6.47

KEY: GP = games in which ratings were earned; **SR** = number of star ratings; **AVE** = average rating.

GABRIELE AMBROSETTI

- **Position:** Midfielder
- **Born:** August 7, 1973 in Varese (Italy)
- **Chelsea Debut:** August 21, 1999 v Aston Villa
- **Total Chelsea League Apps/Goals:** 16/0
- **Transfer:** £3.5 million, August 14, 1999
- **Previous Clubs:** Varese, Brescia, Vicenza
- **Club Honours:** None
- **International Honours:** None

Chelsea first saw Gabriele Ambrosetti in the club's European Cup-Winners' Cup semi-final against Vicenza in April 1998. The coaching staff at Stamford Bridge had been impressed by the winger's pace and skill and monitored the progress he was making in Italy. At the beginning of last season, Gianluca Vialli decided his team needed reinforcements on the left-hand side of midfield and approached Vicenza to see if the player was available. The Blues had an abundance of skill and guile in their forward line but they lacked speed in launching deadly counter-attacks. With Tore Andre Flo and Chris Sutton at the club, Chelsea also needed someone who could deliver quality crosses from the flanks. After signing for £3.5 million in 1999, Gabriele didn't play much of a starring role at Stamford Bridge last season, but don't bet against him making an impact in the first team this season. His position in midfield is occupied by Gustavo Poyet at present, but he provides a different option to the Uruguayan. If Jimmy Floyd Hasselbaink is to score over 20 goals this season, he may require a winger of Gabriele's talent to provide him with service from wide positions.

Lge Games	Total mins	Goals	Star Ratings	Ave Rating
16	747	0	2	5.36

Starts	Subbed off	Subbed on	Yellow	Red
9	7	7	0	0

Cup	Games/Goals	Sub on/off	Star Ratings	Yellow/Red
Champs Lge	5/1	4/1	0	0/0
FA	1/0	1/0	0	0/0
Worthington	1/0	0/0	1	0/0

PIERLUIGI CASIRAGHI

- **Position:** Striker
- **Born:** March 3, 1969 in Monza (Italy)
- **Chelsea Debut:** August 15, 1998 v Coventry City
- **Total Chelsea League Apps/Goals:** 10/1
- **Transfer:** £5.4 million, May 29, 1998
- **Previous Clubs:** Monza, Juventus, Lazio
- **Club Honours:** Italian Cup winner with Juventus (1990); UEFA Cup winner with Juventus (1990, 1993), European Super Cup winner with Chelsea (1998)
- **International Honours:** Senior Italy international

Pierluigi Casiraghi was hailed as the man to shoot Chelsea to the top of the Premiership when he arrived at Stamford Bridge from Lazio for a club record £5.4 million in May 1998. One of the most feared marksmen in Europe, he had vast experience and a proven track record at club and international level. The striker should have been the missing piece in Gianluca Vialli's jigsaw and it seemed just a matter of time before the goals came for the man who had scored consistently throughout his career. But disaster struck in only his tenth game for the club after an accidental collision with Shaka Hislop and Neil Ruddock at West Ham in November 1998 – Gigi snapped his cruciate and medial knee ligaments which immediately ruled him out for the season. Despite the seriousness of his injury, it was predicted that the striker would be back for the start of the 1999-2000 campaign. It wasn't to be. Pierluigi was still on the club's books last season, but after eight operations on his knee, Chelsea accepted a £4 million insurance settlement to compensate for his tragic injury, which means Gigi cannot play professional football ever again. It was a sad end to the career of an immensely talented and popular player.

Lge Games	Total mins	Goals	Star Ratings	Ave Rating
0	0	0	0	0

Starts	Subbed off	Subbed on	Yellow	Red
0	0	0	0	0

Cup	Games/Goals	Sub on/off	Star Ratings	Yellow/Red
All Cups	0/0	0/0	0	0/0

CELESTINE BABAYARO

- **Position:** Defender/Midfielder
- **Born:** August 29, 1978 in Kaduna (Nigeria)
- **Chelsea Debut:** October 18, 1997 v Leicester City
- **Total Chelsea League Apps/Goals:** 61/3
- **Transfer:** £2.25 million, June 20, 1997
- **Previous Clubs:** Anderlecht
- **Club Honours:** Belgian League winner with Anderlecht (1994, 1995); Belgian Cup winner with Anderlecht (1995); European Super Cup winner with Chelsea (1998); FA Cup winner with Chelsea (2000)
- **International Honours:** Senior Nigeria international

Celestine Babayaro became Chelsea's record teenage signing when he joined the club from Anderlecht in 1997 for a fee of £2.25 million. Celestine was a regular in the Anderlecht first team at the age of 16 and Chelsea signed him when he was 18, beating European giants like Juventus, Inter Milan and Deportivo La Coruna to his signature. A versatile performer, the pacy Nigerian is effective in either defence or midfield and is a key member of the current squad. He enjoyed another successful season for The Blues in 1999-2000, playing in all but one of the Champions League games. An integral part of the successful Nigeria international team, he was required on a number of occasions last season for the African Nations Cup and was forced to miss a number of important Chelsea fixtures. While this may have been disruptive for the club, it also provided the promising star with some vital experience at international level, which can only improve his game.

Lge Games	Total mins	Goals	Star Ratings	Ave Rating
25	2048	0	0	6.47

Starts	Subbed off	Subbed on	Yellow	Red
23	1	2	3	0

Cup	Games/Goals	Sub on/off	Star Ratings	Yellow/Red
Champs Lge	15/2	1/1	0	1/1
FA	1/0	0/0	0	0/0
Worthington	0/0	0/0	0	0/0

NEIL **CLEMENT**

- **Position:** Defender
- **Born:** October 3, 1978 in Reading
- **Chelsea Debut:** December 21, 1996 v West Ham United
- **Total Chelsea League Apps/Goals:** 1/0
- **Transfer:** From Trainee, August 1, 1996
- **Previous Clubs:** None
- **Club Honours:** None
- **International Honours:** England Youth & Schoolboy international

Neil Clement's chances were limited last season. The young left-back went on loan to Brentford in November but returned in January to play in the FA Cup win over Nottingham Forest at the City Ground – his only first-team outing of the season. A promising defender with England Youth recognition, Neil left Stamford Bridge for West Brom in the summer for £100,000.

Lge Games	Total mins	Goals	Star Ratings	Ave Rating
0	0	0	0	0

Starts	Subbed off	Subbed on	Yellow	Red
0	0	0	0	0

Cup	Games/Goals	Sub on/off	Star Ratings	Yellow/Red
Champs Lge	0/0	0/0	0	0/0
FA	1/0	1/0	0	0/0
Worthington	0/0	0/0	0	0/0

NICK **CRITTENDEN**

- **Position:** Defender
- **Born:** November 11, 1978 in Bracknell
- **Chelsea Debut:** November 19, 1997 v Southampton
- **Total Chelsea League Apps/Goals:** 2/0
- **Transfer:** From Trainee, July 9, 1995
- **Previous Clubs:** None
- **Club Honours:** None
- **International Honours:** None

Nick Crittenden was tipped as a star in the making when he captained Chelsea's youth team. Unfortunately, the right-sided defender fell down the pecking order at Stamford Bridge and moved to Yeovil Town in the close season on a free transfer.

Lge Games	Total mins	Goals	Star Ratings	Ave Rating
0	0	0	0	0

Starts	Subbed off	Subbed on	Yellow	Red
0	0	0	0	0

Cup	Games/Goals	Sub on/off	Star Ratings	Yellow/Red
All Cups	0/0	0/0	0	0/0

CARLO **CUDICINI**

- **Position:** Goalkeeper
- **Born:** September 6, 1973 in Milan (Italy)
- **Chelsea Debut:** May 14, 2000 v Derby County
- **Total Chelsea League Apps/Goals:** 1/0
- **Transfer:** Undisclosed Fee, July 20, 1999
- **Previous Clubs:** AC Milan, Como, Prato, Lazio, Castel Di Sangro
- **Club Honours:** FA Cup winner with Chelsea (2000)
- **International Honours:** None

The 27-year-old 'keeper is highly rated in Italy but has to wait for his chance at Chelsea behind the consistent Ed de Goey. Carlo nevertheless played in the Champions League last term and made his Premiership debut for The Blues against Derby.

Lge Games	Total mins	Goals	Star Ratings	Ave Rating
1	90	0	0	7.00

Starts	Subbed off	Subbed on	Yellow	Red
1	0	0	0	0

Cup	Games/Goals	Sub on/off	Star Ratings	Yellow/Red
Champs Lge	1/0	1/0	0	0/0
FA	0/0	0/0	0	0/0
Worthington	1/0	0/0	0	0/0

SAMUELE **DALLA BONA**

- **Position:** Midfielder
- **Born:** February 6, 1981 in San Dona di Piave (Italy)
- **Chelsea Debut:** April 12, 2000 v Coventry City
- **Total Chelsea League Apps/Goals:** 2/0
- **Transfer:** Undisclosed Fee, October 28, 1998
- **Previous Clubs:** Atalanta Juniors
- **Club Honours:** None
- **International Honours:** Italy Under-21 international

Plucked from the Atalanta junior side even before he signed professional forms, Samuele Dalla Bona is regarded as one of Italy's hottest young prospects and The Bues can claim something of a coup in tempting the youngster to London from under the noses of a number of Serie A giants. Playing for Chelsea reserves last season, Sam scored an unbelievable 16 goals from midfield – an impressive return for a striker, let alone a player attacking from deep. Although still a teenager, Sam did enough to earn himself a first-team squad number in 1999-2000 and, as captain of Italy's talented Under-21 side, is expected to become a first-team regular before too long. He joins a long list of talented youngsters waiting in the wings at Stamford Bridge, but the precocious talent of this attacking midfielder will soon be too hard for The Blues to ignore.

Lge Games	Total mins	Goals	Star Ratings	Ave Rating
2	82	0	0	6.00

Starts	Subbed off	Subbed on	Yellow	Red
0	0	2	0	0

Cup	Games/Goals	Sub on/off	Star Ratings	Yellow/Red
Champs Lge	1/0	1/0	0	0/0
FA	0/0	0/0	0	0/0
Worthington	0/0	0/0	0	0/0

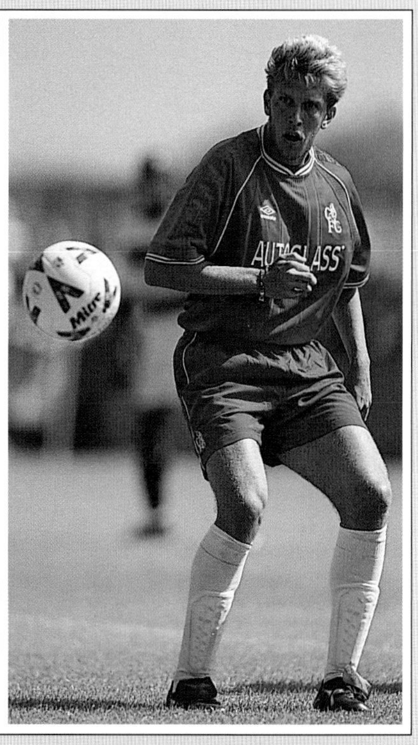

ED **DE GOEY**

- **Position:** Goalkeeper
- **Born:** December 20, 1966 in Gouda (Holland)
- **Chelsea Debut:** August 9, 1997 v Coventry City
- **Total Chelsea League Apps/Goals:** 100/0
- **Transfer:** £2.25 million, June 11, 1997
- **Previous Clubs:** Feyenoord, Sparta Rotterdam
- **Club Honours:** Dutch League winner with Feyenoord (1993); Dutch Cup winner with Feyenoord (1991, 1992, 1994, 1995); League Cup winner, European Cup-Winners' Cup winner & European Super Cup winner with Chelsea (1998); FA Cup winner with Chelsea (2000)
- **International Honours:** Senior, Under-21 Holland international

There were some raised eyebrows when Ruud Gullit signed fellow Dutchman Ed de Goey from Sparta Rotterdam in June 1997, but the former Chelsea boss knew what he was doing. Despite his appearance, Ed is an agile goalkeeper who has proved difficult to beat for even the most prolific marksmen in the Premiership. Standing at an enormous 6ft 6ins, he has quite a presence between the sticks and excels in all aspects of goalkeeping. He is commanding when coming for crosses or corners, he has outstanding reflexes from close-range shots on goal and is virtually impossible to lob from distance.

Ed was brought to the club as cover for injured first-choice 'keeper Dimitri Kharine. When he arrived at Stamford Bridge the huge Dutchman appeared cumbersome and was prone to making the odd embarrassing blunder. Chelsea fans thought Gianluca Vialli had inherited a flop, but he gradually proved the critics wrong to establish himself as one of the best 'keepers in the Premiership. Ed has been capped a number of times for Holland, but he is now behind Edwin van der Sar and Sander Westerveld at international level. Nevertheless, he was one of the club's most consistent performers last season and has become a huge favourite with the Stamford Bridge faithful.

Lge Games	Total mins	Goals	Star Ratings	Ave Rating
37	3330	0	0	6.51

Starts	Subbed off	Subbed on	Yellow	Red
37	0	0	1	0

Cup	Games/Goals	Sub on/off	Star Ratings	Yellow/Red
Champs Lge	16/0	0/1	1	0/0
FA	6/0	0/0	0	0/0
Worthington	0/0	0/0	0	0/0

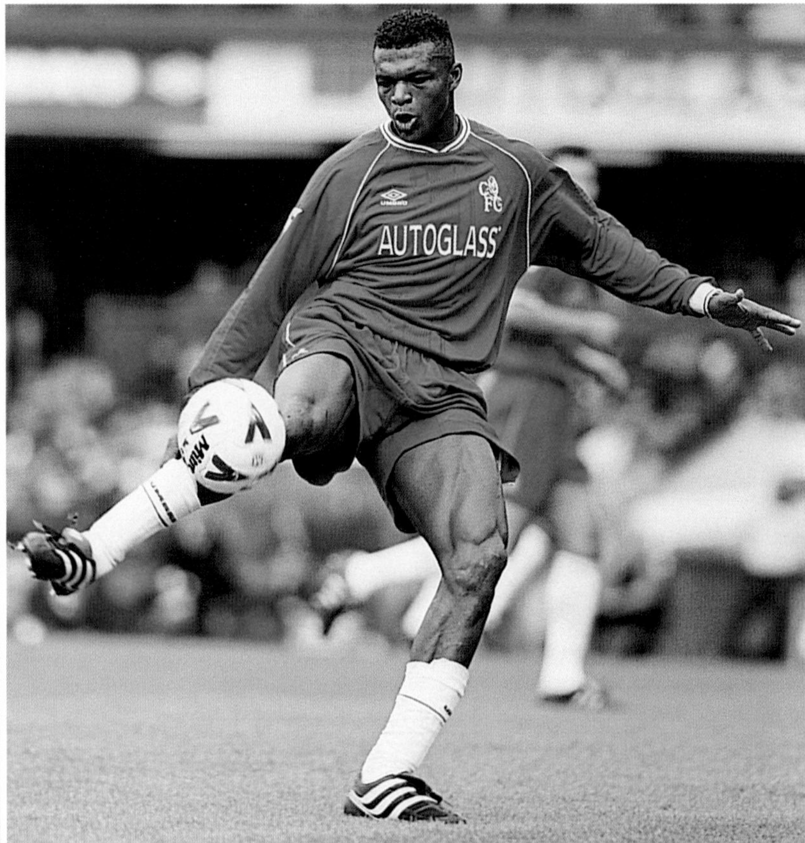

MARCEL DESAILLY

- **Position:** Defender/Midfielder
- **Born:** September 7, 1968 in Accra (Ghana)
- **Chelsea Debut:** August 15, 1998 v Coventry City
- **Total Chelsea League Apps/Goals:** 54/1
- **Transfer:** £4.6 million, June 10, 1998
- **Previous Clubs:** Nantes, Marseille, AC Milan
- **Club Honours:** European Cup winner with Marseille (1993) & AC Milan (1994); European Super Cup winner with AC Milan (1995) & Chelsea (1998); Italian League winner (1996); FA Cup winner with Chelsea (2000)
- **International Honours:** Senior France international

When Gianluca Vialli was looking for a new centre-back before the start of the 1998-99 campaign, there was one prominent name at the top of his list – Marcel Desailly. Vialli was anxious to sign the French centre-back before he joined up with his country's World Cup squad, and it was a good job he did. Marcel was one of the stars of the tournament, proving that his former club had been premature in selling him to Chelsea for £4.6 million. He brought a wealth of crucial experience to Stamford Bridge, having already won the European Cup with Marseille and AC Milan, and clearly saw that The Blues were going in the right direction. Dominant in defence or midfield, he is commanding in the air, strong in the tackle and has an excellent touch for such a powerful player. His sheer presence in The Blues line-up creates an imposing defence, as many opposing strikers have found to their cost since he's been at the club. The fact that Marcel was an ever-present during Chelsea's Champions League campaign last season sums up his importance to the team, and with 'The Rock' at the heart of the back line, anything is possible for the club this term.

Lge Games	Total mins	Goals	Star Ratings	Ave Rating
23	1945	1	2	6.60

Starts	Subbed off	Subbed on	Yellow	Red
23	3	0	3	1

Cup	Games/Goals	Sub on/off	Star Ratings	Yellow/Red
Champs Lge	16/0	1/2	2	0/0
FA	4/0	0/0	0	0/0
Worthington	0/0	0/0	0	0/0

DIDIER DESCHAMPS

- **Position:** Midfielder
- **Born:** October 15, 1968 in Bayonne (France)
- **Chelsea Debut:** August 7, 1999 v Sunderland
- **Total Chelsea League Apps/Goals:** 27/0
- **Transfer:** £3 million, June 21, 1999
- **Previous Clubs:** Nantes, Marseille, Bordeaux, Juventus
- **Club Honours:** French League winner with Marseille (1990, 1992); European Cup winner with Marseille (1993) & Juventus (1996); Italian League winner with Juventus (1995, 1997, 1998); Italian Cup winner with Juventus (1995); Intercontinental Cup winner with Juventus (1996); European Super Cup winner with Juventus (1997); FA Cup winner with Chelsea (2000)
- **International Honours:** Senior France International

Captain of the French side which lifted the 1998 World Cup and the Euro 2000 trophy, Didier Deschamps brought vital experience to Chelsea's midfield, having enjoyed considerable European success during his time at Marseille and Juventus. A holding midfielder whose tireless, unselfish work allowed his team-mates to express themselves, Didier was at his best in the big games – as one would expect for a World Cup-winning captain – and contributed massively to The Blues' impressive Champions League run last season. He wasn't as effective in the Premiership though and moved to Champions League runners-up Valencia for £2.5 million in the close season.

Lge Games	Total mins	Goals	Star Ratings	Ave Rating
27	2050	0	2	6.33

Starts	Subbed off	Subbed on	Yellow	Red
24	8	3	5	0

Cup	Games/Goals	Sub on/off	Star Ratings	Yellow/Red
Champs Lge	14/1	0/7	3	1/0
FA	6/0	0/2	0	1/0
Worthington	0/0	0/0	0	0/0

ALBERT **FERRER**

- **Position:** Defender
- **Born:** June 6, 1970 in Barcelona (Spain)
- **Chelsea Debut:** August 15, 1998 v Coventry City
- **Total Chelsea League Apps/Goals:** 55/0
- **Transfer:** £2.2 million, June 9, 1998
- **Previous Clubs:** Tenerife, Barcelona
- **Club Honours:** Spanish league winner with Barcelona (1991, 1992, 1993, 1994, 1998); European Cup winner with Barcelona (1992); European Cup-Winners' Cup winner with Barcelona (1997); Spanish Cup winner with Barcelona (1997, 1998); European Super Cup winner with Chelsea (1998)
- **International Honours:** Senior Spain International

One of the most consistent players in the Chelsea team since arriving at Stamford Bridge in 1998, Albert Ferrer didn't take long to settle at the club and has carried out his duties with great efficiency. Albert came to England with an impressive list of honours after making over 330 appearances for Barcelona and earning 35 senior Spanish caps. He preferred to defend than attack in Chelsea's defence last season but never let the side down in becoming the first-choice right-back. Albert was devastated to miss out on the FA Cup Final win through injury and now faces a fight for his place from Christian Panucci.

Lge Games	Total mins	Goals	Star Ratings	Ave Rating
25	2109	0	0	6.28

Starts	Subbed off	Subbed on	Yellow	Red
24	2	1	5	0

Cup	Games/Goals	Sub on/off	Star Ratings	Yellow/Red
Champs Lge	14/1	0/3	1	3/0
FA	2/0	0/1	0	0/0
Worthington	0/0	0/0	0	0/0

TORE ANDRE **FLO**

- **Position:** Striker
- **Born:** June 15, 1973 in Strin (Norway)
- **Chelsea Debut:** August 9, 1997 v Coventry City
- **Total Chelsea League Apps/Goals:** 98/31
- **Transfer:** £300,000, August 4, 1997
- **Previous Clubs:** Sogndal, Tromso, SK Brann Bergen
- **Club Honours:** European Cup-Winners' Cup & League Cup winner with Chelsea (1998); FA Cup winner with Chelsea (2000)
- **International Honours:** Senior Norway international

Tore Andre Flo has become a cult hero at Chelsea and has been a mega star in Norway for some time, but the frontman has never really been guaranteed a place in the first team at Stamford Bridge. This has been largely due to Gianluca Vialli's squad rotation system, but also because Tore Andre appeared to be at his most effective from the bench rather than playing the full 90 minutes. Surprisingly, at 6ft 4ins tall, he prefers the ball at his feet where he can use his abundance of skill to run at defences and take them on, which he does well for such a tall player and considering he isn't renowned for his pace.

For a striker with so many apparent drawbacks, Tore Andre is one of the most exciting marksmen in the Premiership and many top British and European sides have tried to prise him away from Chelsea. He faces some tough competition this season with Jimmy Floyd Hasselbaink, Gianfranco Zola and Eidur Gudjohnsen all battling for two places up front, but this won't deter Tore Andre, who was The Blues' top scorer last season with 19 goals in all competitions. If the worst was to happen and he was tempted away from Stamford Bridge one day, Chelsea would undoubtedly receive a substantial amount of money to buy a replacement. A big-money move away from West London would also signify a considerable profit on the £300,000 the club paid for him in August 1997.

Lge Games	Total mins	Goals	Star Ratings	Ave Rating
34	1897	10	3	6.37

Starts	Subbed off	Subbed on	Yellow	Red
20	9	14	1	0

Cup	Games/Goals	Sub on/off	Star Ratings	Yellow/Red
Champs Lge	16/8	2/4	2	0/0
FA	6/1	3/1	0	0/0
Worthington	1/0	0/0	0	0/0

MIKAEL FORSSELL

- **Position:** Striker
- **Born:** March 15, 1981 in Steinfurt (Germany)
- **Chelsea Debut:** January 31, 1999 v Arsenal
- **Total Chelsea League Apps/Goals:** 10/1
- **Transfer:** No Fee, July 31, 1998
- **Previous Clubs:** HJK Helsinki
- **Club Honours:** None
- **International Honours:** Finland Youth & Under-18 international

Finnish striker Mikael Forssell was brought to Chelsea as one for the future and showed his potential with two superb goals in the fourth round of the FA Cup against Oxford in February 1999 – his first start for the club. Mikael found his first-team opportunities limited last term but still enjoyed an introduction to Champions League football. To gain experience and aid his development, Chelsea have loaned him to Crystal Palace.

Lge Games	Total mins	Goals	Star Ratings	Ave Rating
0	0	0	0	0

Starts	Subbed off	Subbed on	Yellow	Red
0	0	0	0	0

Cup	Games/Goals	Sub on/off	Star Ratings	Yellow/Red
Champs Lge	1/0	0/0	0	0/0
FA	0/0	0/0	0	0/0
Worthington	1/0	1/0	0	1/0

BJARNE GOLDBAEK

- **Position:** Midfielder
- **Born:** October 6, 1968 in Nykoebing (Denmark)
- **Chelsea Debut:** November 11, 1998 v Arsenal
- **Total Chelsea League Apps/Goals:** 29/5 goals
- **Transfer:** £330,000, November 9, 1998
- **Previous Clubs:** Schalke 04, Kaiserslautern, TB Berlin, FC Cologne, FC Copenhagen
- **Club Honours:** None
- **International Honours:** Senior Denmark International

Bjarne Goldbaek came to Chelsea after his Danish team, FC Copenhagen, were knocked out at the second round stage of the 1998 European Cup-Winners' Cup by The Blues. On his arrival in West London, few British football fans had heard of the Denmark international, and it was presumed he would provide back-up to Chelsea's talented first team. But Bjarne quickly established himself in The Blues' starting line-up and was a big success on his way to making 23 appearances in the 1998-1999 season, scoring five league goals for the club. He proved a valuable addition and a bargain acquisition by Gianluca Vialli at £330,000 – a snip at today's inflated transfer prices. The direct winger supplied plenty of ammunition for Chelsea's frontmen in his first season at Stamford Bridge and weighed in with his fair share of goals from midfield during his time with the club. However, in the 1999-2000 season Bjarne struggled to command a first-team place as Vialli continued to strengthen Chelsea's squad. He made only two league starts and despite featuring in the early stages of the Champions League he was sold to Fulham in January 2000 for £650,000.

Lge Games	Total mins	Goals	Star Ratings	Ave Rating
6	295	0	0	6.00

Starts	Subbed off	Subbed on	Yellow	Red
2	2	4	0	0

Cup	Games/Goals	Sub on/off	Star Ratings	Yellow/Red
Champs Lge	2/0	1/1	0	0/0
FA	0/0	0/0	0	0/0
Worthington	1/0	0/0	0	0/0

JON HARLEY

- **Position:** Defender/Midfielder
- **Born:** September 26, 1979 in Maidstone
- **Chelsea Debut:** April 5, 1998 v Derby County
- **Total Chelsea League Apps/Goals:** 20/2
- **Transfer:** From Trainee, August 1, 1996
- **Previous Clubs:** None
- **Club Honours:** FA Cup winner with Chelsea (2000)
- **International Honours:** England Under-21 international

Jon Harley enjoyed a fine run on the left of Chelsea's defence towards the end of last season and he impressed enough for some observers to suggest he should be drafted into the full England squad in time for their ill-fated Euro 2000 campaign. That failed to materialise, but it was testimony to the progress the young defender had made since making his debut against Derby in April 1998. Jon still regards himself as a midfielder rather than a defender, so it's no surprise that he likes to get forward when playing at full-back. He did this to great effect last season, creating some vital goals for his team-mates by delivering a steady supply of high-quality crosses from the left wing. He also scored two winning goals – against Leeds away and Watford at home – making him a valuable member of the squad. He provides the same versatility as Graeme Le Saux, the player whose injury contributed to Jon's appearances in the starting line-up last term. A graduate of the FA School at Lilleshall and a former Chelsea Youth captain, he now looks set to develop into one of the finest players of his generation.

Lge Games	Total mins	Goals	Star Ratings	Ave Rating
17	1212	2	4	6.80

Starts	Subbed off	Subbed on	Yellow	Red
13	3	4	1	0

Cup	Games/Goals	Sub on/off	Star Ratings	Yellow/Red
Champs Lge	4/0	3/0	0	1/0
FA	5/0	0/0	0	1/0
Worthington	0/0	0/0	0	0/0

KEVIN HITCHCOCK

- **Position:** Goalkeeper
- **Born:** October 5, 1962 in Custom House, London
- **Chelsea Debut:** March 26, 1988 v Southampton
- **Total Chelsea League Apps/Goals:** 96/0
- **Transfer:** £250,000, March 25, 1988
- **Previous Clubs:** Nottingham Forest, Mansfield Town, Northampton Town (on loan)
- **Club Honours:** FA Cup winner with Chelsea (1997); League Cup & European Super Cup winner (1998)
- **International Honours:** None

Kevin Hitchcock has been a loyal servant to Chelsea since he joined the club in 1988, and he is the longest-serving player at Stamford Bridge. A reliable deputy between the posts, Kevin has had relatively few first-team opportunities since the arrival of current first-choice 'keeper Ed de Goey, but he has never let The Blues down and now helps out on the coaching side.

Lge Games	Total mins	Goals	Star Ratings	Ave Rating
0	0	0	0	0

Starts	Subbed off	Subbed on	Yellow	Red
0	0	0	0	0

Cup	Games/Goals	Sub on/off	Star Ratings	Yellow/Red
All Cups	0/0	0/0	0	0/0

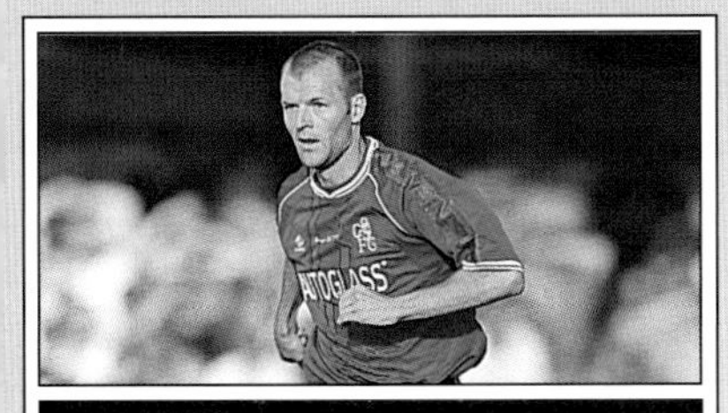

JES HOGH

- **Position:** Defender
- **Born:** May 7, 1966 in Aalborg (Denmark)
- **Chelsea Debut:** September 15, 1999 v AC Milan
- **Total Chelsea League Apps/Goals:** 9/0
- **Transfer:** £300,000, July 8, 1999
- **Previous Clubs:** Aalborg, Brondby, Fenerbahce
- **Club Honours:** 1996 Turkish League winner with Fenerbahce
- **International Honours:** Senior Denmark International

Jes Hogh is turning out to be a bargain buy for Chelsea. The Denmark international defender cost just £300,000 before the start of the 1999-2000 campaign and was a capable deputy whenever he stepped in as cover for the first-choice pairing of Marcel Desailly and Frank Leboeuf in the centre of defence. Jes only made 17 appearances for The Blues last season, but his experience at both club and international level makes him a vital squad member. With over 50 caps for Denmark, he is the perfect example of Chelsea's current strength in depth.

Lge Games	Total mins	Goals	Star Ratings	Ave Rating
9	550	0	0	6.37

Starts	Subbed off	Subbed on	Yellow	Red
6	2	3	0	0

Cup	Games/Goals	Sub on/off	Star Ratings	Yellow/Red
Champs Lge	5/0	3/1	0	0/0
FA	2/0	0/2	0	0/0
Worthington	1/0	0/0	0	1/0

BERNARD LAMBOURDE

- **Position:** Defender/Midfielder
- **Born:** May 11, 1971 in Guadeloupe (French Caribbean)
- **Chelsea Debut:** September 24, 1997 v Manchester United
- **Total Chelsea League Apps/Goals:** 39/2
- **Transfer:** £1.5 million, July 10, 1997
- **Previous Clubs:** Cannes, Angers, Bordeaux
- **Club Honours:** European Super Cup winner with Chelsea (1998)
- **International Honours:** None

After joining the club from Bordeaux for £1.5 million in 1997, Bernard Lambourde has had a mixed three years at Stamford Bridge. Injuries initially hampered his progress as he tried to break into the first team, but he has always proved himself to be a versatile squad member when fit, playing in both defence and midfield. Bernard's injury problems had cleared up by the start of the club's 1999-2000 campaign and he was arguably Chelsea's most improved player by the end of last season, scoring the winning goals in vital away wins at Middlesbrough and Tottenham. Tall and strong, yet impressively comfortable on the ball, he prefers to play in the centre of defence, but his first team appearances have largely been restricted to filling in at right-back. Nevertheless, he deputised admirably when Albert Ferrer was absent from the side last term. Bernard was looking to feature more regularly in The Blues' starting line-up this season but faced strong competition from Ferrer, Christian Panucci and Mario Melchiot. He moved to Portsmouth on loan in September 2000. Although Bernard would like to finish his career in France, he will be offered a permanent deal with the First Division club at the end of his loan spell.

Lge Games	Total mins	Goals	Star Ratings	Ave Rating
15	1136	2	0	6.00

Starts	Subbed off	Subbed on	Yellow	Red
12	1	3	3	0

Cup	Games/Goals	Sub on/off	Star Ratings	Yellow/Red
Champs Lge	2/0	2/0	0	0/0
FA	3/0	0/0	1	0/0
Worthington	1/0	0/1	0	0/0

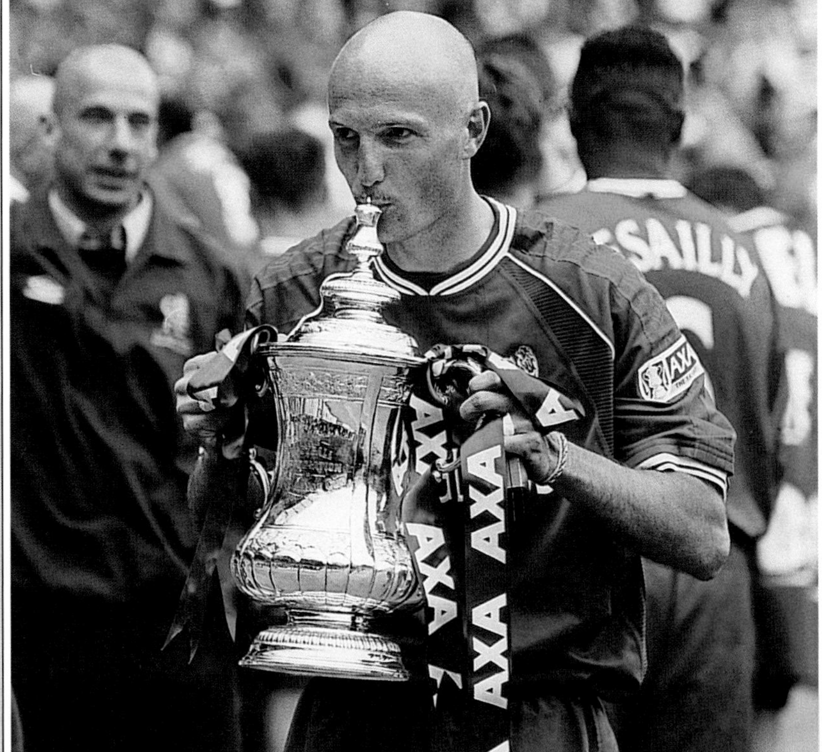

FRANK LEBOEUF

- **Position:** Defender
- **Born:** January 22, 1968 in Marseille (France)
- **Chelsea Debut:** August 18, 1996 v Southampton
- **Total Chelsea League Apps/Goals:** 119/17
- **Transfer:** £2.5 million, July 12, 1996
- **Previous Clubs:** Hyeres, Meaux, Laval, Strasbourg
- **Club Honours:** FA Cup winner with Chelsea (1997, 2000); League Cup winner, European Cup-Winners' Cup winner & European Super Cup winner with Chelsea (1998)
- **International Honours:** Senior France international

Frank Leboeuf and Marcel Desailly have formed a formidable partnership at the heart of the Chelsea rearguard since they came together at the start of the 1998-99 season. No-one had heard of Frank Leboeuf when he arrived at Stamford Bridge in July 1996 from Strasbourg, but he made an immediate impact in Chelsea's defence, displaying many of the attributes that his predecessors had been lacking. In breaking down opposition attacks he has a great reading of the game which allows him to make perfectly-timed challenges. On the ball he is perhaps the most comfortable defender in the Premiership, with the ability to keep it simple or play a defence-splitting throughball from his own half. Frank has a powerful shot and is Chelsea's regular penalty taker, meaning he grabs his fair share of goals as well as stopping opponents from scoring at the other end. He is now set to play a starring role alongside Desailly in the French national side after the retirement of Laurent Blanc.

Lge Games	Total mins	Goals	Star Ratings	Ave Rating
28	2365	2	0	6.42

Starts	Subbed off	Subbed on	Yellow	Red
28	4	0	9	2

Cup	Games/Goals	Sub on/off	Star Ratings	Yellow/Red
Champs Lge	14/1	1/2	0	3/0
FA	4/1	0/0	1	0/0
Worthington	0/0	0/0	0	0/0

GRAEME LE SAUX

- **Position:** Defender
- **Born:** October 17, 1968 in St Pauls (Jersey)
- **Chelsea Debut:** May 13, 1989 v Portsmouth
- **Total Chelsea League Apps/Goals:** 155/9
- **Transfer:** £5 million, August 8, 1997
- **Previous Clubs:** Chelsea, Blackburn Rovers
- **Club Honours:** Premier League winner with Blackburn Rovers (1995); League Cup winner with Chelsea (1998); European Super Cup winner with Chelsea (1998)
- **International Honours:** Senior, Under-21 England international

Graeme Le Saux began his career as a winger at Stamford Bridge and it wasn't until he moved to Blackburn Rovers that he developed into an accomplished attacking defender. After establishing himself as England's first choice left-back, his form tempted Chelsea to re-sign him for £5 million in August 1997. Graeme became a key member of the side as The Blues chased honours at home and in Europe, but the 1999-2000 season was one he would rather forget. An ankle injury kept him sidelined from October until the end of the campaign and he was sorely missed by Chelsea and his country, prompting much debate about England's lack of left-sided players. His return to fitness in time for the new season was a huge boost.

Lge Games	Total mins	Goals	Star Ratings	Ave Rating
8	442	0	0	6.62

Starts	Subbed off	Subbed on	Yellow	Red
6	3	2	3	0

Cup	Games/Goals	Sub on/off	Star Ratings	Yellow/Red
Champs Lge	4/0	1/1	0	0/0
FA	0/0	0/0	0	0/0
Worthington	1/0	0/1	0	0/0

ROBERTO DI MATTEO

- **Position:** Midfielder
- **Born:** May 29, 1970 in Schaffhausen (Switzerland)
- **Chelsea Debut:** August 18, 1996 v Southampton
- **Total Chelsea League Apps/Goals:** 112/15
- **Transfer:** £4.9 million, July 17, 1996
- **Previous Clubs:** Schaffhausen, FC Zurich, Aarau, Lazio.
- **Club Honours:** Swiss league winner with Schaffhausen (1993); FA Cup winner with Chelsea (1997, 2000), League Cup, European Cup-Winners' Cup & European Super Cup winner with Chelsea (1998)
- **International Honours:** Senior Italy international

Italy international Roberto Di Matteo was the club's record signing when he joined Chelsea in 1996 from Serie A giants Lazio for £4.9 million. His impact was stunning. The midfielder shot himself into the record books with the fastest-ever goal scored in an FA Cup Final, coming just 43 seconds into the encounter with Middlesbrough in 1997. Since then, Roberto has struggled to reproduce the same magic on a regular basis and last season was one of frustration. After being sidelined for much of the early part of the campaign with an ankle injury, Robbie found it difficult to break back into the starting line-up, leading to speculation of a move back to Italy. At the start of 2000, after a good run of form in the first team, he broke his arm in the league fixture against Leicester to stall his season even further. Despite this, he made nine Champions League appearances and rounded off the campaign in the best way possible, poaching the winner in a hard-fought FA Cup Final against Aston Villa – the last final to be staged at Wembley before the famous stadium was pulled down. After the game he pledged his future to Chelsea and if he can stay free from injury and recapture his best form, Roberto will have a major influence in Chelsea's quest for silverware this term.

Lge Games	Total mins	Goals	Star Ratings	Ave Rating
18	1298	2	0	6.50

Starts	Subbed off	Subbed on	Yellow	Red
14	3	4	3	0

Cup	Games/Goals	Sub on/off	Star Ratings	Yellow/Red
Champs Lge	9/0	6/1	0	1/0
FA	3/2	0/0	0	0/0
Worthington	1/0	0/0	0	0/0

MARIO MELCHIOT

- **Position:** Defender
- **Born:** November 4, 1976 in Amsterdam (Holland)
- **Chelsea Debut:** April 22, 2000 v Middlesbrough
- **Total Chelsea League Apps/Goals:** 5/0
- **Transfer:** No Fee, June 13, 1999
- **Previous Clubs:** Ajax
- **Club Honours:** Dutch League & Cup winner with Ajax (1998); Dutch Cup winner with Ajax (1999); FA Cup winner with Chelsea (2000)
- **International Honours:** Holland Under-21 international

Mario Melchiot was in danger of becoming the forgotten man at Stamford Bridge because of a series of injuries since his move from Ajax, but the versatile defender endeared himself to Blues' fans with a superb display in the FA Cup Final. Mario proved his worth again with a well-taken Charity Shield goal against Man. United. Capable of playing at centre-back, right-back and in midfield, he will be a useful asset to Chelsea.

Lge Games	Total mins	Goals	Star Ratings	Ave Rating
5	400	0	0	6.40

Starts	Subbed off	Subbed on	Yellow	Red
4	1	1	0	0

Cup	Games/Goals	Sub on/off	Star Ratings	Yellow/Red
Champs Lge	0/0	0/0	0	0/0
FA	1/0	0/0	0	1/0
Worthington	0/0	0/0	0	0/0

JODY MORRIS

- **Position:** Midfielder
- **Born:** December 22, 1978 in Hammersmith
- **Chelsea Debut:** February 4, 1996 v Middlesbrough
- **Total Chelsea League Apps/Goals:** 73/5
- **Transfer:** From Trainee, January 8, 1996
- **Previous Clubs:** None
- **Club Honours:** European Super Cup winner with Chelsea (1998); FA Cup winner with Chelsea (2000)
- **International Honours:** England Under-17 & Under-21 International

A rare commodity at Stamford Bridge, midfielder Jody Morris is a home-grown talent who has more than held his own in the senior side despite the galaxy of foreign stars who have joined the club in recent years. Jody has thrived in the company of his illustrious colleagues and he has already been pencilled in as the natural successor to current skipper Dennis Wise – the ultimate compliment. With this in mind, Jody was handed the captain's armband for the fixture against Coventry, providing vital experience for the young star. A product of the renowned FA School of Excellence at Lilleshall, he has already played for England at Under-17 and Under-21 levels and looks certain to progress to the senior squad in the future. Jody's immediate priority must be to reproduce the form he showed last term, when he featured in 30 league games and made a significant contribution to the club's Champions League campaign. After the departure of Didier Deschamps, he now has the chance to cement a permanent place in the centre of midfield, where his ball-winning skills and passing ability are best suited.

Lge Games	Total mins	Goals	Star Ratings	Ave Rating
30	1769	3	1	6.26

Starts	Subbed off	Subbed on	Yellow	Red
19	4	11	4	0

Cup	Games/Goals	Sub on/off	Star Ratings	Yellow/Red
Champs Lge	11/0	5/0	0	0/0
FA	4/1	3/0	0	0/0
Worthington	1/0	0/0	0	0/0

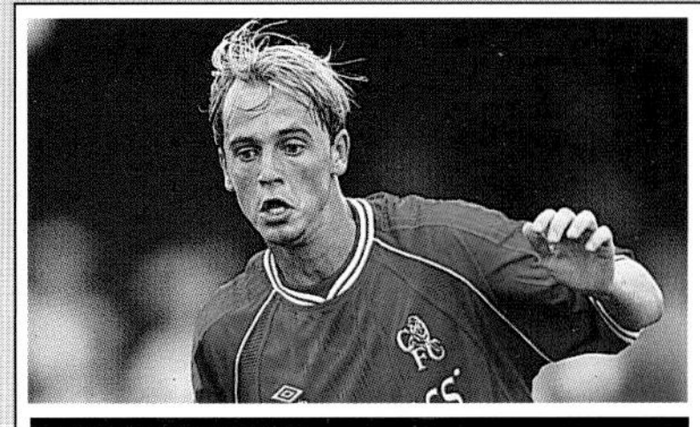

MARK NICHOLLS

- **Position:** Striker
- **Born:** May 30, 1977 in Hillingdon
- **Chelsea Debut:** September 18, 1996 v Blackpool
- **Total Chelsea League Apps/Goals:** 36/3
- **Transfer:** From Trainee, July 1, 1995
- **Previous Clubs:** None
- **Club Honours:** None
- **International Honours:** None

Mark Nicholls is essentially a striker but he has played out wide on his rare first-team appearances. His chances in the starting line-up have suffered with the quality of the strikers who have graced Stamford Bridge in recent years. Despite being on the fringes of the first team last season, Mark only had brief run-outs in the Champions League and Worthington Cup before going out on loan to Reading and Grimsby Town.

Lge Games	Total mins	Goals	Star Ratings	Ave Rating
0	0	0	0	0

Starts	Subbed off	Subbed on	Yellow	Red
0	0	0	0	0

Cup	Games/Goals	Sub on/off	Star Ratings	Yellow/Red
Champs Lge	1/0	1/0	0	0/0
FA	0/0	0/0	0	0/0
Worthington	1/0	1/0	0	0/0

LUCA PERCASSI

- **Position:** Defender
- **Born:** August 25, 1980 in Milan (Italy)
- **Chelsea Debut:** N/A
- **Total Chelsea League Apps/Goals:** 0/0
- **Transfer:** No Fee, July 1, 1997
- **Previous Clubs:** Atalanta Juniors
- **Club Honours:** None
- **International Honours:** None

Luca Percassi, like Samuele Dalla Bona, was signed from the Atalanta junior side after scouts noticed his raw potential. He hadn't even signed professional forms in Italy when The Blues pounced, but he's seen as a big prospect for the future. The young right-back may take time to settle in England, but he has the ability to become another successful Chelsea import.

Lge Games	Total mins	Goals	Star Ratings	Ave Rating
0	0	0	0	0

Starts	Subbed off	Subbed on	Yellow	Red
0	0	0	0	0

Cup	Games/Goals	Sub on/off	Star Ratings	Yellow/Red
Champs Lge	0/0	0/0	0	0/0
FA	1/0	1/0	0	0/0
Worthington	0/0	0/0	0	0/0

DAN PETRESCU

- **Position:** Defender
- **Born:** December 22, 1967 in Bucharest (Romania)
- **Chelsea Debut:** November 18, 1995 v Leeds United
- **Total Chelsea League Apps/Goals:** 150/18
- **Transfer:** £2.3 million, November 18, 1995
- **Previous Clubs:** Steaua Bucharest, FC Olt (on loan) Foggia, Genoa, Sheffield Wednesday
- **Club Honours:** Romanian League & Cup winner with Steaua Bucharest (1989); FA Cup winner with Chelsea (1997); League Cup & European Cup-Winners' Cup winner with Chelsea (1998)
- **International Honours:** Senior, U-21, Romania Youth international

Dan Petrescu can lay claim to being one of Chelsea's most important players in recent seasons. Having joined the club in 1995 under the management of Glenn Hoddle, Dan was involved at the beginning of the Stamford Bridge revolution, playing for Hoddle, Ruud Gullit and Gianluca Vialli. He was one of the team's most consistent performers during his time with Chelsea and was equally comfortable in defence or on the right side of midfield, where he demonstrated his natural attacking instincts and scored his fair share of crucial goals. The Romania international did well enough in the 1999-2000 campaign to be offered an improved contract, but with the close-season arrival of further competition on the right flank in the shape of Mario Stanic, he signed for Bradford City to increase his first-team opportunities. Nevertheless, Dan will be fondly remembered by the Chelsea faithful as one of the first players to turn The Blues into a European force.

Lge Games	Total mins	Goals	Star Ratings	Ave Rating
29	1985	4	4	6.75

Starts	Subbed off	Subbed on	Yellow	Red
24	14	5	2	0

Cup	Games/Goals	Sub on/off	Star Ratings	Yellow/Red
Champs Lge	15/1	2/3	1	1/0
FA	3/0	1/1	0	1/0
Worthington	0/0	0/0	0	0/0

GUSTAVO POYET

Position: Midfielder

Born: November 15, 1967 in Montevideo (Uruguay)

Chelsea Debut: August 9, 1997 v Coventry City

Total Chelsea League Apps/Goals: 75/25

Transfer: No Fee, July 1, 1997

Previous Clubs: River Plate, Grenoble, Bella Vista, Real Zaragoza

Club Honours: Spanish Cup winner with Real Zaragoza (1994); European Cup-Winners' Cup winner with Real Zaragoza (1995); European Cup-Winners' Cup & European Super Cup winner with Chelsea (1998); FA Cup winner with Chelsea (2000)

International Honours: Senior Uruguay International

Gustavo Poyet must be one of the most popular players to have arrived at Stamford Bridge in recent years, despite the fact that he seems to have spent half of his Chelsea career on the treatment table struggling with injury. The Uruguay midfielder showed flashes of his ability in his first two years with The Blues before picking up a bad injury in each term. However, Gus remained virtually injury-free in the 1999-2000 campaign and confirmed his status as a true crowd favourite with some memorable moments. His acrobatic scissor-kick in the 4-0 win over Sunderland may have been on the opening day of 1999-2000, but many Chelsea fans considered it the club's best goal of the season. It was a spectacular strike, but not his most important – his double in the FA Cup semi-final against Newcastle sent The Blues to Wembley. Gus is now set to be a key figure in 2000-2001. He is loved by the supporters because of his obvious passion for the game and his goals from midfield will be vital as Chelsea challenge for honours.

Lge Games	Total mins	Goals	Star Ratings	Ave Rating
33	2338	10	6	6.77

Starts	Subbed off	Subbed on	Yellow	Red
25	6	8	5	0

Cup	Games/Goals	Sub on/off	Star Ratings	Yellow/Red
Champs Lge	14/2	2/6	1	0/0
FA	6/6	0/0	3	1/0
Worthington	0/0	0/0	0	0/0

CHRIS SUTTON

Position: Striker

Born: March 10, 1973 in Nottingham

Chelsea Debut: August 7, 1999 v Sunderland

Total Chelsea League Apps/Goals: 28/1

Transfer: £10 million, July 5, 1999

Previous Clubs: Norwich City, Blackburn Rovers

Club Honours: Premiership League winner with Blackburn Rovers (1995)

International Honours: Senior, Under-21 England International

When Chris Sutton was prized away from Blackburn in July 1999 for a club record fee of £10 million, he was seen as the missing piece of the jigsaw, the man who could finally bring the Premiership title to Stamford Bridge. He was expected to score at least 20 goals but struggled to find his best form in Chelsea's cosmopolitan team, scoring just once in the league last term, a header in the 5-0 romp over Manchester United. Chris was immediately under close scrutiny due to his price tag, which seemed to weigh heavily on the striker's shoulders. While he was always a committed and honest performer in the Chelsea side, he seemed to lose his touch and confidence in front of goal. Sutton must have known the writing was on the wall when he was omitted from the club's FA Cup Final squad to face Aston Villa at Wembley and a £6 million move to Celtic in the summer was seen as good business for all parties. He gladly took the opportunity to leave his troubles at Stamford Bridge behind him and relaunch his career in Scotland.

Lge Games	Total mins	Goals	Star Ratings	Ave Rating
28	1828	1	0	5.54

Starts	Subbed off	Subbed on	Yellow	Red
21	9	7	7	0

Cup	Games/Goals	Sub on/off	Star Ratings	Yellow/Red
Champs Lge	7/1	4/1	1	1/1
FA	4/1	1/2	0	1/0
Worthington	0/0	0/0	0	0/0

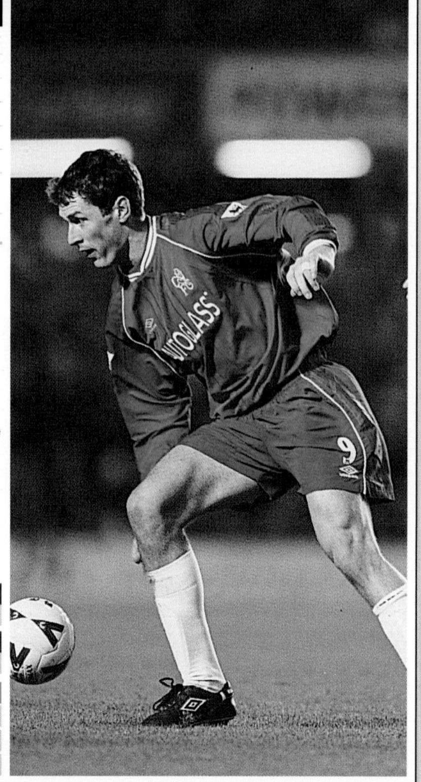

JOHN TERRY

Position: Defender

Born: December 7, 1980 in Barking

Chelsea Debut: December 26, 1998 v Southampton

Total Chelsea League Apps/Goals: 6/0

Transfer: From Trainee, August 1, 1997

Previous Clubs: None

Club Honours: None

International Honours: None

If John Terry was at a smaller Premiership club than Chelsea he would have made bigger strides in the first team by now. Unfortunately for John, two world class centre-backs are currently ahead of him in the starting line-up. But John has impressed whenever he has been called upon by Chelsea and remains an exciting prospect for the future. Much will depend on whether he gets a good run in the side, but he is bound to learn from the likes of Marcel Desailly and Frank Leboeuf.

Lge Games	Total mins	Goals	Star Ratings	Ave Rating
4	260	0	0	6.25

Starts	Subbed off	Subbed on	Yellow	Red
2	0	2	0	0

Cup	Games/Goals	Sub on/off	Star Ratings	Yellow/Red
Champs Lge	0/0	0/0	0	0/0
FA	4/1	1/1	0	0/0
Worthington	1/0	0/0	0	0/0

EMERSON THOME

- **Position:** Defender
- **Born:** March 30, 1972 in Port Alegre (Portugal)
- **Chelsea Debut:** December 26, 1999 v Southampton
- **Total Chelsea League Apps/Goals:** 20/0
- **Transfer:** £2.7 million, December 23, 1999
- **Previous Clubs:** Benfica, Sheffield Wednesday
- **Club Honours:** Portuguese Cup winner with Benfica (1996)
- **International Honours:** None

Emerson Thome moved to Chelsea from Sheffield Wednesday after impressing Blues' scouts with his pace and his ability to bring the ball out of defence. Emo was essentially brought to the club as back-up for Marcel Desailly and Frank Leboeuf, but despite making 18 starts last season, he found himself out of the reckoning at the start of 2000-2001. The club needed to recoup some of the money they had spent on new signings in the summer, so Emo was sold to Sunderland for £4.5 million.

Lge Games	Total mins	Goals	Star Ratings	Ave Rating
20	1693	0	5	6.47

Starts	Subbed off	Subbed on	Yellow	Red
18	0	2	0	0

Cup	Games/Goals	Sub on/off	Star Ratings	Yellow/Red
Champs Lge	1/0	0/0	0	0/0
FA	0/0	0/0	0	0/0
Worthington	0/0	0/0	0	0/0

GEORGE WEAH

- **Position:** Striker
- **Born:** October 11, 1966 in Monrovia (Liberia)
- **Chelsea Debut:** January 12, 2000 v Tottenham Hotspur
- **Total Chelsea League Apps/Goals:** 11/3
- **Transfer:** On Loan, January 11, 2000
- **Previous Clubs:** Monaco, Paris St Germain, AC Milan
- **Club Honours:** French League winner with Paris St Germain (1994); French League & Cup winner with Paris St Germain (1995); Italian League winner with AC Milan (1996, 1999); FA Cup winner with Chelsea (2000)
- **International Honours:** Senior Liberia International

George Weah, the World Player Of The Year in 1995, had an immediate impact when he joined Chelsea in a loan deal from AC Milan in January 2000. The Liberia striker scored on his debut against Tottenham after coming on as a second-half substitute. From then on he proved a valuable addition to the Chelsea line-up, even helping Chris Sutton to find some form, if not goals, in the second half of the season. George's arrival marked an upturn in Chelsea's league form in the 1999-2000 campaign and the club went 16 games unbeaten around the time of his arrival. George wasn't eligible to play in Chelsea's Champions League campaign, but he scored some vital goals in the FA Cup to earn himself a place in the starting line-up at Wembley in May. Sadly, the final was his last contribution in a Chelsea shirt but he still left the club with a winner's medal. He joined Manchester City in a permanent deal in the summer of 2000 and will be guaranteed a good reception whenever he returns to Stamford Bridge.

Lge Games	Total mins	Goals	Star Ratings	Ave Rating
11	876	3	6	7.36

Starts	Subbed off	Subbed on	Yellow	Red
9	1	2	0	0

Cup	Games/Goals	Sub on/off	Star Ratings	Yellow/Red
Champs Lge	0/0	0/0	0	0/0
FA	4/2	0/3	1	0/0
Worthington	0/0	0/0	0	0/0

DENNIS WISE

- **Position:** Midfielder
- **Born:** December 16, 1966 in Kensington
- **Chelsea Debut:** August 8, 1990 v Derby County
- **Total Chelsea League Apps/Goals:** 296/50
- **Transfer:** £1.6 million, July 3, 1990
- **Previous Clubs:** Southampton, Wimbledon
- **Club Honours:** FA Cup winner with Wimbledon (1988) & Chelsea (1997, 2000); League Cup, European Cup-Winners' Cup & European Super Cup with Chelsea (1998)
- **International Honours:** Senior, Under-21 England International

A Chelsea side without Dennis Wise must be like a Christmas without cards, cake and carol singers. The crafty midfielder is the captain and heartbeat of the team and the 1999-2000 campaign – his tenth season since signing from Wimbledon in 1990 for £1.6 million – was one of his best. In a side of foreign stars, Dennis is often the most influential player on the pitch, an Englishman who directs operations from the anchor role in midfield. Wisey is far more than just a brutal ballwinner – he has the ability to control games with his incisive and creative passing. At his brilliant best in the Champions League, he put in some commanding displays and scored some crucial goals, such as his strike in AC Milan's San Siro stadium which was a real collector's item. At the end of last season, Wisey lifted the third FA Cup of his career and earned himself a recall to the England squad for Euro 2000. Instead of slowing down, Wisey just gets better, which is fantastic news for The Blues.

Lge Games	Total mins	Goals	Star Ratings	Ave Rating
30	2614	4	4	6.70

Starts	Subbed off	Subbed on	Yellow	Red
29	3	1	6	1

Cup	Games/Goals	Sub on/off	Star Ratings	Yellow/Red
Champs Lge	15/4	1/0	1	2/0
FA	5/2	0/0	0	1/1
Worthington	0/0	0/0	0	0/0

ROBERT **WOLLEASTON**

- **Position:** Striker
- **Born:** December 21, 1979 in Perivale
- **Chelsea Debut:** December 12, 1999 v Sunderland
- **Total Chelsea League Apps/Goals:** 1/0
- **Transfer:** From Trainee, August 1, 1998
- **Previous Clubs:** None
- **Club Honours:** None
- **International Honours:** None

Robert Wolleaston's first-team experience in the 1999-2000 campaign was limited to a meagre 14 minutes of action as a substitute in Chelsea's 4-1 league defeat to Sunderland at The Stadium Of Light. In such a disappointing game, Robert didn't get much of a chance to shine, but he will gain some encouragement by being included in the first-team squad, which means the staff at Chelsea believe he has the potential to be a success in the Premiership. A powerful and athletic forward, he has been a great success at youth level and has played in midfield when necessary. Robert went on loan to Bristol Rovers in March 2000, playing in four matches for the Second Division outfit. Only time will tell whether the pacy young striker has what it takes to play at the highest level, and, for the forseeable future at least, Wolleaston may have to bide his time and show patience before getting his chance.

Lge Games	Total mins	Goals	Star Ratings	Ave Rating
1	14	0	0	N/A

Starts	Subbed off	Subbed on	Yellow	Red
0	0	1	0	0

Cup	Games/Goals	Sub on/off	Star Ratings	Yellow/Red
Champs Lge	0/0	0/0	0	0/0
FA	0/0	0/0	0	0/0
Worthington	1/0	1/0	0	0/0

GIANFRANCO **ZOLA**

- **Position:** Striker
- **Born:** July 5, 1966 in Oliena (Sardinia)
- **Chelsea Debut:** November 16, 1996 v Blackburn Rovers
- **Total Chelsea League Apps/Goals:** 120/34
- **Transfer:** £4.5 million, November 15, 1996
- **Previous Clubs:** Nuorese, Torres, Napoli, Parma
- **Club Honours:** European Super Cup winner with Parma (1994) & Chelsea (1998); FA Cup winner with Chelsea (1997, 2000); League Cup & European Cup-Winners' Cup winner with Chelsea 1998
- **International Honours:** Senior Italy international

For a man who made such a huge impact when he came to Chelsea from Parma in 1997 – wowing crowds with his deft touches, clever flicks and intelligent passing on the way to winning the Footballer Of The Year award after six months – Gianfranco Zola was in a worrying position at times during the 1999-2000 season. The diminutive Italian striker feared for his place in the side under pressure from Tore Andre Flo, Chris Sutton and George Weah, and he struggled to produce goals on a consistent basis to back up his claims for a regular spot. Undeterred by the pressure, Gianfranco stuck to the challenge before him and his quality eventually shone through. By the latter half of the season he was playing some superb football, particularly in Europe, where he ran AC Milan ragged in the Champions League and scored a magical free-kick in the 3-1 home win over Spanish giants Barcelona. However, his best performance of the season was saved for last, as an inspired display in the second half at Wembley helped Chelsea win the FA Cup Final against Aston Villa. Before the start of the new campaign, rumours started to circulate that Franco wanted a move back to Italy, but he insisted that he intended to stay at Stamford Bridge and challenge for honours.

Lge Games	Total mins	Goals	Star Ratings	Ave Rating
33	2247	4	2	6.61

Starts	Subbed off	Subbed on	Yellow	Red
25	10	8	0	0

Cup	Games/Goals	Sub on/off	Star Ratings	Yellow/Red
Champs Lge	15/3	0/7	3	2/0
FA	5/1	1/2	0	0/0
Worthington	0/0	0/0	0	0/0

TRANSFER ROUND-UP

Chelsea have always been a major force in the transfer market and the summer of 2000 was no different. After winning the FA Cup in May, The Blues acted quickly in an attempt to solve their problem in front of goal. The first signing announced Chelsea's intent to launch a serious challenge for the title. Jimmy Floyd Hasselbaink, the former Leeds striker who had finished as the top scorer in Spain's Primera Liga, arrived for £15 million. He was joined by sought-after Bolton striker Eidur Gudjohnsen and Croatian midfield ace Mario Stanic, giving The Blues several fresh attacking options.

But Chelsea were careful not to neglect the defensive department of the squad. The huge spending spree may have finished with Jimmy, Eidur and Mario, but the club still managed to sign two more world class defenders for the start of the new season. In came experienced Italian full-back Christian Panucci on a year's loan, and versatile defender Winston Bogarde, who signed from Barcelona on a free transfer.

Leaving Stamford Bridge were Chris Sutton, transferred to Celtic, Didier Deschamps – to Valencia – and Emerson Thome, who left for Sunderland. George Weah's loan spell expired and he returned to Italy with AC Milan, before negotiating a switch to Premiership new boys Manchester City. The popular Dan Petrescu was signed by Bradford, Bjarne Goldbaek made the short trip to Fulham and Pierluigi Casiraghi retired after his injury nightmare. Youngsters Neil Clement and Nick Crittenden moved to West Brom and Yeovil respectively.

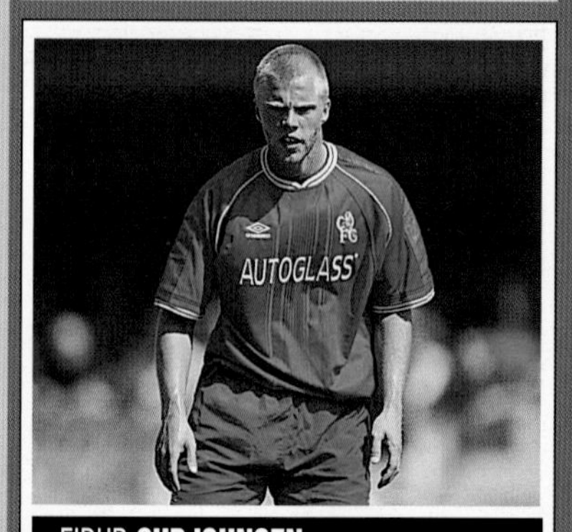

EIDUR **GUDJOHNSEN**

- **Position:** Striker
- **Born:** September 15, 1978 in Reykjavik (Iceland)
- **Chelsea Debut:** August 13, 2000 v Manchester United
- **Transfer:** £5 million, June 20, 2000
- **Previous Clubs:** PSV Eindhoven, Bolton Wanderers
- **Club Honours:** None
- **International Honours:** Senior Iceland International

Chelsea beat several top clubs to sign young Icelandic star Eidur Gudjohnsen for £5 million after his outstanding season with First Division Bolton Wanderers in 1999-2000. Eidur started his career playing alongside Ronaldo at PSV Eindhoven under the guidance of ex-England boss Bobby Robson, but after suffering a serious ankle injury he moved to Bolton to make a fresh start. As the striker regained his fitness he alerted Premiership clubs with some fantastic goals, particularly in the FA Cup as he inspired Wanderers to a place in the semi-final. At 22 years of age, Eidur has a sparkling future lying ahead of him at Stamford Bridge.

JIMMY FLOYD HASSELBAINK

- **Position:** Striker
- **Born:** March 27, 1972 in Paramaribo (Surinam)
- **Chelsea Debut:** August 13, 2000 v Manchester United
- **Transfer:** £15 million, June 2, 2000
- **Previous Clubs:** Campomaio, Boavista, Leeds, Atletico Madrid
- **Club Honours:** None
- **International Honours:** Senior Holland International

Chelsea smashed their transfer record in August 2000 to bring highly-rated marksman Jimmy Floyd Hasselbaink to Stamford Bridge. However, if the Dutch international can help to deliver the Premiership title to West London he will have been worth every penny of the £15 million. A prolific hitman with Leeds in 1998-99, Jimbo did his reputation no harm by finishing as the top scorer in Spain's Primera Liga last term with 24 goals, despite the relegation of his club, Atletico Madrid. Jimbo has all the qualities a top-class striker needs – powerful shooting, instinctive finishing, electric pace and controlled aggression.

WINSTON BOGARDE

- **Position:** Defender
- **Born:** October 22, 1970 in Rotterdam (Holland)
- **Chelsea Debut:** N/A
- **Transfer:** No Fee, August 31, 2000
- **Previous Clubs:** Sparta Rotterdam, Ajax, AC Milan, Barcelona
- **Club Honours:** Dutch League, Dutch Cup, European Cup, European Super Cup & World Club Championship winner with Ajax (1995); Dutch League winner with Ajax (1996); European Cup-Winners' Cup winner with Barcelona (1997); Spanish league winner with Barcelona (1998, 1999); Spanish Cup winner with Barcelona (1998)
- **International Honours:** Senior Holland International

Winston Bogarde's pedigree as an experienced player at both club and international level is undeniable. His lengthy honours list shows how many trophies he's won with some of the best clubs in Europe. A Holland international who played in Euro '96 and the 1998 World Cup, Winston is a left-sided defender who can also play in a central role, although he has played in midfield when required and actually began his football career as a striker. The Blues snapped him up on a free transfer from Spanish giants Barcelona after Winston expressed his desire to play in the Premiership. He will be an important defensive acquisition after Emerson Thome's move to Sunderland.

CHRISTIAN PANUCCI

- **Position:** Defender
- **Born:** April 12, 1973 in Savona (Italy)
- **Chelsea Debut:** August 13, 2000 v Manchester United
- **Transfer:** On Loan, August 10, 2000
- **Previous Clubs:** Genoa, AC Milan, Real Madrid, Inter Milan
- **Club Honours:** Italian League winner with AC Milan (1994, 1996), European Cup winner with AC Milan (1994) & Real Madrid (1998); European Super Cup winner with AC Milan (1995), Spanish League winner with Real Madrid (1997)
- **International Honours:** Senior Italy International

Chelsea pulled off a transfer coup by luring Christian Panucci to Stamford Bridge on the eve of the new season. Christian is a solid defender who has enjoyed phenomenal success in his career with AC Milan and Real Madrid. The Blues signed him on a one-year loan deal from Inter Milan and have an option to make the move permanent at the end of this season. The Italian has already hugely impressed his colleagues.

MARIO STANIC

- **Position:** Midfielder
- **Born:** April 10, 1972 in Sarajevo (Croatia)
- **Chelsea Debut:** August 13, 2000 v Manchester United
- **Transfer:** £5.6 million, June 28, 2000
- **Previous Clubs:** Zeliznicar, Sporting Gijon, Benfica, FC Brugge, Parma
- **Club Honours:** Italian League winner with Parma (1999); Italian Cup winner with Parma (1999); UEFA Cup winner with Parma (1999)
- **International Honours:** Senior Croatia international

Croatia international Mario Stanic could prove to be one of the club's shrewdest signings if his early showings in the blue of Chelsea are anything to go by. Having played in the World Cup for his country and in Italy's Serie A with Parma, the man they call 'Super Mario' is a player of proven quality and another fine addition to the squad at Stamford Bridge. His ideal position is on the right of midfield, but he can also play as an emergency striker and has a good goalscoring record. Skilful on the ball and dangerous from crosses and set-pieces, Mario announced himself to the Chelsea supporters in some style on his debut with an awesome volleyed goal from 30 yards in The Blues' 4-2 Premiership victory against West Ham.

THE SQUAD

1. Ed **de Goey**
2. Christian **Panucci**
3. Celestine **Babayaro**
4. Jes **Hogh**
5. Frank **Leboeuf**
6. Marcel **Desailly**
7. Winston **Bogarde**
8. Gustavo **Poyet**
9. Jimmy Floyd **Hasselbaink**
10.
11. Dennis **Wise**
12. Mario **Stanic**
13. Kevin **Hitchcock**
14. Graeme **Le Saux**
15. Mario **Melchiot**
16. Roberto **Di Matteo**
17. Albert **Ferrer**
18. Gabriele **Ambrosetti**
19. Tore Andre **Flo**
20. Jody **Morris**
21. Bernard **Lambourde**
22. Eidur **Gudjohnsen**
23. Carlo **Cudicini**
24. Samuele **Dalla Bona**
25. Gianfranco **Zola**
26. John **Terry**
27. Rati **Aleksidze**
28. Robert **Wolleaston**
29. Neil **Clement**
32. Mikael **Forssell**
33. Luca **Percassi**
34. Jon **Harley**
35. Leon **Knight**

Mario Stanic points where Chelsea are heading – the top of the Premiership.

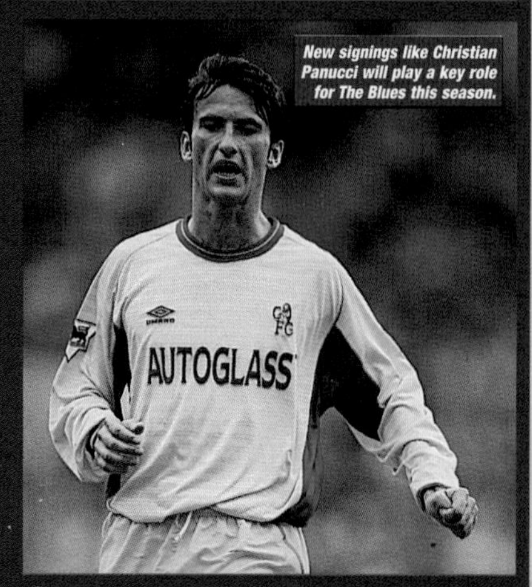

New signings like Christian Panucci will play a key role for The Blues this season.

CHELSEA FIXTURES

Date	Opponent	H/A
Aug. 19	**West Ham United**	H
Aug. 22	Bradford City	A
Aug. 27	Aston Villa	A
Sept. 6	**Arsenal**	H
Sept. 9	Newcastle United	A
Sept. 17	**Leicester City**	H
Sept. 23	Manchester United	A
Oct. 1	**Liverpool**	H
Oct. 14	Sunderland	A
Oct. 21	**Coventry City**	H
Oct. 29	**Tottenham Hotspur**	H
Nov. 4	Southampton	A
Nov. 12	**Leeds United**	H
Nov. 18	Charlton Athletic	A
Nov. 25	Everton	A
Dec. 3	**Manchester City**	H
Dec. 9	**Derby County**	H
Dec. 16	Middlesbrough	A
Dec. 23	**Bradford City**	H
Dec. 26	Ipswich Town	A
Dec. 30	West Ham United	A
Jan. 1	**Aston Villa**	H
Jan. 13	Arsenal	A
Jan. 20	**Ipswich Town**	H
Jan. 31	**Newcastle United**	H
Feb. 3	Leicester City	A
Feb. 10	**Manchester United**	H
Feb. 24	Liverpool	A
Mar. 3	Coventry City	A
Mar. 17	**Sunderland**	H
Mar. 31	**Middlesbrough**	H
Apr. 7	Derby County	A
Apr. 14	**Southampton**	H
Apr. 16	Tottenham Hotspur	A
Apr. 21	**Charlton Athletic**	H
Apr. 28	Leeds United	A
May 5	**Everton**	H
May 19	Manchester City	A